D0450171

 Mack, Glenn Randall,
1963-
   Food culture in
Russia and Central
Asia

JUL 0 7 2005

# Food Culture in
# Russia and Central Asia

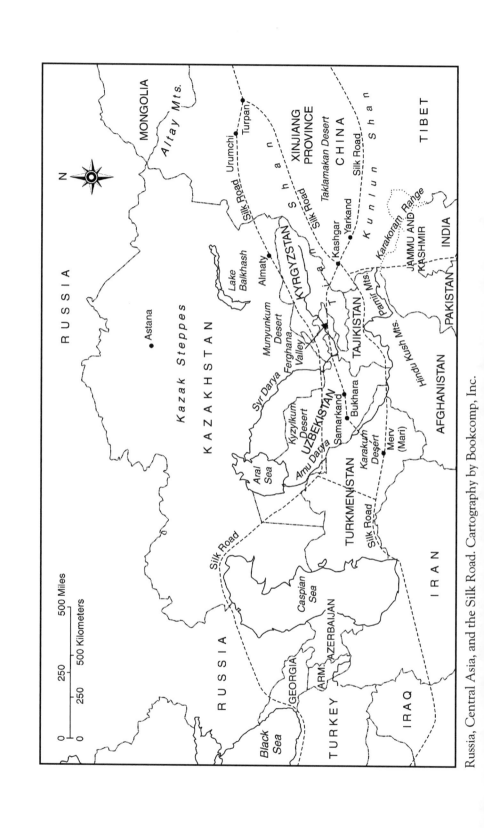

Russia, Central Asia, and the Silk Road. Cartography by Bookcomp, Inc.

# Food Culture in
# Russia and Central Asia

## GLENN R. MACK AND ASELE SURINA

Food Culture around the World

Ken Albala, Series Editor

GREENWOOD PRESS
Westport, Connecticut · London

**Library of Congress Cataloging-in-Publication Data**

Mack, Glenn Randall, 1963–
   Food culture in Russia and Central Asia / Glenn R. Mack and Asele Surina.
     p. cm. — (Food culture around the world, ISSN 1545–2638)
   Includes bibliographical references and index.
   ISBN 0–313–32773–4 (alk. paper)
   1. Cookery, Russian. 2. Cookery—Asia, Central. 3. Food habits—Russia (Federation). 4. Food habits—Asia, Central. 5. Dinners and dining—Russia (Federation).
6. Dinners and dining—Asia, Central. I. Surina, Asele. II. Title. III. Series.
TX723.3.M2356 2005
394.1'2'0958—dc22     2005004192

British Library Cataloguing in Publication Data is available.

Copyright © 2005 by Glenn R. Mack and Asele Surina

All rights reserved. No portion of this book may be
reproduced, by any process or technique, without the
express written consent of the publisher.

Library of Congress Catalog Card Number: 2005004192
ISBN: 0–313–32773–4
ISSN: 1545–2638

First published in 2005

Greenwood Press, 88 Post Road West, Westport, CT 06881
An imprint of Greenwood Publishing Group, Inc.
www.greenwood.com

Printed in the United States of America

The paper used in this book complies with the
Permanent Paper Standard issued by the National
Information Standards Organization (Z39.48–1984).

10  9  8  7  6  5  4  3  2  1

The publisher has done its best to make sure the instructions and/or recipes in this book
are correct. However, users should apply judgment and experience when preparing recipes, especially parents and teachers working with young people. The publisher accepts no
responsibility for the outcome of any recipe included in this volume.

*To Dasha and Gregory, our inspiration for attempting to live and eat well.*

*"The joys of the table belong equally to all ages,*
*conditions, countries and times; they mix with all other*
*pleasures, and remain the last to console us for their loss."*
*Jean-Anthelme Brillat-Savarin in*
*The Physiology of Taste (1825).*

# Contents

# Series Foreword

The appearance of the Food Culture around the World series marks a definitive stage in the maturation of Food Studies as a discipline to reach a wider audience of students, general readers, and foodies alike. In comprehensive interdisciplinary reference volumes, each on the food culture of a country or region for which information is most in demand, a remarkable team of experts from around the world offers a deeper understanding and appreciation of the role of food in shaping human culture for a whole new generation. I am honored to have been associated with this project as series editor.

Each volume follows a series format, with a chronology of food-related dates and narrative chapters entitled Introduction, Historical Overview, Major Foods and Ingredients, Cooking, Typical Meals, Eating Out, Special Occasions, and Diet and Health. Each also includes a glossary, bibliography, resource guide, and illustrations.

Finding or growing food has of course been the major preoccupation of our species throughout history, but how various peoples around the world learn to exploit their natural resources, come to esteem or shun specific foods and develop unique cuisines reveals much more about what it is to be human. There is perhaps no better way to understand a culture, its values, preoccupations and fears, than by examining its attitudes toward food. Food provides the daily sustenance around which families and communities bond. It provides the material basis for rituals through which people celebrate the passage of life stages and their connection to divinity.

Food preferences also serve to separate individuals and groups from each other, and as one of the most powerful factors in the construction of identity, we physically, emotionally and spiritually become what we eat.

By studying the foodways of people different from ourselves we also grow to understand and tolerate the rich diversity of practices around the world. What seems strange or frightening among other people becomes perfectly rational when set in context. It is my hope that readers will gain from these volumes not only an aesthetic appreciation for the glories of the many culinary traditions described, but also ultimately a more profound respect for the peoples who devised them. Whether it is eating New Year's dumplings in China, folding tamales with friends in Mexico or going out to a famous Michelin-starred restaurant in France, understanding these food traditions helps us to understand the people themselves.

As globalization proceeds apace in the twenty-first century is it also more important than ever to preserve unique local and regional traditions. In many cases these books describe ways of eating that have already begun to disappear or have been seriously transformed by modernity. To know how and why these losses occur today also enables us to decide what traditions, whether from our own heritage or that of others, we wish to keep alive. These books are thus not only about the food and culture of peoples around the world, but also about ourselves and who we hope to be.

*Ken Albala*
*University of the Pacific*

# Acknowledgments

First and foremost, many thanks are in order to Ken Albala, series editor, who provided us the opportunity to write this book, and editor Wendi Schnaufer, who guided us every step of the way, patiently waiting as both our manuscript and children grew ever so slowly. We owe lifelong appreciation to Irma and Ella Abdurahmanova, Asele's mother and aunt, respectively, who taught us the pleasures of Uzbek and Russian cuisine and hospitality. Asele's great aunt in Uzbekistan, Raisa-hola, too, unselfishly revealed all her Uzbek and Tatar kitchen secrets during an unhurried year in Tashkent, the majority of which was spent relaxing in the family courtyard or sweating in her kitchen. Needless to say, without the countless sacrificing hosts who opened their homes to us over the past two decades in every republic of the former Soviet Union, we would never have had the inspiration to pick up a pen. Ergun Çağatay taught us the importance of not only documenting Turkic culture through photography but also cherishing the daily fleeting moments while experiencing another way of life. Many other dear people assisted us over the years in our research, openly sharing their time and expertise: Rachel Lauden, Darra Goldstein, Russell Zanca, Uli Schamiloglu, Daniel Waugh, Charles Perry, Joyce Toomre, Lynn Visson, Robert Arndt, Inci Bowman, Nazhie Ebubekirova, Ken Rubin, Maria Wade, and Andy Smith. The indefatigable Sharon Hudgins somehow found time to extensively review the entire manuscript. We raise a toast to all of you.

Furthermore, I am forever indebted to Rashid Ushurov, the Central Asian noodle master, who entrusted to me his life's written work on Uighur culinary culture and indulged my obsession for the mysteries of gluten. Special recognition goes to Michael Katz, my friend, mentor, and former professor, who demonstrated the breadths and depths of intellectual rigor and curiosity. Without the unfaltering support and encouragement of food historian Alice Arndt I would have long ago given up on culinary history. I am also eternally grateful to the Culinary Trust of the International Association of Culinary Professionals for their grant to continue my noodle research and to the Mirzo Ulugbek Culinary Institute in Tashkent for the opportunity to study not only cuisine but also their educational system. And, of course, to my mother, Greta Mack, who humored my culinary adventures while "proper" children were "building their careers." To all those upon whose shoulders we stand and whose traditions we maintain, we acknowledge and appreciate you more than you will ever know.

*Glenn R. Mack*

# Preface

Documenting the foodways of Eurasia is a formidable task, one we undertook with great trepidation. It is too easy to fall into the trap of presenting culinary culture as a static phenomenon. Russian and Central Asian cuisine and food-related customs are continually evolving, as do all ethnic or national cuisines. This book serves as a snapshot of contemporary food culture in a rapidly changing region, with a touch of historical context for illumination. It highlights the unexpected cultural similarities across vastly different cultures. Our intention is to provide the reader with an extensive outline of the directions and possibilities for culinary exploration in the former Soviet Union beyond the usual collection of recipes and anecdotes found in many cookbooks. It is our hope that students, culinary professionals, scholars, and enthusiasts may find here a starting point for more detailed research and systematic exploration of the subjects described in this reference. We have tried to avoid sweeping stereotypical statements and to refrain from including unnecessary minutiae, resigning ourselves to the unwritten law of publishing: "It is never done, it is just due." Although Russian cuisine has been well documented in the current literature, we are honored to add the first comprehensive examination of Central Asian food culture to be published in the West.

This book has also provided us an opportunity to express our own life experiences and our curiosity for the diverse cultures of Eurasia. Growing up in Moscow, Asele, with her mix of Russian, Uzbek, and Tatar heritage, could scarcely imagine a day when foes (United States and Russia) become friends and an entire world of cuisine could be intimately shared with the Western world. When I chose to study Russian language and literature at the height of President Ronald Reagan's anti-Soviet, "evil empire" rhetoric in the early 1980s, the idea that food and culture would dominate my life was absurd. My classmates in Moscow made fun of excursions to the regional markets, grungy cafés, and the home kitchens of hospitable acquaintances. What began as a graduate student's search to maintain a full belly grew to a full-time preoccupation.

Asele has the advantage of viewing Eurasian foodways from both perspectives—as an insider and an outsider. Coming from a family of professionals, Asele experienced a moderately privileged Soviet existence. But that status was not sufficient enough to shield her from the blatant inequities of the Communist system, the shortages, and the inconveniences of daily life. After my first visit to the Soviet Union in 1984, the most lasting impression was that this country was not a homogeneous land of vile Russians but an incredible ethnic and cultural patchwork empire with scores of distinctly un-Slavic peoples. Though naïvely unaware of the crucial role of food as a defining element of culture, I vaguely recognized that there might be a greater significance to cuisine than pure nourishment.

The first exposure to another culture for many people often comes in the form of food. *Culinary culture* is a shorthand term encompassing the products, techniques and tools, and, of course, the cultural and historical context of a cuisine for a particular nation or a cultural group across nations. The notion of culinary culture crystallized for me in 1989 after an enlightening journey from Moscow to Beijing on the Trans-Siberian Railroad. Continuing on from Xian, the terminus of the Silk Road, into Chinese Central Asia, then farther down through Pakistan to the border of Afghanistan and on to India, I experienced several distinct culinary cultures within the span of four months. Before even setting foot in Soviet Central Asia, I unwittingly had tasted the cultural influences surrounding the region. The scent of cumin and freshly baked flat breads still linger in the air in the Islamic cultural areas of China. My exposure to savory stews and Persian-influenced sweets began in Pakistan and India. Eastern style noodles and dumplings and the pervasive heritage of hospitality were found everywhere along the old Silk Road. Circumnavigating Soviet Central Asia only reinforced the cultural similarity and continuity with their neighbors in other countries. More than a century ago, Lord Curzon remarked: "Central Asia has its charm for the historian, the archeologist, the artist, the man of science, the dilettante traveler, for every class—from the erudite to the idle. A wide field of research and a plentiful return await the explorer in each of these regions."[1] To this day, his words could not ring more true. Living in Moscow and Tashkent during the tumultuous period of imperial collapse in the 1990s, Asele and I witnessed firsthand the role that culture and cuisine played for Russians and Central Asians in formulating new identities. The countries attentively explored their culinary heritage as part of national self-awareness and reawakening, questioning their distorted past and pondering an indeterminate future. Russians and Central Asians are not only seeking to establish their national character, they are also striving to confirm their culinary distinctiveness.

## NOTE

1. George N. Curzon, *Russia in Central Asia in 1889 and the Anglo Russian Question* (London: Longmans, Green, New, 1889), x–xi.

# Introduction: Russian and Central Asian Culinary Culture

## REGIONAL OVERVIEW

Among the world's most vibrant civilizations, Russia and Central Asia possess cuisines as complex and contradictory as their respective histories. History continuously attempts to define and label Russia primarily in political and economic terms. The designations are endless: Kievan Rus', Muscovy, All the Russias, Third Rome, dictatorship of the proletariat, Great Socialist Experiment, Evil Empire, New Klondike, and so forth. Central Asia is equally challenging for categorization. The post-Soviet area includes the newly independent states of Kazakstan, Kyrgyzstan, Tajikistan, Turkmenistan, and Uzbekistan. It has been identified by and large in geographic terms: Tartary, Transoxiana, Turkestan, imperial playground for the Great Game, Russian and Chinese Turkestan, Soviet Central Asia, and now, collectively and derisively, the "Stans." When viewed through a cultural lens, invariably the eyepieces for Russia and Central Asia are Eastern Orthodox Christianity and Islam. Few efforts, though, have been made to describe this vast region in terms of culinary culture.[1]

Russia is an inscrutable land on many levels. It is difficult to comprehend the size of its territory, the number of ethnic groups within its borders, and the depths of its history. Russia's varied cuisine, too, defies neat description. As outsiders looking in, it is tempting to simply christen certain Russian dishes as authentic or traditional. For decades, the West maintained that the Soviet Union was the same thing as Russia and ignored the nuances and hues of reality. U.S. president Ronald Reagan labeled the Soviet Union in pure black-and-white terms as "The Evil Empire." Sir Winston Churchill at least allowed for some shades of gray imagery when uttering his famous phrase about Russia—"It is a riddle, wrapped in a mystery, inside an enigma." In actuality, Russia is full of color, not just the whites of driving snow and the blacks of impeding mud. The root cellar, the cornucopian pantry, and the rustic table of Russia, though at times in history depicted as dark as the country itself, can vibrantly glimmer when food and camaraderie overlap.

It has become canonical that the cookery of a region plays an integral role in identity formation, both for an individual and for a nation. In recent years, Russia and Central Asia have ventured out from the culinary backwaters to join the swift rapids of global gastronomic interaction. Moscow has become a center of culinary innovation in the early twenty-first century, quickly erasing bitter images of empty food shelves and state-run restaurants. Russia is renowned for its literature, not its larder, more famous for its ballet than its borscht. In times past, Central Asia enriched the West more frequently with its carpets than with its fragrant melons. Yet, the cuisines of Eurasia have always offered their people a splendid and wholesome variety of flavors, complemented by munificent hospitality. Russians approach every meal with gusto and sincere appreciation, be it beer and crayfish or champagne and caviar. Centuries of scarcity, deprivation, and hardship have shaped the culinary aesthetics in the Slavic consciousness. Central Asians, though equally unpretentious, raise hospitality to an utmost art form and performance, nearly embarrassing the guest with excess and praise. The foods of the region, nonetheless, have had little positive exposure to the rest of the world due to geographical as well as self-imposed political isolation in recent memory.

Today, the remarkable Eurasian cuisines are accessible in restaurants, cafés, markets, and as home-cooked meals. This work explores the role of cuisine and food rituals (collectively described as *foodways*) placed within their cultural and social context in contemporary Russia and Central Asia. It ambitiously attempts to make known some of the dishes, customs, and regional differences obscured by the stereotypes of Russia as an arctic wilderness and Central Asia as a forbidding desert. The appeal of their cuisines is due to several factors: their diversity, their novelty, and the intriguing evidence of cultural exchange over the ages. This culinary terra incognita is now open for all to partake and enjoy.

Throughout its history, Russia was no straightforward place for foreigners to visit or to reside. Lengthy, ruthless winters, the sheer expansiveness of the country, and the seemingly barbaric customs of the populace (based on medieval accounts) hindered frequent and long-term contact with the West. For the entire twentieth century, the Communist Party, with its revolutionary zeal, shrouded Russia and Central Asia in obscurity. It was a closed society from top to bottom—distrustful of the West and fearful for its own stability as a piecemeal nation bound together through force and terror.

Central Asia is among the most isolated areas of the planet, halfway between Europe and China. Travelers along the ancient Silk Road, the network of trade routes connecting east and west, appreciated the grandeur of the civilizations and the opulence of the royal courts that grew up with the increasing trade. Their exotic tales became myths and legends in the manner of *Arabian Nights*. Few Europeans fully understood its people or its lands. When imperial Russia gained control of Central Asia by the eighteenth century (only to be taken over again by the Soviets in the twentieth), the region became even further removed from Western eyes.

Why, after the region unwillingly endured 150 years of Russian influence and control, should Central Asia be again lumped back together with Russia? In terms of cuisine and culinary culture, centuries of contact and conflict among peoples of Eurasia produced undeniable elements of a common cultural history. Russian culinary culture cannot be fully understood without a Central Asian context. Central Asian cuisine becomes less obscure when the Russian influence in the area over the past century and a half is taken into account.

On the most elementary level, Russian and Central Asian cuisines share ingredients, dishes, and customs. For example, hot tea, grilled skewered meats, and festive hospitality are the culinary foundations of both areas. Even more compelling is the idea that just as Russia mimicked Europe in developing its national identity, Central Asia then modeled its national institutions and symbols on Russia. Today both areas follow, to varying degrees, the global model of cultural commodification in the marketing of their national cuisines. As in the rest of the world, glossy magazines glamorize the food, cookbooks recall the ancient culinary heritage, restaurants capture the national essence on a plate, food festivals celebrate the local culinary traditions, and chefs find their way into the spotlight. Yet, the most distinctive aspect of culinary culture in Russia and Central Asia is the hospitality. Hospitality, the largest service industry in the West, remains in the East a way of life.

More importantly, both regions share cultural rifts and upheavals that have resulted in certain commonalities. Russia and Central Asia both experienced wholesale religious conversions in the Middle Ages, suffered Mongol conquests in the thirteenth century, and forcibly became one nation under Russian and then Soviet control. Central Asia adopted Islam beginning in the eighth century A.D., which transformed the region in ways that continue to this day. Eastern Orthodox Christianity became the altering cultural force for the Slavs shortly thereafter, from the tenth century onward. The horror and humiliation of Mongol destruction and dominance are still a painful memory for peoples of both regions. The Soviet political and social experiment, though Moscow-centered and more fleeting than the Mongol period, remains as the overwhelming cultural determinant of both contemporary Central Asia and the new Russian Federation. It forcibly brought the regions together while eventually exposing their fundamental cultural disparities.

By the beginning of the twenty-first century, however, experiments with a market economy exposed the colorful cuisines of the former USSR to an astonished international audience expecting the drab uniformity of the austere Soviet period. Once considered a gastronomic badlands, its remarkable and delectable cuisines are again finding their way onto a world stage through travel, commerce, immigration, and media coverage. Russians and Central Asians now travel abroad, experiencing and adapting global culinary models. Some immigrate and share their cuisine through the medium of restaurants. Cookbooks about the region are proliferating. Foreigners, too, now freely delve into the richness of the culinary culture as guests in someone's home or in the ever-sprouting cafés. Writers, journalists, and other visitors have begun to share the secrets of this new culinary frontier in feature articles, documentaries, and cookery shows.[2]

After decades of oblivion, mockery, and isolation, the vast Eurasian continent once again divulges its intense history, cultural heritage, and food customs to the international community. Over the centuries, Western conceptions of the Russian Empire and the Soviet Union oscillated variously as a venerable wasteland, an ominous threat, a helpless bungler, and a convenient ally. In the post-Soviet era, the West tries to reinterpret the Newly Independent States (NIS) while each country struggles to reassert or create its national identity. Led by cultural nationalists, these newfound political entities attempt to define or reconstruct their nation's history and culture. This includes the identification and promotion of an authentic national cuisine, which incongruously at times comes to symbolize the identity of a nation or ethnic group. A search for the authentic, essential, or genuine cookery of any single country is an elusive, dodgy, and quixotic exercise. Cuisine, even within a homogeneous society, can greatly vary. So imagine the food disparity and diversity within the former USSR, claiming over a hundred distinct nationalities—each with its own language, culture, history, and cuisine.

The dreaded Soviet Union disintegrated with nary a shot fired in 1991. Though 15 new nations arose from the skeleton of the former USSR, the Russian Federation and Central Asia together still compose 95 percent of that territory.[3] Few twentieth-century commentators made the distinction between Russia and the USSR, despite the fact that ethnic Russians made up only half of the entire population. Part of this misperception is due to *Russianization*—the promotion of the Russian language in education, government, and diplomacy, beginning with the Russian Empire in the seventeenth century. By the twentieth century, the other 14 Soviet republics perforce accepted Russian in an equal and official status with their indigenous languages. This policy laid a foundation for *Russification* and later *Sovietization*—the process of establishing Russian culture as the basis for cultural and political identity, disguised as Socialist brotherhood or friendship among peoples in the Soviet era.

Twenty-four million ethnic Russians now live outside the Russian Federation proper in the Near Abroad, the Russian designation for the former Soviet republics. In a greatly abridged independent Russia, the number of official nationalities nonetheless jumped from 136 a decade earlier to 160 by 2003.[4] Most people (80% or 116 million) counted themselves as ethnically Russian. Tatars are the second most numerous ethnic group, making up only 5 percent of the total 143 million citizens of the Russian Federation. The other 150-odd nationalities make up the remaining 15 percent of the population. With declining economic prospects in their new countries, more Azeris, Armenians, and Tajiks have migrated to Russia. Chinese and North Koreans are also adding to the influx, especially in the Russian Far East. Russia experienced a net increase of 5 million citizens from all over the world through immigration since independence in 1991, making it the third most popular destination for relocation after the United States and Germany.[5] This makes Russia among the most ethnically diverse countries in the world. The resulting cultural mosaic, beyond question, enriches the cuisine.

Drawing a triangle on the map—with the endpoints of Stockholm, Beijing, and Istanbul—neatly conveys the major cultural influences, not to mention the populated territory of Eurasia itself. From the second century B.C., the Silk Road connected China and the Mediterranean and on to Rome, with the bulk of its routes passing through Central Asia and northward into Russia. Even before the Vikings in the ninth century, the

"Amber Road" functioned as a network of waterways for ancient trade between the Baltic and Black Seas. Though Byzantium, the Vikings, and Marco Polo are easy conventions for attributing cultural diffusion, the truth of the matter is that the process of contact and conflict was gradual and continual through the ages, affecting in no small way the culinary cultures of Russia and Central Asia.

Cultures clearly evolve over time through contact with other groups. Cuisines change by the same process. Combining a steady influx of ideas, products, and techniques with existing foodways is the standard process of culinary evolution. Recipes, dishes, and traditions passed down from generation to generation evolve through a natural course of assimilation and acculturation. With Russia and its borderlands, there were additional forces that affected the cuisine. Perhaps the twentieth-century Soviet experience has left the most indelible mark on national foodways. The first major factor influencing cuisine was the centrally planned economy's penchant for standardization and prescription. Food was no exception, and recipes and restaurant menus were planned in detail by ministries in Moscow. Combining cultures and imposing party-approved representations of cuisine have had large-scale consequences on the foodways of all nations, cultures, and peoples in the region.

The most important factor influencing culinary cultures, obviously, was the compulsory population redistribution within the Soviet Union. Unlike traditional European expansion to overseas territories, Russia broadened its borders almost without interruption for three hundred years over contiguous terrain. In contrast, European colonists in foreign lands were generally few in number and rarely integrated with the local culture. Nor did the European empires experience massive emigration from the colony to the mother country. Granted, there are considerable Indian, Middle Eastern, and Caribbean communities in England and North African communities in France. But those resettlements poorly compare with the population redistribution experienced in the USSR. Russians, Ukrainians, and Belarusians emigrated to the non-Slavic republics as party hacks, teachers, bureaucrats, and technical advisers. The military purposely sent conscripts far away from their homeland. People migrated from rural areas to the cities for work and study. Ostensibly for political and economic reasons, Soviet leader Joseph Stalin uprooted millions of cultural groups and disbursed them throughout the country. Populations and cultures were intermixed, resulting in cuisines liberally borrowing from one another. *Tabaka*, a Georgian chicken dish, became as common in Russia as borscht has become in Moldova.

Scholars tend to amplify the differences and uniqueness of peoples and environment. This book seeks to underscore the similarities and constants within the massive and disparate remnants of the empire. Admittedly, on a purely political basis, combining Russia and Central Asia is fraught with controversy. Even ethnically, the stark cultural contrast is obvious when comparing the Slavs of the north to the Turks of the east and south. Religion, geography, and language conventionally serve as suitable partitions to generate tidy and simplistic divisions among groups. Through repeated cultural contact, however, communities adopt or adapt certain culinary characteristics, at times leaving observable patterns and traceable origins as is clearly evident on the Eurasian continent. Food and foodways, it may be argued, more than any other element of culture—language, religion, clothing, ethnicity, ceremonies, symbols, and so forth—are the most enduring cultural aspect within a society. People move, migrate, and experiment. Nevertheless, the familiar foods of childhood and community are among the most powerful sources of comfort and identity for an individual and a cultural group.

## LEARNING FROM EURASIAN FOODWAYS

The Russian Empire, which included Ukraine, the Baltic nations, the Caucasus, Central Asia, and Siberia, was blessed with an abundance of fish from its seas, oceans, rivers, and lakes; fresh and dried fruits and nuts from the southern regions; endless variations of grains and hearty breads; the wild game of the forest; and the rewarding berries and mushrooms of the woods. The ingredients for an extraordinary cuisine are still there through centuries of trade and migration. Once Russian and Central Asian food producers and restaurateurs learn the intricacies of international trade and safety standards, Eurasian foodstuffs and restaurants will make their way around the world. Language and political barriers are disappearing, and these countries have plenty of hospitality to share with the rest of the world. The cuisines of Russia and Central Asia certainly deserve a place on the global culinary stage.

Russia and Central Asia are still in the midst of tremendous social, economic, and cultural upheaval. With regard to gastronomy—the art of eating excellent food—it is nigh impossible for Americans to imagine the Russian and Central Asian attitude toward food after the hardships suffered through famines, revolutions, world wars, starvation, rationing, shortages, and an inefficient and inequitable centralized economy under Communism. For those ever-increasing numbers of Russians and Central Asians who can afford the luxury of dining out, the novelty of the experience must be staggering. In the West, the restaurant industry incrementally matured and consumers became more knowledgeable and demanding over the course of two hundred years. Russia and Central Asia missed almost half of that developmental stage under the Soviets, and in the process lost a respect for the customer, emphasized quantity over quality, and squelched the entrepreneurial spirit. As the pendulum swings to the other extreme, to reach any permanent conclusions about Russian and Central Asian restaurants in the period of transition is extremely difficult. Only time will tell when new "national" cuisines in these countries will develop with the help of cookbooks, restaurants, and the mass media.

After a century of stereotyping Russia as a wasteland of potatoes and vodka, it is difficult to imagine Moscow as a new center of culinary innovation, leading an entire country in culinary changes. Russians love extremes. Now that they have turned their attention to cuisine, it may rise to national prominence and pride on a level with Russian literature, ballet, and science. Unlike the traditional Russian restaurants of the Soviet era or those outside of Russia, the new Moscow restaurants are leading the nation in both novelty and the rediscovery of a national cuisine.

## STRUCTURE OF THE BOOK

This reference focuses principally on the food itself, although the production, preferences, and preparation also merit significant attention. No other single work has attempted to describe the cuisines of Russia or the nations of Central Asia within a historical, geographic, social, and aesthetic context. The historical framework includes ethnicity, religion, family and social structure, culinary heritage, and regional influences. Geography encompasses the climate, topography, natural resources, and proximity of the regions to other areas. Social and aesthetic concerns include typical daily meals, as well as special occasions, setting and presentation, who actually does the cooking at home, and the experience of dining out.

A review of the background of people, agriculture, food sources, and attitudes toward food is found in the historical overview in chapters 1 and 2. Russian history may be viewed as a history of hardships, which the nation both endured and brought upon itself. Since the defeat of the Russian Imperial army by Western forces in the Crimean War, Russia has suffered as difficult a century and a half as can be imagined. Central Asia, too, in this same turbulent time frame was colonized, conferred nominative republic status within the USSR, and then left to its own tarnished devices with independence in the 1990s. This led logically to the invention or redis-covery of suppressed culture and tradition, as well as the production of na-tional ideologies. Moreover, both regions experienced a highly stratified society, with a miniscule elite and an extensive pitiable underclass. This situation has its parallels in the cuisine of the eighteenth and nineteenth centuries, with the high aristocratic dishes in Russia and the royal court cuisine of the Central Asian khanates juxtaposed with the meager meals of the serfs, petty traders, agricultural laborers, and nomads.

For the uninitiated, the quantity and quality of foodstuffs in Eurasia are purely staggering. Chapter 3—covering the major foods and ingredi-ents—can only scratch the surface of the diversity and richness of nature's bounty and the profuse ethnic culinary traditions. Here, for example, the reader will discover that pickles and pilaf are not merely dishes with a set recipe. Pickles to a Slav go far beyond brined cucumbers. They symbolize familial relations, ties to the countryside, and culinary heritage, and are a perfect complement to a shot of vodka. For Central Asians, pilaf signifies hospitality, celebration, and solemnity, and is a weekly ritual.

The cooking of Eurasia is the domain of womenfolk, as clearly illus-trated in chapter 4. Wives and grandmothers spend much of their day procuring ingredients and preparing meals for their families. The rare exception, much like in American society, is the cookout. Both Rus-sian and Central Asian men pride themselves on preparing grilled shish kebab (*shashlyk*) over glowing coals. Men in Central Asia also prepare pilaf, *samsa* (savory pastries), and bread—all the items prepared over an open flame or in tandoor (*tandir*) ovens. In the public domain, men pre-dominate as street vendors and in the preparation of food for restaurants and cafés.

Documenting typical meals in earlier eras was considered so mundane or obvious that there is a tremendous gap of knowledge of what most peo-ple ate in all societies of every epoch. Written or iconographic documen-tation naturally overemphasizes the extravagant rulers and the wealthy. It elevates gastronomy over sustenance, which is the necessity and practice of daily life. While it is unavoidable to generalize and stereotype, at least an attempt has been made in chapter 5 to record the standard fare of the hoi polloi, or common folk.

Eating outside the home is as old as civilization itself, yet modern res-taurant culture has globally transformed eating habits. Chapter 6 traces the development of dining out—from the public eateries in the Middle Ages, its opulent zenith during the late nineteenth century, and the trend toward communal and institutional cookery of the Soviet period. Particular attention is paid to the wild and ever-fluctuating free-market establishments of the post-Soviet period.

Special occasions during the Soviet period were almost exclusively secular. For almost a century the region officially embraced atheism. As described in chapter 7, it is only with independence in the late twentieth century that people began to openly celebrate religious and ethnic holidays again. The religious diversity of the population is expressed in its ritual foods. Russia has believers from all of the world's great historical religions (with the sole exception of Hinduism)—Christianity, Islam, Judaism, and Buddhism. Central Asia, on the other hand, has endeavored to glorify its nomadic and Islamic culinary traditions.

Diet and health for the entire population of Eurasia dramatically improved in the twentieth century despite, or perhaps thanks to, a Communist system. Even with the Communist system's dreadful reputation for inefficiency and shortages, the basic nutritional standards improved for a greater proportion of inhabitants than in previous centuries. Chapter 8 documents that subsistence diets slightly improved for the majority, contrasted with the precipitous demise of the opulence on privileged tables.

In such a colossal geographic area with so many ethnic groups, it is impossible to touch on every cuisine in the region equally. Therefore, endnotes, a glossary, a resource guide, a timeline, and an extensive bibliography can assist those who want to learn more about the many cultures of the former USSR. Beyond the major English-language works on the subject, the back matter also provides relevant Web sites, films, and organizations to pursue further research.

## CONCEPT OF NATIONAL CUISINE AND IDENTITY

The description of a culture of any group is essentially an attempt to establish an identity. *Culture* and *identity*, however, are among the most contentious words in the English language, with contradictory definitions that range from the mundane to the sublime. *Culture* applied to food typically entails an element of style or judgment, specifically culinary refinement or haute cuisine—the elaborate and sophisticated preparation of a cuisine. In this work, however, *culture* simply means the attitudes and behaviors of a social group. *Culinary culture* here entails a most basic description of everyday cookery, knowledge, and values shared by a particular society, in this case contemporary Russia and Central Asia. In the most basic terms, it includes the products, techniques and tools, and, of course, the cultural context for preparing and consuming meals on a daily basis.

A country's cuisine has become the calling card of its culture, perhaps not as formal as a coat of arms or the flag, but more amenable, accessible, and understandable to outsiders than any national symbol. It is also the source for debatable claims about certain dishes and numerous disagreements if taken at face value. One purpose for describing a national cuisine is to explain the greatness or meagerness of a particular cultural heritage in comparison to another group. Whether it is an outsider commenting on what makes a certain group different from the one to which the writer belongs, or whether a member of a particular group tries to justify the uniqueness of his or her community, it is usually an exercise in cultural supremacy or affirmation.

Though the process began many decades ago in the former USSR, now more than ever, Russia and Central Asian countries are striving to reassert their national identity in a new, unfamiliar global world. The common indices of culture—language, ethnicity, religion, dance, folklore, folk heritage, and certainly cuisine—must be acknowledged and validated. Cultural nationalism is essentially a reaction to the perceived erosion of traditional identities, status, and order disturbed by the modernization process. In culinary terms, food festivals and celebrations, restaurants that serve national cuisine, and cookbooks that codify a national cuisine all play into the process of nation building and national identity construction.

The opinion that it is possible or even appropriate to identify and describe a national cuisine is no more than a residual practice of modern intellectuals and politicians who place undue significance on the nation-state. It is nearly impossible to distinguish a single characteristic common to *all* members of a society who claim to belong to one culture or one nation. The same holds true for food, especially in a global world with regular commercial contact. The availability of foodstuffs is no longer dependent on season, climate, or locale, and is mainly limited only by lines of transportation, demand, and disposable income. The dishes, cuisine, and food habits even within a distinct culture can be far from homogeneous. Yet the romantic notions of a unique folk heritage and national identity linger on. In many ways, it is convenient and reassuring to categorize the world into geographical and political entities imbued with certain cultural characteristics and traits. One food historian points to nineteenth-century English and American tourists in Paris as among the first to assume that, in some inexplicable yet reasonable way, "national character" revealed itself in restaurant dining rooms.[6]

This concept of an authentic national cuisine, which somehow contains the "essence" of a particular nation or culture, has only gained speed and adherents in the past few decades. Publishing houses and the food-service industry are marketing culture and authenticity to a nostalgic audience, who sense that traditional cuisines are being lost in the modern mad dash for mass production, efficiency, and standardization. Cookbooks systematize and prescribe how to make genuine ethnic cuisine. All of these sources deliver heritage on some level within the context of global flows of tourism, media, and advertising. Heritage, tradition, and culture are often taken as something resilient and perpetual. On the other hand, it has been suggested that all of these values are actually new modes of cultural production that give a second life to dying ways of life, economies, and places.[7] In other words, restaurants continuously parade the national cuisine of the moment, while cookbooks transform dishes from the ephemeral to the eternal.

This phenomenon often results in a national cuisine being judged solely by its manifestation in restaurants and cookbooks. While perhaps unjust or merely shortsighted, both instruments are commercial ventures and artificial re-creations. Consumers can read, experiment, and prepare various ethnic recipes in a cookbook. The restaurant in many ways is more powerful and has a more direct impact on the consumer than cookbooks. For cookbooks to be transmitted globally with their adoring portrayal of a national cuisine, they require wistful authors, translators, and a literate, interested audience. With restaurants, however, experiencing the culinary "Other" is much easier. There is no need to seek exotic ingredients, to follow daylong preparations, or to clean up the kitchen afterward. With the possible exception of the waitstaff, there are few language barriers at the table. Simply order from the menu and the illusion of national culinary culture is delivered on a plate. International travelers and visitors carry with them bizarre notions of authenticity, bred and polished in the major metropolitan cultural centers.[8] Having eaten at a Russian or Central Asian restaurant, be it in that country or in another country, they cannot help but depart with a sensation of experiencing the essence of a national cuisine.

Globalization, too, shapes the world's cuisines. In some instances, these pervasive exchanges in the international sphere of culture and economics make cuisine more uniform (processed, frozen food, for example), and in other ways, they create the conditions for discovering, defining, or seeking out ever more exotic foods, recipes, and traditions. Many cultural groups clamor to prove their culinary uniqueness and heritage with representative cookbooks, culinary tourism, and restaurants that purportedly offer a sample taste of their territories.

With regard to food and foodways, it may just be that there are limited ways in which nations and ethnic groups can symbolize their identity. Western conceptions and definitions of cuisine, cookery, and hospitality constrain understanding of those cultures that do not fit the mold. As Western culture predominates worldwide, it is as if the world is reading off the same basic, globalized menu. By increasingly mimicking each other, cultural groups may actually be reducing the possibilities of culinary expression.[9] We expect coffee with dessert, anticipate that a guest will bring a bottle of wine when invited to dinner, and take for granted prompt and attentive service in restaurants. Why should every cuisine be forced into the francophone menu format of hors d'oeuvres, main course, salad, and dessert? Why does a glass-and-brass interior signify upscale dining, whereas fake cultural props in an ethnic restaurant ironically trigger the anticipation of real ethnic cuisine? Why continually seek out novel culinary experiences while being guided mainly by mainstream travel guides and restaurant reviews?

Customary food habits and the designation of what constitutes high cuisine become narrower and narrower. People can observe other culinary cultures only from the standpoint of what is considered "normal" based on their life experiences. Most of the world finds it highly unusual to eat a meal in a car, to throw away leftovers, and to use a microwave oven to prepare an industrially processed frozen meal. The depiction of foodways for Russia and Central Asia should provide a sense of their collective attitude toward food, as well as providing glimpses of their national and ethnic identity. Those instances that seem unusual or distinctive to Americans only underscore the point at which various food cultures part ways. Those differences then allow groups to create symbolic boundaries. Defining Russian or Central Asian cuisine not only prescribes their identity but actually reaffirms the identity of the outsider. The following chapters should provide a sizable mirror for the examination of both U.S. and Eurasian culinary cultures. And the view is enormous, compelling, and delightful.

## NOTES

1. Anya von Bremzen and John Welchman's, *Please to the Table: The Russian Cookbook* (New York: Workman Publishing Company, 1990) and *Russian Cooking*, by Helen and George Papashvily, Foods of the World Series (New York: Time-Life Books, 1969) are two attempts.

2. During the past five years the obscure culinary cultures of the former Soviet Union made their way into the U.S. consciousness through popular culture. Some examples include Food TV's spots in 2004—*Tastes of Russia, From Russia with Love, 30-Minute Passport to Russia, Weak in the Knees,* and *To Russia with Love; Gourmet* magazine's 2000 issue about the Almaty market in Kazakhstan; *Saveur's* 1998 articles "Caviar Dreams" and "Preserving Summer"; *Gastronomica's* "My McDonald's" in 2000, and major newspaper articles such as Susan Glasser's "Russian Evolution Hip Dining in Moscow? We Had Reservations," *Washington Post,* 27 January 2002.

3. Out of the 22,402,200 square kilometers of the USSR, the Russian Federation made up about 77 percent of the total area. Kazakhstan was just over 12 percent, and the other four countries of Central Asia combined added another 6 percent. NationMaster.com, "Map & Graph: Geography: Area," http://www.nationmaster.com/graph-T/geo_are_tot.

4. ITAR-TASS, "Census Shows Shift in National Identity within Russia," *News Wire Service,* 10 November 2003.

5. ITAR-TASS, "Census Explodes Immigration Myths," *News Wire Service,* 10 November 2003.

6. Rebecca Spang, *The Invention of the Restaurant: Paris and Modern Gastronomic Culture* (Cambridge, MA: Harvard University Press, 2000), 2.

7. Eric Hobsbawm, *The Invention of Tradition* (Cambridge: Cambridge University Press, 1992) and Barbara Kirshenblatt-Gimblett, *Destination Culture: Tourism, Museums, and Heritage* (Berkeley: University of California Press, 1998).

8. Arjun Appadurai, "How to Make a National Cuisine: Cookbooks in Contemporary India," *Comparative Studies in Society and History* 30, no. 1 (1998): 19.

9. For a further discussion of how cultures reduce their uniqueness through mimicry, see Simon Harrison, "Cultural Difference as Denied Resemblance: Reconsidering Nationalism and Ethnicity," *Society for the Comparative Study of Society and History* 45, no. 2 (2003): 343–61.

# Timeline

| | |
|---|---|
| 7th century B.C.–3rd century A.D. | Scythians trade grain, livestock, and cheese with the Greek colonies on the Black Sea in exchange for wine, luxury goods, fine ceramics, and jewelry. |
| 5th century B.C. | Towns of Bukhara and Samarqand appear as centers of administration and culture. |
| 2nd century B.C.–15th century A.D. | The Silk Road, a collective description of trade routes connecting east and west, helped disperse culture, ideas, and merchandise from China to Italy and from India to the Baltics, and vice versa. |
| 5th or 6th century A.D. | Slavs begin to arrive in central Europe, displaced by Turkic groups originating on the Asian plateau. |
| 8th–10th centuries | The cultural golden age of Iran, refining an already sophisticated court cuisine made with products from the Mediterranean to China, building on their culinary heritage beginning twenty-five hundred years ago. The major settlements of Central Asia fall under the cultural sway of Iran, which greatly influences their cookery. |
| mid-8th–10th centuries | Byzantine Greek and Scandinavian traders are well established in Russia with extensive trade routes along the Volga River between the Baltic and Caspian Seas and beyond, introducing exotic spices, fruits, and nuts. |

| | |
|---|---|
| 8th–12th centuries | Various Uighur Islamic kingdoms rule most of Central Asia. The Uighur Turkic language is the lingua franca of Central Asia, giving the region a semblance of cultural homogeneity. |
| 8th–15th centuries | Religious conversion of Central Asians to Islam, changing their diet with food prohibitions. |
| 988 | Kievan Rus' Prince Volodimer (St. Vladimir) accepts Christianity. The religious conversion of the Slavs greatly affects their diet with church-mandated fasting and food prohibitions. |
| 13th–14th centuries | Mongol invasion and establishment of empire of Golden Horde, which controlled most of present-day Ukraine, southern Russia, and Central Asia. |
| 1326 | Center of the Russian Orthodox Church is moved from Kiev to Moscow. The Russian Orthodox seat of religious power, or the Metropolitan See, is officially transferred from Vladimir to Moscow two years later. Moscow is now the center of the Eastern Slavic cultural world. |
| 1448 | Russian Orthodox Church breaks with Rome. |
| 15th century | Buckwheat is introduced and becomes mainstay of Russian diet. |
| 1552 | Russians capture Kazan from Tatars and start the trek east to the Pacific Ocean. |
| 1580 | A push to colonize Siberia begins with Russia establishing a string of fortresses along the Eurasian steppe. |
| 16th century | *Domostroi*, a Russian household management manual that also includes recipes and other information about domestic cookery, is written for wealthy Muscovites. |
| 1694–1725 | Peter the Great begins modernization of Russia with Western European technology and ideas. |
| 16th–18th centuries | The Lithuanian-Polish Commonwealth commands significant portions of Slavic territory. |
| 17th century | Tea from China arrives in Russia via Siberian trade routes. |
| | Great Russia annexes much of the lands of its Slavic neighbors, Ukraine (sometimes referred to as "Little" Russia) and Belarus ("White" Russia). |

|  | The beginning of Russianization in the Russian Empire gives cuisine and other cultural elements a common framework within the Russian language. |
|---|---|
| 1762–1796 | Reign of Catherine the Great, who expands Russia south to the Black Sea, bringing slavs into permanent cultural contact with numerous ethnic groups. |
| 18th century | Imperial Russia gains control of northern parts of Central Asia. Russian nobility intermarry with the royal houses of the European continent and adopt fashions from Germany and France. New World foods—potatoes, tomatoes, peppers, and chocolate—slowly begin to spread throughout Russia and Central Asia. |
| mid-18th century | French culture and language dominate in Russian aristocratic circles, including French adjustments to Russian cuisine, giving it world renown and many of its present characteristics. |
| late-18th century | Almost 94 percent of the Russian population lives as serfs. |
| 18th–19th centuries | High aristocratic dishes in Russia and the royal court cuisine of the Central Asian khanates pose a sharp contrast to the meager meals of the serfs, petty traders, agricultural laborers, and nomads. |
| 1847 | Russians successfully grow tea in the semitropical climate of Georgia on the shores of the Black Sea |
| 1861 | Russian serfs are freed, which has enormous agricultural and political implications. Elena Molokhovets writes *Gift to Young Housewives*, a classic guide for household management for the Russian elite, along the lines of *Domostroi*. It contains more than one thousand recipes. |
| 1865–1885 | Decisive Russian battles for southern fringe of Central Asia. By the end of the nineteenth century, Russia firmly controls the region. |
| 1876 | Chinese forces attack Eastern Turkestan to quell Muslim uprisings. After this invasion, tens of thousands of Uighurs, Kazaks, and Dungans fled China into Russian Central Asia. |

19th century

Rice dishes become common in Russia, adopted from the territories of Central Asia and the Caucasus that were absorbed into the empire. The potato overtakes the turnip in Russia as the main vegetable in the diet. Russians begin to commercially produce sunflower oil as this was the only kind of oil the Orthodox Church did not forbid during Lent.

19th–20th centuries

Slavs begin unprecedented migration into Central Asia, with one million peasants alone relocating to the region in the late nineteenth century after the abolition of serfdom. Especially lucrative were the farming areas of northern Kazakstan as well as the Russian military fortresses and parallel European-style settlements which were created alongside major non-Slavic urban areas.

1917

Russian Revolution fundamentally alters the economic and social conditions of the former Russian Empire. Thousands of Turkish peoples and White Russians migrate across Central Asia and Siberia into China or throughout the world.

1920

Civil war continues in Ukraine and Siberia.

1920s

Central Asian republics are given their own distinct ethnic profile, language, and history.

1921

Vladimir Lenin implements the New Economic Policy (NEP)—temporary postponement of Socialist measures to improve agriculture and commerce.

1922

Soviets establish full control over Central Asia, Ukraine, and the Caucasus region.

1928

End of NEP. Joseph Stalin begins enforced collectivization of agriculture. Millions of peasants resist and are killed.

1930

Temporary halt to agricultural collectivization.

1933

Widespread famine, especially in Ukraine, caused by collectivization.

1935

Stalin acknowledges the right to a prosperous life, which includes food: "A distinctive feature of our revolution is that it gave the people not only freedom, but also material goods and an opportunity for a wealthy and civilized life."[1]

| | |
|---|---|
| 1937 | Record harvest in Russia. |
| 1937–1944 | Stalin deports Koreans of the Russian Far East to Central Asia; Turks and Kurds are removed from the Caucasus. By the start of World War II, one million Germans who had farmed the Volga region since the time of Catherine the Great are also sent to Central Asia. Conveniently accused of Nazi collaboration, Crimean Tatars, Meskhetian Turks, Ingush, Chechens, and Kalmyks, among others, follow the familiar road to the no-man's-land of Soviet Central Asia. |
| 1939 | The first Soviet cookbook, *Book of Delicious and Healthy Food,* is published. The recipes and illustrations in the cookbook become symbols of a Communist utopia. |
| 1940 | Baltic nations of Latvia, Estonia, and Lithuania are forcibly incorporated into the USSR. |
| 1949 | Chinese Communists cause the final migration flood of Uighurs, Kazaks, and Dungans to Soviet Central Asia by defeating the Nationalist Chinese government in China. |
| 1954 | Premiere Nikita Khrushchev launches project to plow up the "virgin lands" of Kazakstan and southern Siberia. |
| 1958 | The publication of the first book on Uzbek "national" cuisine, written by Karim Makhmudov, a philosopher, professor, cultural nationalist, and avid cook. |
| 1990 | Opening of first Pizza Hut and McDonald's in Moscow. Hundreds of European, American, and American-style restaurants open during the decade. |
| 1991 | Breakup of Soviet Union into 15 sovereign nations, all practicing variations of a market economy that would dramatically influence their foodways. |
| 1992 | Turkish, Chinese, and Iran products flood the Central Asian markets, including food items. |
| 1998 | Russian economic crash and financial crisis threaten reforms and dampen culinary extravagance. |
| 20th century | Russians encourage commercial production of the potato, beet, and tomato in Central Asia. |

| | |
|---|---|
| 2000 | Foreign food products and ethnic restaurants are commonplace in major metropolitan areas of Russia and Central Asia. |
| 2001 | Russian financial recovery. |
| 2004 | Moscow recognized in Europe as culinary capital of innovation. Russian billionaires are third on the Forbes' World list behind the United States and Germany. |

## NOTE

1. Joseph Stalin, frontispiece to *Book of Delicious and Healthy Food*, by USSR Ministry of Food Industry (Moscow: Pichshepromizdat, 1952), iii.

# 1
# Russia Historical Overview

Until recently, defining cultural phases within a national history often meant forcing the square peg of culture into the round hole of dynastic timelines. History tends to favor a periodization based on major events or the reigns of individual leaders. Rulers, wars, and treaties continue to dominate the historical literature. Russia's past is arranged, accordingly, on the basis of power and control: Kievan Rus', Muscovy, Tsarist imperial Russia, Soviet Communism, and currently the newly independent Russian Federation. Central Asia follows a similar pattern: Persian Empire, Golden Horde, Tamerlane, Turkic Khanates, Russian rule, Soviet regime, and now, five newly independent states. The character of the Russian food system is determined by its society, economy, and geography. As with any region, a cuisine evolves through additions from other cultural groups as well as adaptations and innovations of the dominant culture. A regional cuisine generally develops in proportion to the size and strength of its economy. It is also limited by the yields of its earth and a nation's ability to transport foodstuffs to its people. Viewed within this historical context, it becomes clear that Russian food may very well be the quintessential cuisine of the Eurasian territory. This is based on Russia's ability to freely adopt foodstuffs, cooking methods, and dishes from other cultural groups found within its empire and incorporate them as its own.

## RUSSIAN CULINARY CULTURE

Russian cultural identity is difficult to reconcile considering its tumultuous history and current national borders. In December 1991, 24 million

Russians awoke to find themselves living in foreign nations. The 14 other non-Russian republics of the former USSR had declared themselves independent, and finally, with the annulment of the 1922 union treaty that had established the Soviet Union, a new Russian Federation was born. Russians had been scattered over the empire for several centuries, and the new declarations of independence left over 20 percent of ethnic Russians outside their country. Moreover, Russians are among the 56 officially recognized ethnic groups in China. There are still more than ten thousand Russians in China, living mostly in northern Xinjiang, Inner Mongolia, and Heilongjiang. Tens of thousands more have immigrated to Europe and the United States. How does Russia grapple with the geographic realities that reverted the map of the Russian world back to the seventeenth century? How can Russians now rediscover an identity within the new boundaries of the new Russian Federation?

The Soviet Union, despite its politics of internationalization and fraternal brotherhood, could never publicly reconcile the fact that its borders roughly matched the extent of the Russian Empire. In terms of national identity, some argue that it was only in the eighteenth century that Russian thinkers began to envision themselves as a nation and culture distinct from Europe and China.[1] Later, the fierce debate of the nineteenth century between the *Slavophiles* and the *Westernizers* began to mark the true meaning of Russianness.[2] Slavophiles considered their version of culture to be superior to the West, and their patriotism was defined by the ideological and educational policy of Tsar Nicholas I—"Orthodoxy, Autocracy, and Nationality." This debate is still relevant in Russia, whether the subject involves politics, economics, or culture.

Instead of attempting to identify a single national identity and cuisine, it may be more useful to view Russian haute cuisine and peasant food as two separate and distinct entities. A common source of current identity is to return to the pre-Soviet era. The dynastic appeal is still strong for those who consider the Communist era an aberration and an easy, if not problematic, path to the Russian essence. Is aristocratic haute cuisine of the nineteenth century really representative of an entire nation? In culinary terms—for the Westernizer—French, Dutch, and German influences were the necessary refinement to create the finest food in the world. Still others, in Slavophile fashion, look to the peasantry for the roots of Russianness. Peasant cuisine may be viewed as simple and earthy food, a contrast of the traditional against the modern. From there, it is an effortless step to the use of caviar and cabbage as tropes of Russian culture and cuisine, blotting out the nuances separating high and low, the aristocracy from the peasants.

The recent conversion from a Communist regime to a nascent capitalist market has had tremendous effects on Russian food production and consumption, as well as every other part of the food system. In addition, Russian cuisine and foodways continue to change with the new emerging political and national identities. When President Boris Yeltsin pulled Russia out of the USSR in 1991, the country declared itself a democratic state with a republican form of government.[3] Russian is the state language, although the federal republics may establish their own language for use in addition to Russian. Vladimir Putin was appointed acting president by Yeltsin in 1999, elected in 2000, and reelected in a landslide in 2004. While presidential critics claim that he is leading the country down an authoritarian path, others praise the relative economic and social stability that are necessary for a functional capitalist system. Among Putin's first reforms was to divide Russia into seven new federal megaregions (*okrugs*), further centralizing the power of the Russian state. If Russia can maintain civil order, it has the natural and human resources to become a major world leader again. To reflect the new realities, the government actively promotes a revival of Russian national spirit, one that is clearly manifested in the culinary realm by developing the kind of national pride that leads its citizens to purchase native foodstuffs and to frequent Russian-style restaurants.

## PEOPLE

How do the ideas of nation, ethnicity, and identity affect cuisine and vice versa? Before defining Russian cuisine, there must be agreement on the use of the term *Russian*. This includes the question of *where* Russia is. The next issue is whether it is possible to "become" Russian. "Russia" is an extremely complex concept. Though nationalists like to paint a picture of one thousand years of ethnic and political continuity since the time of Kievan Rus', the reality is much less clear-cut. Politically, Russia is the prodigious remnant of the Russian and Soviet empires, now officially named the Russian Federation. Geographically, it stretches from the Baltic Sea to the Pacific Ocean and spans 11 time zones. It is difficult to truly comprehend the scale of Siberia alone—10 percent of the earth's inhabited land area. Culturally, Russia is larger still, exceeding the limits of imperial boundaries via Russian-language media, established trade patterns from the past centuries, and the presence of its military on the borders of the former USSR.

## Roots of Russian Identity

Russian identity places great emphasis on religion, at times a more powerful self-defining characteristic than language or politics. Today, about 80 percent of the citizens of the Russian Federation consider themselves Orthodox Christian, even though atheism was the official state religion barely a decade ago.[4] Ethnic Russians, not surprisingly, also make up 80 percent of the population.[5] Russia ruled for several centuries as the only independent Orthodox regime with its messianic mission to defend Christianity. Aside from the Soviet era with its own peculiar fanaticism, the issue today is whether it is possible to be a Russian without professing Orthodoxy. Even though it is an adopted faith, from the East no less, Orthodox Christianity has united Russians since the tenth century A.D. It gives them a sense of destiny and provides the distinctive marker that sets them apart from neighboring peoples and cultures. By the late medieval period, several populations were recast into a single distinguishable Russian cultural group. A common liturgical language and the power of the Orthodox Church held the society together in ways that the multiple ruling principalities could not.

The USSR maintained and expanded the Russian national idea through inventive Marxist acrobatics. Russian nationalism has always had multiple and changing forms, but the heart of Russian identity is tied to the sacred and fertile black earth as well as the power of the Russian soul. Today, Russia toils to recapture the essence of both a national character and cuisine. Certain foods are tagged as authentic for the purpose of both identity and marketing. Yet the nature of Russian cuisine is as difficult to describe as the people themselves.

Who then are Russians? It may be argued that Russians are people who merely identify themselves as such, similar to the American attitude that places more emphasis on a shared culture than on an ethnicity. What then is Russian food? Russian food (*pishcha*), in a comparable manner, is any food immediately and inherently familiar to and embraced by Russians as *nasha*, the Russian word for "our," be it spicy Korean carrot salad or Crimean Tatar meat pies (*chebureki*).

## Ethnicity in Russia

Centuries of migration and assimilation with other ethnic groups, so the argument goes, means there is no such thing as a pure Russian.[6] The oft-repeated saying attributed to Napoleon Bonaparte, "Scratch as Russian and find a Tatar," refers to the 350 years of Mongol-Tatar dominance, not to mention a disparaging allusion to Russian barbarism. Ethnicity, in its broader and more accepted use, denotes a society that shares a language and culture. Language is relatively easier to classify and evaluate. Culture, on the other hand, is a more ambiguous abstraction. A single identifiable culture often may overlap contiguous political territories containing multiple ethnic and religious groups, as is the case with Russia. The persistent and futile question arises: Are certain customs or habits—particularly as they relate to food—Soviet, Eastern European, European, oriental, Slavic, northern, or strictly Russian? What about specific foods? When does a non-Russian dish such as *kharcho*, Georgian lamb or beef soup, become "Russian"? This is part of the process of how some dishes make the transition from "customary" non-Russian to "traditional" Russian.

Russians actually have two separate words to describe themselves—*russkiy*, an ethno-linguistic categorization, and *rossiyskiy*, a citizen of Russia. The term *Rhosia*, the Byzantine Greek root for Russia (*Rossiya*), describes the vast and undefined religious territory with the city of Kiev as its cultural capital. The Eastern Orthodox Church in Constantinople assigned Kiev as a *metropolitanate*, the Orthodox equivalent of a diocese.[7] Rossiya and "All the Russias" regained imperial currency after Great Russia annexed the lands of their Slavic brothers, Ukraine ("Little" Russia) and Belarus ("White" Russia) in the seventeenth century. By the end of the nineteenth century, Russia counted 128.2 million citizens, and its territory ballooned to 22.5 million square kilometers, roughly the size of the USSR that was to follow. At that point "ethnic" Russians made up less than half of the population. The empire incorporated people from almost a dozen distinct linguistic families, the four most numerous among them were Indo-European (Slavic, Baltic, Germanic, Greek, Indo-Iranian, Armenian), Altaic (Turkic, Mongolian), Uralic (Finnish, Estonian, Mordvin, Karelian), and Caucasian (Georgian, Chechen, Ingush). For the next two centuries, Russians undertook specific measures to increase the Russian, or at least the Slavic, portion of the total population.

### Slavs

Russian is a Slavic language within the Indo-European family of languages. Slavs share similar cultures and languages, although migrations, intermarriages, and population dislocations over time have transformed Slav identity. Traditionally, linguists divide Slavs into three main geographic groups: East, West, and South. Eastern Slavs include Russians, Ukrainians, and Belarusians; among the Western Slavs are Poles, Czechs, and Slovaks; and Bulgarians, Croats, Macedonians, and Serbs make up the Southern Slavic group. Taken together as a linguistic family, Slavs are the largest group in Europe.

The genesis of Slavic peoples is associated with the Great Migration in the first millennium A.D. Classical historians refer to various tribes that some scholars identify as proto-Slavs.[8] However, there is no firm linguistic, literary, or archaeological data on Slavs before the mid-fifth century A.D., when they are mentioned as a component of Attila's army. Archaeological evidence supports the theory that by the fifth or sixth century A.D. Slavs began to arrive in central Europe, pushed westward by erratic movements of the seemingly endless flow of Turkic groups from the Asian plateau. The mutual cultural influence and assimilation, especially between the Slavic and Turkic peoples, are particularly evident in geographic and family names, loan words, and, of course, cuisine. The early population of Russia also included Balts and Finns, as well as other non-Slavic groups. There existed no Slavic political entity in the modern sense of the word. These groups lived near the great forests and woods that provided food, shelter, and protection. As subsistence farmers, Slavs also relied on hunting, fishing, and the gathering of berries, nuts, and mushrooms to supplement their diet.

### Demographics

Obviously, the greater the number of cultural groups within a country, the more likely that the nation's cuisine will be enriched by the diversity of culinary offerings and traditions. In 1897, the Russian Empire completed its first (also to become its last) full census.[9] In the twilight of the empire, Russians still only made up 43 percent of the total population. Adding Ukrainians, Poles, and Belarusians, however, pushes the Slavic total to almost 72 percent. Turkic peoples supplied another 10–15 percent, and Jews numbered roughly 4 percent. In spite of its obvious deficiencies, the 1897 census remains the most reliable source of ethnic, religious, tribal, and cultural groups of Russia at the end of the nineteenth century. It also richly illustrates how the nation of Russia journeyed from a loose confederation of princes and a predominantly Slavic population in the ninth century to a multiethnic world empire by the nineteenth century. The twentieth century saw Russia shrink back to civil war and chaos, only to rise to world prominence as a revolutionary leader. The century closed with the nation jettisoning its periphery, settling on a Russia composed chiefly of Russian citizens.

To further compound the ambiguities of identity, the first Soviet census in 1926 obliged the respondents to designate their ethnicity, or in Soviet terminology, their "nationality." The result identified almost two hundred distinct ethnicities, with each ethnic group ranging in number from a few hundred to several million members. These ethnic affiliations were based on everything from mother tongue to tribal or religious affiliation. Though citizenship was Soviet, the official ethnic nationality was noted in the internal passport. Through the process of acculturation, many groups also assimilated or accepted ethnic Russian identity out of convenience, coercion, or compliance. In the late nineteenth century, Jews could become ethnic Russians simply through baptism in the Orthodox Church. Non-Slavs commonly married ethnic Russians and raised their children as Russians. Others merely Russified their names. In the case of mixed marriages, children could choose their nationality according to their parents' label. If both parents were Uzbek, the child was automatically designated Uzbek. If, however, the father was Russian and the mother Tatar, the child could choose, at age 16, to "become" Russian or Tatar. Despite this mixed ethnic ancestry, Russians have a deeply held sense of self, based on their culture, religion, and literary language.

### Population Dislocations

There is no denying the atrocities that the Russian and Soviet empires inflicted on their own people. Planned hunger directed against the "wealthy" peasants and collectivization of agricultural farmland were the first state attempts of the Soviets to control or realign the population balance in favor of Russians. Deportations began as early as the 1920s, in particular clearing the non-Slavic populations from Ukraine, southern Russia, and Kazakstan. Untold millions perished through starvation and relocation. Deportations of specific ethnic groups began in 1937 with the Koreans of the Russian Far East, when two hundred thousand were scattered throughout Central Asia. Later that year, Turks and Kurds were systematically removed from the Caucasus. By the start of World War II, millions of Germans who had farmed the Volga region since the time of Catherine the Great were also sent to Central Asia. Immediately after the war, unfairly accused of Nazi collaboration, Crimean Tatars, Meskhetian Turks, Ingush, Chechens, and Kalmyks, among others, followed the familiar road to no-man's-land of

Soviet Central Asia. As in the case of Crimea and other regions that had a governmental territory based on non-Slavic ethnicity, deported groups lost their political autonomy and new administrative units were created.[10]

To further complicate the turnover, Soviet republics were flooded with Slavic refugees and migrant workers after World War II. The upsurge in the Slavic populations dramatically affected the cuisine nationwide, since the dominant culinary culture was Russian, all part and parcel of the Russification policy. Despite concerted efforts to increase the Slavic population throughout the USSR, Turkic groups actually experienced an almost threefold increase in population during the 30-year span from 1959 to 1989. The Soviet era instead witnessed an unexpected change in ethnic composition resulting in a net loss in the Slavic population. Not surprisingly, Turkic culinary preferences spilled over into the produce markets of the USSR.

Similar to the upsurge recorded in the numbers of ethnic groups of the early Soviet census, the 2002 census counted 160 nationalities, an increase of 24 more groups compared with the census just three years earlier.[11] Compare that with an average of only nine nationalities each currently in countries of Europe. As mentioned, roughly 80 percent of the 145.3 million total citizens of the Russian Federation are Russians. Kazan Tatars are the second most numerous ethnic group with almost 6 million constituents. Other ethnic groups in Russia that top 1 million people include Ukrainians, Bashkirs, Chuvash, Chechens, and Armenians.[12] Another 23 ethnic groups have a population over 400,000 including Mordovians, Belarusians, Kazaks, Udmurts, Germans, and Ossetians.[13] This demographic diversity allows Russians to claim most any dish as their own, such as pilaf, dumplings (*pelmeni*), eggplant caviar, or Baltic herring—much like pizza, Swedish meatballs, or salsa in American cuisine.

### Culinary Influences of the Periphery

There are innumerable specific cultures that significantly affected the foodways of Russia and Central Asia. Ukraine and the Baltic region served as a conduit for ideas and cultural influence from Europe, specifically from Scandinavia, Germany, and Eastern Europe. Ottoman Turkish and Iranian control over the Caucasus Mountains also had repercussions in Russia. These areas were buffer regions, borderlands, and areas of cultural exchange and experimentation. Over time, the empire gradually incorporated the far-flung territories into the Russian and Soviet food system, which covered all phases—from production to distribution to consumption. Furthermore, the dispersals of Ukrainians, Caucasians, Balts, Tatars, and Koreans throughout the Russian and Soviet empires have made their cuisines familiar and accepted by all.

Operating as restaurants, however, only Georgian and Central Asian establishments have had notable commercial success in Russia. Yet Koreans and Crimean Tatars have permeated the markets and street food of Russia, respectively. No discussion of Russian or Central Asian foodways would be complete without acknowledging the influence and contributions of these groups.

### Ukrainians

Although Ukraine was one of the 51 charter member-nations of the United Nations in 1945, the country marks its independence with the demise of the USSR in 1991. Although Kievan Rus' is generally regarded as the motherland of the first Slavic state in the ninth century A.D., Ukraine has usually been defined from a Russian perspective and, therefore, marginalized. Its very name, *Ukraina,* means "near the edge," "fringe," or "border" (U = near, *krai* = edge) of Russia. Ukrainian culture was on the verge of extinction within the Russian Empire and the Soviet Union as a result of the state policy promoting Russian language and culture. The pendulum has swung in the opposite direction since independence, with Russian language banned in national advertising, and all things Ukrainian encouraged and celebrated. The cultural pervasiveness of its larger neighbor, however, remains considerable, with the reality of Russian-language media, economic interests, and family ties shared by Russia and Ukraine. Ukrainian cuisine as a distinct entity is usually traced from the mid-eighteenth century through the beginning of the nineteenth century, coinciding with cultural and political movements in Ukraine. Naturally, there was also a close affinity with Polish and Belarusian cuisine, given the two hundred years where much of Ukraine existed within the Polish-Lithuanian Commonwealth (1569–1795).[14]

Ukrainian food, however, has never bowed to Russian cuisine, and some of the best so-called Russian dishes can rightfully be claimed as being Ukrainian. In fact, because of the climate, longer growing season, and its fertile soils, the country produces a wider variety of agricultural products than Russia. This forms the basis for a rich and distinct culinary culture. Those foods that have been co-opted into Soviet or Russian cuisine, such as borscht or cabbage rolls (*holubtsy*), will forever have a shared heritage.[15] With almost 11 million Ukrainians living in Russia and another 14 million in the Newly Independent States (NIS),[16] their cultural influence in the region is undeniable. And the fact that Russia and Ukraine, off and on, have been part of the same "country" for almost a millennium makes it all the more difficult to extricate dishes from the Russian table and prove that they were on the Ukrainian table all along. But these are concerns for the cultural nationalist. Wherever the Ukrainians have shared their pantry and culinary ingenuity, their neighbors are undoubtedly grateful.

### Georgians

Under Communism, Georgia was considered one of the wealthiest and most privileged of the republics, and many Russians treated its Black Sea coast as their Riviera. At the beginning of the nineteenth century, 83 percent of the population consisted of Georgians and Abkhazians, a percentage that decreased to 63 percent by 1939, mainly due to Soviet Russification and collectivization. There were also no shortages of Georgians in Russia. From 1959 to 1988, almost two hundred thousand Georgians immigrated to other Soviet republics.[17] Georgian restaurants were prevalent in Russia throughout the twentieth century, no doubt assisted by the fact that Stalin (birth name of Iosif Vissarionovich Dzhugashvili) was a Georgian and particularly fond of his native food and drink. Certainly many of Stalin's minions necessarily emulated his taste in red wine—the semisweet Khvanchkara and the fruity Kindzmarauli have both been attributed as his preferred drink. The famous Georgian restaurant Aragvi on Tverskaya Street—Moscow's ritziest thoroughfare leading to the Kremlin—not surprisingly opened its doors in the 1930s during Stalin's reign. Other cafés followed suit, and Georgian cuisine became exceedingly familiar to Russians. In the major cities of today's Russia, there are many Georgian restaurants, and Russian restaurants often carry Georgian dishes on their menus. The fresh, flavorful, and exotic foods from the Caucasus remain a Russian passion.

### Volga Tatars

The Volga, or Kazan, Tatars have food products and a climate similar to Russia (obviously, since they are located in the same country), but their dishes are closer to those of Central Asia. Mutton is the meat of choice, and horse meat is made into sausage (*kazylyk*). At first glance, soups (*ashlar*), baked and fried savory pastries, fermented dairy products, pilaf, and tea are the symbolic foods representative of the Volga Tatars—almost identical to the main foods of Central Asia.

In terms of culture, language, and politics, the Volga Tatar influence on Russia was immense. The Golden Horde controlled Muscovy from the thirteenth to the sixteenth century. In the fifteenth century, the Golden Horde split into the Khanates of Siberia, Kazan, Astrakhan, and Crimea. The first three were incorporated into the new state of Russia in the sixteenth century under Ivan the Terrible. The Crimean Khanate aligned itself with the Ottoman Empire and continued in power until the Russian occupation of the peninsula in 1783.

Volga Tatars were largely farmers and herders from the ninth to the fifteenth century, although they gained a reputation as traders due to their location between Europe and Asia. By the fourteenth century, they had converted to Sunnite Islam. Four centuries later, Catherine the Great granted Kazan merchants special privileges in Central Asia.[18] Kazan Tatars, in many cases, acted as Russian front men for the eventual conquest of Kazakstan and Central Asia. Their work in Central Asia, however, was far from insidious. Central Asia did not have a single publishing house, even at the beginning of the twentieth century. Books, written in Tatar using Arabic script, were published in the printing houses of Kazan and Orenburg and distributed throughout Central Asia. The influence of two centuries of the Tatar written and spoken word on the daily language of food cannot be overestimated.[19] Working mainly as translators, merchants, craftsmen, religious educators, and teachers, Kazan Tatars attained a position of eminence in Central Asia, only to be replaced by the conquering Russians in the nineteenth century. Exemplifying the Russian condescension toward Turkic peoples in the country, Soviet census reports in Central Asia after World War II counted Crimean Tatars and Kazan Tatars as one and the same people, although they are two distinctly different Turkic groups.

### Crimean Tatars

Crimean Tatars have lived on the Black Sea peninsula of Crimea at least since the thirteenth century. They are descendants of the settled Turkic groups in and around Crimea—Khazars, Pechenegs, and Kipchacks—with significant genetic influence from the Golden Horde. Some estimates put the Crimean Tatar population at more than 5 million during the height of the Khanate rule, decreasing to fewer than 300,000 by the time of the Bolshevik Revolution in 1917. On May 9, 1944, Stalin unjustly accused the remaining Crimean Tatars of being Nazi collaborators and deported them to Central Asia, forever changing their identity and the politics of Crimea. In the early 1990s, many Crimean Tatars decided to resettle in Crimea after nearly five decades of exile, despite considerable economic and political obstacles. Approximately a quarter of a million Crimean Tatars have returned to their homeland, which officially became a part of the Ukrainian Soviet Socialist Republic in 1954, thanks to Khrushchev, himself a Ukrainian. However, they remain a minority on the peninsula, making up only about 12 percent of the population. Another 5 million Crimean Tatars live in Turkey and approximately 25,000 in Romania after fleeing their land during the two centuries of Russian domination of Crimea.

Crimean Tatar culinary influence has at least four layers. First, when Russia claimed this territory and the Russian royal family and aristocracy made the Crimean coast their costal resort in the nineteenth century, they had several tales to share about their experiences with the exotic Orient. Many travelers' accounts of Crimea make reference to the savagery of the locals, as well as a few, mostly unfavorable, references to the indigenous food.[20] Second, the Crimean diasporas of the eighteenth through the twentieth centuries spread their cooking methods to Turkey, the Balkans, Central Asia, and beyond. Third, while in exile in Central Asia, Crimean Tatars adopted many Uzbek dishes that are now promoted in Crimea as Crimean Tatar national cuisine. Uzbek *samsa*, *laghman*, and pilaf are sold in most Tatar roadside cafés. Finally, Crimean kiosks or cafeterias are found throughout major cities in Russia, selling chebureki and other "Eastern" cuisine. For a small cultural group with such a heavy history, the cuisine of the Crimean Tatars has traveled widely and adapted well considering its unusual circumstances.

### Koreans

For any foreigner who has spent time in the former Soviet Union and explored the produce markets there, the discovery of Korean-style food has to be among the greatest of culinary thrills and surprises. It is surprising, first, because Koreans do not immediately come to mind when thinking about Russia and Central Asia; second, it is thrilling because the spicy flavors of Korean food are decidedly different from the local fare. Korean salad vendors may be found in almost any vegetable market of a medium-sized city of the NIS and Moscow supermarkets. The most well known dish is peppered julienned carrots, available in many Russian and Central Asian restaurants and even in the United States. Many other Korean salads are made from pickled or fermented vegetables and fish. Some of the most common dishes are made with eggplant, mushrooms, string beans, kidney beans, beets, squash, seaweed, and fish. Traditional *kimchi*, made with Chinese cabbage, garlic, and red pepper, which is the national dish

Korean salad at market.

of North and South Korea, is rarely found, however, beyond the Russian Far East. The cabbage salads for sale in most of the NIS are usually much more subdued than their spicy counterparts on the Korean peninsula.

There are an estimated 2.5 million ethnic Koreans in China, Japan, and the NIS. The current count of "Soviet Koreans" is almost a half million, with approximately ninety thousand in Uzbekistan alone.[21] Nearly 70 percent of Koreans in the NIS live in Central Asia and refer to themselves as *koryo saram*. Koreans first began migrating north of the Korean border to the Russian Empire in 1860 in search of better farming land and quality of life. A second migration wave came during 1910–1945, to escape the Japanese occupation of Korea. Stalin began his massive population deportations in 1937 by dispersing throughout the USSR two hundred thousand Koreans whom he labeled as spies living in the Russian Far East. Most were sent to Central Asia, where they worked primarily on state collective farms. Not all Koreans in Russia today, however, are there because of Stalin's deportations. Thirty-five thousand Koreans and their descendants remain on Sakhalin Island, where they were initially resettled as forced Japanese laborers during World War II. Russia took the island as war compensation from Japan in 1945. Another heterogeneous and more recent group of Koreans in Russia is made up of North Korean citizens who are a mixture of guest workers, former students, and illegal immigrants, living mostly in the Russian Far East and in major urban areas.

After the death of Stalin, Koreans began to move more freely in the USSR and began to sell their culinary delights on a greater scale. Given their agricultural prowess in northern climes, Koreans ventured to sell their excess produce in the local markets. Milder derivations of their prepared traditional side dishes (*banchan*) were also sold. For Russians and Central Asians alike, the unusual combinations of sesame oil, soy sauce, salt, garlic, ginger, and, most importantly, *gochujang*, fiery red-pepper paste, were accepted with pleasure. Korean carrot salad is almost unknown outside the former Soviet Union, even though Russians believe it to be the prototypical Korean dish.[22] Korean cuisine is genuinely appreciated and widely popular in Russia and Central Asia. While Korean restaurants are still few and far between, many supermarkets and even small shops carry commercially produced and packaged Korean salads. Even gas-station quick marts sell prepackaged Korean salad spice mixes.

## ECONOMY

Russia is a study in contrasts. The country is third on *Forbes'* world list for the total number of billionaires, yet 75th in gross domestic product per capita, a few slots behind Trinidad and Tobago.[23] If one accepts the premise that human development and progress proceed roughly on an upward linear path, Russia defies all economic and sociological theory. The European cultural renaissance from the fourteenth through the middle of the seventeenth century as well as the Industrial Revolution of the eighteenth and nineteenth centuries mostly bypassed Russia. Many argue that Russia remained a medieval, feudal society until 1917. The Soviet period was marked by decades of violence, chaos, and decay. The country lost millions of citizens to wars and purges, and the West openly undermined Soviet economic development and foreign relations. Still the USSR industrialized, defeated the Nazis, put men in space, and created a massive modern military. The centrally planned economy laid transportation and communication lines, housed the majority of its citizens, and reluctantly brought a society into the modern era, all without the aid of computers, the Internet, and reliable telephony. Russia is again faced with starting over and catching up with a global economy. The infrastructure is crumbling or obsolete. Its people have experienced neither a democracy nor a market economy, and the country lacks the institutions necessary to support them. Russia lost half of its economic potential with the faltering of the USSR. Still the country retains tremendous assets in its natural resources and educated workforce. Russia possesses deposits of oil, natural gas, coal, and strategic minerals, as well as prodigious forestland for timber. It boasts a 99 percent literacy rate, not to mention highly skilled scientists and engineers. Given Russia's past record of accomplishment in the face of overwhelming obstacles, it is not a far-fetched bet that the country will adapt, refine, and thrive in a globalized world.

Approximately three-fourths of all Russian citizens live in cities, and the remaining one-quarter lives in rural areas. According to the latest figures, the process of urbanization has essentially stopped.[24] One-fifth of the nation lives in the 13 cities of Russia with a population of 1 million or more. Most city dwellers live in two- or three-room apartments, often in enormous, squalid complexes that encircle the urban center. Freedom of relocation is still limited by an archaic registration system of residential permission. Many urbanites have a countryside cottage (dacha) with a small garden plot, emulating their rural cousins while supplementing their nutrition and budget.

Agriculture is the major economic activity outside the urban areas. Under the Communists, village life revolved around collective or state farms. Farm laborers were among the least paid and least respected members of society. Students and young pioneers regularly assisted the farmers at harvest time. Soviet agricultural bureaucrats and managers were generally lured from the administrative centers to maintain ideological stringency. Rural lifestyles in Russia have changed little over the centuries. Small villages and households, the basis of the tsarist economic system, were destroyed by collectivization. A centrally planned economy directed collectivization, which began alienating people from their work and environment, separated them from nature, and made them dependent on centrally apportioned supplies. Given that the economy is an inextricable part of culture, these actions have precipitated the decay of the national culture.

Rural life is harsh, austere, yet uncomplicated. Houses are generally constructed of wood and contain a larger living area than city apartments. The rural family, a source of pride and wealth for the peasant society, is decaying. Young people move to the city for education and seldom return. With no Communist social-net guarantees, villages are simply dying. The few villages close enough to major urban areas may be temporarily bolstered by the arrival of New Russians, who purchase and renovate homes for use as dachas. They may also hire the locals for construction, the harvest, and security. But these situations are too rare to sustain the countryside for the long term. The 2002 census estimates that more than half of Russia's villages have been virtually abandoned by death and migration over the past two decades.[25]

## Bifurcated Social Structure

Social stratification is the single most important factor in understanding Russian society throughout its history. The clearly divided social structure—the extremely wealthy or privileged on the one hand, and the serfs or working poor on the other—defines imperial Russia, Communist Russia, and contemporary Russia. It is not a great exaggeration to claim that the peasant diet remained essentially the same for the past several hundred years. Only the royalty, aristocracy, and wealthy merchants enjoyed abundance and refinement in their cuisine until the 1917 revolution.

Nineteenth-century Russia reached its zenith as a European power. Starting in the eighteenth century, Russian nobility intermarried with the royal houses of the continent and adopted fashions from Germany and France. The aristocracy made up only a miniscule percentage of the entire population, yet today imperial style and culture are still considered by many to contain the Russian essence. In 1796, almost 94 percent of the population lived as serfs in bondage, though by 1859, four years before emancipation, the numbers had decreased to only three-quarters of the nation.[26] The classical Russian literature of Pushkin, Chekhov, Goncharov, and Tolstoy contains numerous references to food, frequently portrayed in the framework of the Slavophile-Westernizer debate. The general plot often pits a Westernized protagonist against a provincial Russian antagonist.[27]

Already by the seventeenth century, French culture and language dominated in aristocratic circles of Europe. This affliction became particularly acute for the Russian patricians in the mid-eighteenth century. The Russian bourgeois class, like the rest of the elite of Europe, looked to France as a model not only for its political and military power but also for its self-assured national consciousness. The French possessed a "potent and richly developed symbolism of national identity."[28] The more French cultural trappings a nobleman acquired, the easier it was to distinguish himself from the minor nobility and, of course, local peasantry. The great Russian houses entertained in lavish style, importing French, German, and Swiss chefs as early as the eighteenth century. European chefs working for noble houses in Russia adapted French cuisine to indigenous ingredients. In the early nineteenth century, even Tsar Alexander I enjoyed the services of Marie-Antoine Carême, dubbed "King of Chefs, and the Chef of Kings." Carême, founder and architect of French haute cuisine, also served as chef to Talleyrand, George IV of England, and Baron James de Rothschild. As the Europeans applied the codified French cuisine model to their indigenous cookery, they ultimately reduced the variety of their own culinary expression, differentiating themselves from the French in only superficial and constrained ways. Menus adopted the standardized French menu and cookbook order of appetizers, soup, main entrée, and dessert. Banquets and meals were expected to adhere to an accepted format of presentation, service, and style. While the French chefs used Russian ingredients, they also flattened the richness and diversity of the indigenous cuisine by forcing the cuisine into the rigid classical cooking system. This is generally referred to as the process of French refinement.

Observance of the Marxist economic doctrine led to a fundamental break with Western consumerism and consumption. Food was frequently scarce, with the country sporadically plunging into famine and hunger from the years just prior to the revolution in 1917 until well into the 1950s. During that dreadful period, it is estimated that more than 33 million people perished as a result of World War I, revolution, civil war, epidemics, famines, purges, and World War II. With the deaths of Lenin and Stalin, the fear of repressions somewhat subsided. The conflict-weary party hacks dropped their ardent guard and increasingly indulged in gustatory pleasures. While the masses were busy building Communism, the Soviet Party elite established perquisites and privileges. Most survived in cramped communal living quarters while spending untold hours in line to buy food and other basic goods. The corrupted party system of patronage, or *nomenklatura*, evolved to the point of essentially creating a secret, parallel economy. The elite had their own schools, shops, restaurants, banquet halls, dachas, health resorts, and hospitals. They were even allowed to travel abroad. The powerful enjoyed brandy and fine chocolate while the rest of the country filled up on bread and low-grade Georgian tea. The nomenklatura swiftly adopted the lifestyle of the vilified prerevolutionary rich and powerful, all the while maintaining appearances of equality and progress.

### The New Elite

With the breakup of the USSR in the early 1990s, the nomenklatura in many instances used their power and influence to acquire state-owned industries or property at minimal cost. A new class of billionaire oligarchs—especially from industries of petroleum, natural gas, and metal deposits—replaced the Communist elites. As Western advisers were urging the immediate privatization of state sectors, the Russians accommodated by turning state monopolies into private ones. A former prime minister under Yeltsin in the 1990s, Viktor Chernomyrdin, for example, simply privatized the natural-gas industry he earlier oversaw as a bureaucrat. Again, the reptilian elite molted into the nouveau riche. This group, dubbed the New Russians, also includes powerbrokers in business, finance, entertainment, and services, as well as the Mafiosi. The social and economic dysfunction that followed the demise of the USSR resulted in widespread poverty, corruption, and capital flight.

Without ideological or ethical constraints, the goal of the super wealthy quickly became conspicuous consumption in swank restaurants, perpetual nightclubs, and outrageous casinos. Turkey, Spain, and other European tourist destinations responded to the flood of well-heeled Russian travelers by printing menus in Russian, hiring Russian-speaking waitstaff, and, of course, serving Russian cuisine. Cyprus, above all, has lured wealthy Russians on a more permanent basis, thanks to minimal tax rates, balmy shorelines, and, most importantly, no visa requirements. Every year, more than 150,000 Russian tourists visit the island. Russians also are now the second-largest group of visitors to Turkey, after Germans. Russians experience Western-style service, atmosphere, and taste abroad then return home as more demanding consumers, creating competition for ever-so-phisticated restaurants, cafés, pubs, and nightlife. One Moscow restaurant, aptly called Snob's, offers an eclectic menu made from produce flown in daily from France. Dinners start above $100 per person; this, of course, does not include a collector's bottle of vodka, for $400, or a brut champagne, for $600. Just another night out on the town.

Estimates for the number of New Russians fall somewhere between 5 and 10 percent of the adult population, with a great majority below the age of 40.[29] The middle class, which occupies the economic position above poverty but below the New Russians, varies from 20 to 30 percent of the population. For the food industry, catering to this group offers true growth potential. For restaurants, it means quick service, a family-friendly atmosphere, or new locations in the suburbs. Food stores fill the gap by providing low-cost quality Russian products or imports from the near abroad.

Although more foodstuffs and eating-out options are available, they are still beyond the means of the typical worker. Russians, on average, spend more than one-third of their budget on food, much higher than in Britain or the United States.[30] Seventy percent of citizens in Russia live near or below the poverty line. According to most polls, Russians across the board believe that the main problems of the country are poverty and a low standard of living. The cruel and stark contrast between the availability of food and the few who can actually afford it is the most distasteful aspect of the new "capitalistic" Russia. Sectors such as agriculture, education, culture, science, and health care generally consist of the lowest wage earners in Russia, not too surprising since many of these sectors are still state owned. Whether examining the Russian masses of today, or the serfs and peasants from a couple of centuries ago, the story line varies little. A very small few at the top continue to hold sway over the cultural, political, and economic life of the country and have the means to enjoy its full bounty.

## GEOGRAPHY AND AGRICULTURE

Russia's agricultural promise is clearly constrained by geography and climate. Because of its sheer size, the country endures a continental climate: it experiences temperature extremes in summer and winter, and low precipitation, generally during the summer. Therefore, it is joked, the country experiences only two seasons—winter and July. More than half of Russia's territory lies above 60 degrees north latitude, which is roughly where Anchorage, Alaska, falls. Permanently frozen subsoil is common in many regions that experience six months of snow cover per year. Winter has an enormous impact on almost every aspect of life in Russia. It affects mood, diet, and work. Weather controls settlement patterns, industry development, and crop types. Great quantities of food have traditionally been smoked, pickled, or otherwise preserved to survive the winter season. Given regular physical activity in low temperatures, caloric intake must increase in the winter to produce enough heat to keep the body warm. Therefore, Russian cuisine is renowned for adding rich butter, sour cream, or nonlean meats. It also justifies hot tea and cold shots of vodka. Despite the myths of vodka's many magical properties, alcohol actually causes blood vessels to dilate, causing a loss of body heat, even though it may produce the illusion of, among other things, warmth.

A little over 7 percent of the country's total land area is arable, with around 60 percent of that area dedicated to cropland; the remainder is left for pasturage.[31] Agriculture engages about 10–15 percent of the workforce. No part of the country has a year-round growing season. The most fertile agricultural region is found in the south, between Ukraine and Kazakstan. This is the area referred to as *chernozem*, literally "black earth." The southernmost part of Russia is situated along the same latitude as Chicago with similar-length growing seasons.

### Private Agricultural Plots

While the remnants of the Soviet collective farms, now called joint stock companies, still control most of the land for agriculture (up to 90%), individual private plots produce a staggering percentage of the total output. Individual plots include rural household plots, private farms, and dacha plots. This little-studied phenomenon goes far in explaining how a

Individual plot at dacha.

country can survive when more than two-thirds of its population subsists near the poverty line. It also explains the freshness and full flavor of the produce that hits the market daily. In the early 1990s, Soviet (*sovkhoz*) and collective (*kolkhoz*) farms accounted for three-quarters of the total agricultural product. By 2003, more than half of the nation's produce was supplied by private farms.[32]

In 2002, Russian citizens produced 53.8 percent of the nation's produce. Specifically, private plots accounted for 93 percent of potatoes, 82 percent of vegetables, and 89 percent of fruits and berries. Furthermore, private farmers produced 12 percent of the country's grain, 20 percent of the sunflowers, and 7 percent of sugar beets. In other sectors, the private citizen farmer produced 55 percent of the livestock and poultry and 50 percent of the milk.[33] No developed country in the world comes close to such active participation in feeding itself. People are able to supplement their meager incomes by selling the produce at market. The priceless benefit of such close ties to the land, however, is that Russians are able to provide flavorful and wholesome food for their families.

### Crops

About half of the total Russian farmland is devoted to grain production. Joint stock companies account for the bulk of the production since grains are machine-intensive crops. Wheat dominates in the grain-producing areas. Winter wheat thrives in southern Russia, while spring wheat predominates in the region that stretches from northern Ukraine, along the

Kazakstan border, to Lake Baikal in Siberia. Khrushchev's Virgin Lands Campaign, a dream to grow corn in the vast steppe areas of Kazakstan and southern Siberia, achieved little success. Corn grows only in southern Russia and is mainly used as livestock feed. Russia is the world leader in both production and consumption of rye, oats, and barley. Barley is primarily used for beer and livestock feed.

Potatoes are widely grown in the northern regions. Though associated with vodka production, vodka began as a rye-based liquor. As the potato became more common, it was easier and less expensive to distill than grains. Today almost all brands of Russian vodka are distilled from rye, wheat, barley, and, most commonly, corn. Any Russian will say that grain-based vodkas are by far superior to potato vodkas, which are made mainly in Poland. Cucumbers, tomatoes, cabbage, and carrots are the most common vegetable harvest. Sugar beets thrive in the fertile soils of European Russia. Flax, sunflowers, and soybeans produce the components of vegetable oil. Livestock is a sizable component of Russia's agricultural sector. Although the country ranks fifth worldwide in meat production, it generates 10 times less than China and 7 times less than the United States.[34] Cattle, pigs, sheep, and chickens are the main animal protein.

## HISTORY

### Early Peoples (to the Tenth Century A.D.)

People have inhabited parts of present-day Russia from the earliest period of human development. Scythians occupied the steppes of Russia and Ukraine and as far east as the Altai Mountains from the seventh century B.C. to the third century A.D.. They have received significant archaeological attention, thanks to their elaborate burial mounds, replete with splendid golden ornaments and other artifacts. Scythians engaged in the slave trade with the Greek colonies on the Black Sea, but eventually they grew grain and exported wheat, livestock, and cheese. The Greeks sold them wine, and the Scythians traded wheat flour and yeast to the Slavs, or at least to their ancestors. The Scythians drank their wine without adding water, which appalled the Greeks, who noted that, "to get drunk is to behave like a Scythian."

From the first to the eighth century A.D., migrating tribes passed through, conquered, and settled parts of Russia and Ukraine. Slavic material culture clearly arises by the seventh century A.D. in central Russia, including remains of earthen fortifications of their settlements. Scandinavian traders became well established in Russia by the mid-eighth century with extensive trade routes along the Volga River between the Baltic and Caspian Seas and beyond. They also founded of the first Slavic political entity, Kievan Rus'. Slavs were sedentary agriculturists, but they later engaged in trade on great north-south river routes with Persian and Byzantine merchants.

Speaking generally, the diet of the inhabitants of the central European plain included grains, milk products, nuts, and berries. Written sources from the pre-Mongol invasion period list only cabbage and turnips as definitive Russian vegetables. Porridge (kasha) provided the staple food of the poor, using coarse millet, barley, and oats. Kasha is infinitely flexible—served sweet or savory, a meal unto itself, or as a side dish. Rye grew as the principal grain, but wheat, suitable for cultivation mainly in the southern regions, was still a luxury item. Kvas was the drink of choice. A fermented beverage made from rye or barley and similar to beer, kvas was easy to make, refreshing, and safer than pond or well water since the water used in making the drink was often boiled in the production process. Eggs and dairy products were commonly accessible. In leaner times, Russians ate a dish called ty-urya, consisting of stale breadcrumbs mixed with water or kvas, sometimes jazzed up with garlic or hemp oil.[35] Mushrooms, wild plants, and game from the dense woodlands supplemented daily sustenance. For seasonings, dill and poppy seeds are also part of the historical record. Famine and disease persistently menaced the population, as was the case elsewhere in medieval Europe. Russians still equate hospitality with abundance. Extremes are part of the Russian character and an alternating culinary pattern of deprivation in lean times and overeating during feasts developed.

Because wood was plentiful (and winter was long), Russians designed a stove that not only kept the house warm but led to the creation of the basics of Russian cuisine.[36] The stove could sustain varying cooking temperatures based on the placement of the food inside the oven. The dry heat produced crusty and sustaining breads, soups and stews in their characteristic earthenware containers, and numerous dishes suited to long, low-heat cooking methods. One dish served was "baked milk"—left in the oven all day until it acquired a brown crust. Perfected over generations, the Russian stove burns wood extremely efficiently and requires fueling only a couple of times during the day. The intense heat of the fire is absorbed by the thick brick walls, which radiate heat all day long. Russia is justifiably famous for the amazing variety and flavor of its breads. On special occasions, breads such as bobalki, a Byzantine-inspired pastry made with honey and poppy seeds and still popular in Eastern European Slavic cookery, were made. The stove served as a slow-bake oven; a dryer of berries, herbs, and mushrooms; and an accelerator in the fermentation of doughs and kvas. The stove also doubled as a clothes dryer and heated bed. Sleeping lofts were constructed adjacent to or above the stove, creating a cozy platform for children, the elderly, and the infirm.

The preservation of food, mainly through pickling and drying, was a year-round preoccupation. Slavs used brine to pickle cabbage, cucumbers, and other vegetables. Over time, the flavor of smoke and brine imparted to foods came to be valued as a characteristic of Russian cuisine. Salt throughout world history has been an extremely valuable commodity. One of the earliest industries on Russian territory was salt production, dating back to the second millennium B.C.[37] The coastal areas of the Black and Azov Seas produced most of the salt in the Middle Ages. Some Russian cities, Solvychegodsk, for example, incorporated the word *salt*, or "*sol*'" in Russian, into their names.[38] This city is renowned as the original source of wealth for the influential Stroganov family, of beef-dish fame, who established a salt extraction and distribution industry there in the sixteenth century.

### Kievan Rus' (Ninth to Fifteenth Century)

Ukraine, Belarus, and Russia all trace their hallowed political and cultural roots to Kievan Rus'. Russia's state origins spring from the Nordic leader Rurik, who established a dynasty in the northern Russia town of Novgorod in the mid-ninth century A.D. Oleg, his successor, moved the capital to Kiev. Prince Volodimer (St. Vladimir) is credited with the conversion of the Slavs to Christianity in 988, according to the *Primary Chronicles*, a twelfth-century history of Kievan Rus'. Adopting the Orthodox faith had profound effects on the national diet due to the prodigious amount of holy or fasting days in the Christian calendar. Kievan Russia dissolved into petty principalities in the eleventh century and was overrun (1237–40) by Batu Khan, grandson of Genghis Khan. The Mongols established the empire of the Golden Horde and controlled the southern lands from 1240 to 1480. There was surprisingly little Mongol culinary influence in relation to the duration of overlordship because of the lack of direct contact between Novgorod and the Mongols. The center of Slavic power shifted to the north regions of Novgorod and Muscovy, and the Rurik line of princes continued to rule Russia until 1598.

The diet of the lower class has remained exceedingly simple and remarkably constant over the centuries. The main cooking methods were boiling and baking. Peasant cuisine was generally filling, though greatly impacted by the dietary restrictions of the Orthodox Church doctrine.

Although wine was allowed, there were almost two hundred fasting days a year. Even wealthy peasants maintained a predominantly vegetarian diet common to the average peasant. Food was the chief item of expenditure, and the poor prided themselves on adhering to the austere peasant life-style in the manner of the Christian monks.[39] This entailed a life of privation and fasting, wasting no trifle on oneself, and living off the land and tilling it with their own hands. Family meals were communally served on wooden plates or bowls. Ceramic vessels were common, even as bottles and pitchers. Metal dishes—usually copper, sometimes cast-iron—were also widely used but were not as common as wooden or ceramic ones. Glass was rare until recent times. Even in affluent homes, while they may have additional ceramic dishes and metal goblets, people still shared a common dish. Barrels and baskets were used for storage of dry goods, and liquids were kept in ceramic containers. For cooking pots, the main materials were ceramics and metal, particularly iron.

Most of the peasant and serf population lived in the countryside in muddy villages strewn across the steppe and plain. Most of the food was derived from small farm plots, the woods, and nearby waterways. Peasants lived in relatively squalid conditions, but their simple hearty cooking is still a source of inspiration for Russian cooking today. Garden plots were part of every household and wild greens were close at hand. Buckwheat from Asia became firmly established by the fifteenth century and is now one of the foods most commonly associated with Russia. The list of recorded vegetables is more modest and includes the inevitable: cabbage, onions, garlic, and turnips. Early seventeenth-century travel journals describe garlic and onions as especially prevalent, on the Russian breath as well as in the cuisine.[40] Turnips, an important and abundant staple, have been thoroughly replaced in the Russian diet by potatoes. Cucumbers, carrots, beets, pumpkins, and string beans round out the most common vegetables.[41] Fruit, fresh and dried, was found in the form of cherries, apples, plums, pears, raspberries, currants, raisins, and prunes. Other southern fruits came up from the Byzantine areas around the Black Sea. Berries were preserved with honey for use in the winter. Fungi were also preserved, dried on a string. Hemp seed and flax-seed were used, from early times, both directly and as a source of oil.[42] Some of the main early seasonings were cinnamon, nuts, mint, anise, and black pepper.[43]

Peasants customarily ate meat on Sundays for the main weekly meal, but meat was never consumed on a daily basis. The meat of domesticated animals was a luxury item, taking 5–10 times more energy than was necessary to produce cereals alone. The high price of meat, coupled with the fact that peasants could not hunt on private land, limited meat consumption. The primary restriction of meat eating, however, was the church, banning its consumption on Wednesdays and Fridays, as well as Lent and dozens of other religious holidays. This prohibition also included animal byproducts—butter, milk, eggs, and cheese. The main meats included beef, pork, mutton, goat, chicken, duck, and goose.[44] Game meat ranged from the flesh of bison, elk, stag, and boar to the fowl of pheasant, partridge, and quail. The eating of horse meat, a custom most likely adopted from Turkic tribes, was not uncommon as inferred in the *Primary Chronicles*, but its low price may indicate a relatively small demand for it.[45] This dish, however, did not remain with the Russians into the modern era.

Fresh fish from the teaming inland lakes and mighty rivers offered a crucial protein alternative. Fish was salted, smoked, and dried for preservation. A sixteenth-century source mentions about three dozen common species of fish in Russia. A dried, powdered fish for stock, smoked salmon, and caviar are all mentioned in early sources.[46] *Ukha* is a universal fish soup, made by simmering a whole fish in seasoned broth. When food was in short supply, all parts of the fish were eaten, including the softened bones. In more prosperous times the solid ingredients were strained out to make a clear broth. Sometimes low-quality fish with many troublesome bones were used to make a broth; then they were removed and better fish were added to poach for a few minutes before the soup was served. Russians believe that ukha is best when made from several kinds of fish. Smoked, dried, and pickled herring and mackerel from the Baltic Sea became increasingly popular with greater trade from the north.

Drinking has a long history in Russian culture. The early alcoholic drinks included mead, kvas, *kumiss* (fermented mare's milk), and barley beer. Hops (*khmel'*) were used to flavor beer from the eleventh century onward. Hops grew wild in northern Russia and from the thirteenth century onward, they were a regular item of trade in Novgorod and Pskov.[47] Honey was used as a sweetener, a food preservative, and also in the preparation of mead. Mead was very common and in such supply that it was even exported; it was found in several varieties such as sweet, dry, and peppered.[48] Wine was imported from Byzantium and Europe. Even at such an early date, Russian hosts exhorted guests to eat heartily and drink repeated toasts. Prince Volodimer, as the tale goes, received religious delegations imploring his majesty to accept the faith of Muslim Bolgars, Catholic Germans, Jewish Khazars, and Orthodox Greeks. He was neither overjoyed with the prospects of circumcision nor willing to abstain from pork as proscribed by Jewish and Islamic tradition. But Islamic prohibitions from wine broke the deal. "Drinking," he said, "is the joy of Rus'. We cannot exist without that pleasure."[49] Practicing what he preached, Volodimer dedicated the majestic Cathedral of St. Sophia with three hundred kettles of mead for the celebrants.[50]

The Hanseatic League, a coastal trade monopoly throughout Northern Europe and the Baltics beginning in the twelfth century, established a trading post as far east as Novgorod. Scandinavians and Byzantine Greeks brought trade across Russia in the tenth century on to the Abbasid Caliphate in Baghdad, introducing exotic spices, fruits, and nuts. Walnuts to this day are still called *gretskie orekhi,* or "Greek nuts." Almonds, olive oil, dried figs, and preserved lemons poured in from Central Asia and the Middle East.[51] Lemon rinds were a snack in the early seventeenth century.[52] Russia mainly exported fur pelts, wax, honey, slaves, and some finished products such as linen cloth and jewelry. The Mongol appanage period, from the thirteenth to the fifteenth century, disrupted the commercial routes and exchanges. Novgorod, however, was never under direct Mongol rule. Therefore, the commercial relations between this region and its Western partners continued throughout the Mongol period.

### Imperial Russia (Fifteenth to Twentieth Century)

In 1480, the grand duke of Moscow, Ivan III (the Great, First Sovereign for all Russia; ruled 1462–1505) ceased paying tribute to the Tatars and went on the offensive. Ivan IV (the Terrible, 1547–1584) claimed the title "Tsar of All the Russias" and soon thereafter defeated and incorporated the territory of the Kazan and Astrakhan Tatars into Muscovy. The single most recognizable iconographic symbol of Russia—St. Basil's Cathedral on Red Square in Moscow—was built on the order of Tsar Ivan to commemorate the seizure of Kazan. As Slavs migrated into these new areas, the Turkic cultural influence increased dramatically. One reason the Mongols introduced so few culinary changes, however, was the distance that separated them from northern Russia. The Mongols were mainly located on the southern steppes for pasturage and extracted their tribute. Though Mongol and Turkic administrative and financial words entered the Russian language, the basic foodways for Slavs continued uninterrupted.

Asian influence is a constant throughout Russian history. Tea must be considered the ultimate Eastern culinary contribution to Russia, given its importance in the daily routine. The earliest written record notes the drinking of tea by Russian tsars in the seventeenth century, a gift from a

Chinese ruler. In 1667, Russia sent its first trade caravan to Beijing.[53] In addition to the endless nomadic intruders from the east and the settled Turkic groups on the periphery, the oriental inspiration of the Byzantine Greeks was the preeminent conduit of ideas and culture for the ancient Rus'. Spices and seasonings in the cuisine of the wealthy were varied in medieval Russian cooking with some of the main products imported from Byzantium and the East. Already from the ninth through the thirteenth centuries, professional cooks were hired by the monasteries and nobility.[54]

The *Domostroi,* a Russian household management manual written in sixteenth century Muscovy, provides a hint of which spices may have been found in the affluent households. Saffron, garlic, hops, cloves, nutmeg, ginger, hemp seed, lemons, horseradish, and mace are all mentioned.[55] The *Domostroi* is a priceless historical account of the social world of the nobility and wealthy during the time of Ivan the Terrible. The amount of imported spices increased throughout the sixteenth and seventeenth centuries. In 1667, the tsar presented 381 pounds of spices to the Polish embassy in Moscow, including loaf sugar, cinnamon, saffron (18 pounds), nutmeg, cloves, cardamom, ginger, pepper, anise, and caraway.[56] From these seasonings, only dill, pepper, garlic, horseradish, poppy seeds, cloves, and cinnamon are commonly utilized in Russian cookery today. Many early travel accounts of Russian cuisine remarked on its blandness. Part of this may be explained by the tremendous cost of spices at the time, yet seasonings were also separately served for the guests to add at their discretion and to their taste.

European influence, too, was nothing new in Russia. Scandinavians appeared as early as the ninth century; the Hanseatic League promoted trade via the Baltic region; the Lithuanian-Polish Commonwealth commanded significant portions of Slavic territory from the sixteenth to the eighteenth century; and English merchants established a formal trading organization in the city of Arkhangelsk on the White Sea and in Moscow by the mid-sixteenth century. In time, it became an English overland trade route from the White Sea in the north of Russia all the way to Asia and lasted until 1917. In 1555, the same year Ivan was subduing the Kazan and Astrakhan territories, a Moscow company was set up in London and lasted for over three hundred years. Dutch merchants, too, docked their trade ships in the White Sea.

With the ascendancy to the throne of Mikhail I in 1613, the Romanov dynasty began. The Romanovs ruled Russia until 1917 with the abdiction of Nicholas II. During these three centuries, increased contact and conflict with Europe and Asia dramatically altered eating habits. Peter the

Great implemented a well-known program of Westernization and moved the capital from Moscow to St. Petersburg in the early eighteenth century. He also expanded autocratic tendencies and further entrenched the institution of serfdom.

Francophilia, or an infatuation with France, swept across Europe in the seventeenth century, offering the noble houses a refined culture to emulate. During this time, thousands of Europeans flooded into Russia, though the country was still taken by a "cult of all things English" among the upper classes.[57] French cultural influences overtook English mannerisms by the mid-eighteenth century and persisted well into the nineteenth century. Russia became a great European and Asian power during the reign of Catherine the Great (1762–96), stretching its borders in the west and south. The French under Napoleon I captured a deserted Moscow in 1812, though Alexander I marched the Russian army triumphantly into Paris two years later. After Bonaparte abdicated, the tsar's affection for France returned and he personally intervened to limit European demands for vengeance. The serfs were freed in 1861 (two years before Lincoln's Emancipation Proclamation went into effect), which had enormous agricultural and eventually political implications. Even after emancipation, land was sold to communes rather than individuals, maintaining a centuries-old communal system of agriculture. Meanwhile, Russia's expansion continued

Tsar's golden tableware, Moscow. Library of Congress, Prints and Photographs Division (reproduction number LC-USZ62-117003).

into the Caucasus, Central Asia, and the Far East. Wars, civil conflict, and revolutions ravaged the country from 1904 to 1922, when the Soviet Union was finally consolidated under the Bolsheviks.

The increased contact with the West during the imperial period had significant cultural consequences. By the eighteenth century, Russia was becoming a major player among the royal houses of Europe, and trade brought new foodstuffs and cooking techniques. New World foods—potatoes, tomatoes, peppers, and chocolate—slowly began to spread throughout the region. Foreigners flooded in, trade increased, and the nobility refined their culinary customs, accelerating the gastronomic evolution that forms the basis for what is considered haute Russian cuisine today. This food, however, was available only to a tiny percentage of the population. Only aristocrats and wealthy merchants could afford the luxuries of imported delicacies, bountiful tables, and sophisticated service.

Three hundred years after the *Domostroi* handbook appeared, Elena Molokhovets wrote a comparable classic guide for household management for the Russian elite. First published in 1861, this manual for Russian homemakers offers an accurate glimpse of household conditions and domestic social history with instructions on kitchen arrangement; management of servants; and food acquisition, storage, and preservation, along with over one thousand recipes. Molokhovets' *Gift to Young Housewives*, with its references to domestic help and a wide range of luxury foodstuffs, became irrelevant in the Soviet period, and it was not until 1991 that it was republished in Russian for an audience receptive to recovering an obscured past.

### Soviet Union (1917–91)

While the USSR dominated the politics and history of the twentieth century, in retrospect that episode may prove to be but a noxious blip in the one thousand years of Russian history. In the name of Marxist Socialism, an entire society was turned inside out. The revolution did not eliminate poverty, nor did it provide universal gastronomic bounty to the peasants and workers. In fact, for a number of years the situation deteriorated. The civil upheaval, repressions, deportations, genocide, war, occupation, and ethnic and social experiments in the USSR were horrific. Given this backdrop, the concern was not for fancy foods or refined dining, but rather for the "bread and peace" that Lenin had originally promised in 1917.[58] The Soviet Union was not only trying to reform an entire economic and social system, it was simultaneously pursuing industrialization, urbanization, and modernization. The state both owned and controlled industry and agriculture. Private property was abolished

Soviet propaganda poster, "Down with kitchen slavery," 1931.

and land was divided into state and collective farms. Fortunately under Khrushchev, small, life-sustaining garden plots were again encouraged. Nevertheless, the changes in eating habits during the Soviet era will have lasting repercussions on the culinary heritage and attitudes.

Religious practices that influenced diet were curbed and traditional cookbooks abolished. Special dishes prepared on holidays fell from practice. Twentieth-century Soviet Russia is associated with breadlines, shortages, famines, and even starvation. After decades of deprivation and hardship, the Communists emphasized the improvement of the national diet through public canteens and institutions.[59] Dining as a leisure activity was practically nonexistent until 1935, when Stalin acknowledged the right to a prosperous life.[60] Fine food was associated with the oppressors of the previous regime. In 1939, the first Soviet cookbook, *Book of Delicious and Healthy Food*, was the state's initial foray into the construction of Soviet culinary culture. Stalin's frontispiece in the four-hundred-page volume outlines the linkage between Communist modernity and prosperity. "A distinctive feature of our revolution is that it gave the people not only freedom, but also material goods and an opportunity for a wealthy and civilized life."[61] The recipes in the lavishly illustrated cookbook became symbols of a Communist utopia, well beyond the reach of the ordinary citizenry. After World War II, more public restaurants slowly appeared but did not proliferate until the 1970s with an influx of foreign visitors. In drab, cavernous halls, a notorious lack of service was the single constant among Soviet restaurants. After all, dining out was strictly for special occasions or exceptional people—weddings and birthday parties, Communist dignitaries, and tourists.

While Soviet cuisine was struggling to gain a modicum of respect, three phenomena of the twentieth century heightened Russian culinary awareness worldwide. First, thousands of Russian émigrés settled in France, England, China, New York, and California after the revolution, bringing with them an aristocratic culinary heritage and memory. Second, the modern restaurant and hospitality industry, with emphasis on consumption and thematic concepts, came to full bloom. Third, in the 1970s Brighton Beach in Brooklyn, New York, attracted thousands of Soviet Jewish immigrants. Its restaurants and nightclubs are still a draw for gourmands, melancholy Russian speakers, and Eastern European Jews. The global perception of Russian cuisine was abbreviated and degraded to little more than black bread, ice-cold vodka, and caviar.

### Contemporary Russia (1986–Present)

The post-Soviet era may be considered to begin with Soviet premier Mikhail Gorbachev and his reform policies of *perestroika* (rebuilding) and *glasnost'* (openness) in 1986. Obviously, the most significant event was the breakup of the USSR in 1991 into 15 new countries. Yeltsin led Russia through the turbulent but surprisingly peaceful 1990s. Some doubt that true democracy will ever take root in the region. Economically and socially, Russia has stabilized since independence. This era also witnessed the greatest culinary change for the region in several centuries. In a little over a decade, tons of forgotten and exotic foodstuffs poured into Russia; new restaurants appeared like autumn mushrooms; and many Russians had, for the first time in generations, an opportunity to travel abroad and experience other culinary cultures. Events, however, are changing with such speed that it is impossible to describe the current situation, much less predict the future trends.

Moscow has become the Las Vegas of the East—full of glitz, bluster, and illusion. Will the whole country follow the same path, or will Moscow just be Moscow—the magnificent devil-may-care city of the ages? In 2004 the latest tourism initiative bandied about is the creation of a Russian Heritage Highway Foundation from Moscow to St. Petersburg.[62] Sites along this route would include birthplaces, academies, residences, principal performance venues, and final resting places of cultural icons such as Tchaikovsky, Dostoevsky, Rachmaninov, Pushkin, Chekhov, Rimsky-Korsakov, Stravinsky, Tolstoy, and many other luminaries of international stature. It is not hard to imagine the theme-park atmosphere and attendant hotels and dining facilities that could bury the very cultural heritage the Russians are trying to protect and exhibit.

Yet somehow the genius of the country rises up to meet its greatest challenges at the last moment. Russia now enters into globalization as an active participant, not as an imitator. Russians will borrow, improvise, and create something uniquely Russian to fit their needs and circumstances. Over the next couple of decades, the "new" Russian cuisine will evolve and come into full form. This will be a period of trial and error—of mixing, matching, and inventing past culinary traditions. These efforts are an attempt to re-create an authentic Russian cuisine, one Russians long to enjoy and are proud to share with the outside world.

## NOTES

1. Robert Williams, *Russia Imagined: Art, Culture, and National Identity, 1840–1995* (New York: Peter Lang Publishing, 1997).

2. For further discussion of Russian identity, see David Laitin, *Identity in Formation: The Russian-Speaking Populations in the Near Abroad* (Ithaca, NY: Cornell University Press, 1998), 301; Catriona Kelly and David Shepherd, eds., *Constructing Russian Culture in the Age of Revolution, 1881–1940* (New York: Oxford University Press, 1998); and Robert L. Belknap, *Russianness: Studies on a Nation's Identity: In Honor of Rufus Wellington Mathewson, 1918–1978* (Ann Arbor, MI: Ardis, 1990), 62.

3. The Russian Federation includes the following autonomous republics: Adygeya, Altai, Bashkortostan, Buryatia, Chakasya, Chechnya, Chuvasia, Dagestan, Ingushetya, Kabardino-Balkarya, Kalmykia, Karacha-Cherkesia, Karelia, Komi, Mari El, Mordovia, North-Ossetia, Sakha (Yakutia), Tatarstan, Tuva, and Udmurtia. Chechnya and Tatarstan have yet to sign the federation treaty.

4. Rosbalt News Agency, "About 80% Russians Say They are Orthodox Christians," *News Wire Service*, 25 January 2004.

5. Rosbalt News Agency, "First Results of 2002 Census Published," *News Wire Service*, 29 October 2003.

6. From a strictly biological perspective, indeed, there are no pure ethnic groups anywhere in the world. Most people now reject the pseudoscience of physiognomy and generally rebuke the notion that certain physical human characteristics such as hair, skin color, and the shape of the eyes or nose predetermine individual temperament and societal culture.

7. An Eastern Orthodox metropolitanate is an ecclesiastical jurisdiction under the direction of a metropolitan bishop where his cathedral is located.

8. Veneds are mentioned by Tacitus, Ptolemy, and Pliny, among others. Some authors are convinced that these were early Slavs, while others make them Turks or Balts.

9. Tsentral'niyi statisticheskii komitet [Central Statistical Committee], *Pervaia vseobshchaia perepis naseleniia Rossiiskoi imperii, 1897 g* [Statistical Summaries of the First Complete Census of the Population of the Russian Empire, 1897] (Washington, DC: Library of Congress, 1977), microfilm. The first Russian census (household and tax) was conducted in 1710.

10. By the time of Stalin's death in 1956, the total number of deportees constituted 2.7 million people, including 1.2 million Germans, 316,000 Chechens, 84,000 Ingush, 165,000 Crimean Tatars, 100,000 Lithuanians, 81,000 Kalmyks, 63,000 Karachai, 52,000 Greeks, 50,000 Meskhetian Turks, 45,000 Moldavians, 40,000 Letts, and 20,000 Estonians. These figures do not include those imprisoned or executed, or those who died of hunger or disease. Other sources indicate that 3.5 million people were forcefully removed from their homelands between 1936 and 1956.

11. ITAR-TASS, "Census Shows Shift in National Identity within Russia," *News Wire Service,* 10 November 2003.

12. Bashkirs are Turkic peoples living in the southern part of the Ural Mountains and in adjacent plains. Bulgar-Turkic Chuvash live in the Volga-Kama region, about 600 kilometers due east from Moscow. Ossetians are a people of mixed Iranian origin who reside in the northern Caucasus Mountains.

13. Mordovians and Udmurts are Finno-Ugric–speaking peoples living in the Volga-Kama region.

14. V. V. Pokhlebkin, *Bol'shaya entsiklopediya kulinarnogo iskusstva. Vse retsepty V.V. Pokhlebkina* [Great Encyclopedia of Culinary Arts. All the Recipes of V. V. Pokhlebkin] (Moscow: Tsentrpoligraf, 2003), 340.

15. Chicken Kiev is intentionally excluded as a Ukrainian dish since its origins are still disputed. Also called *kotleta* or *tsiplyonok po-Kievski,* it is a dish made from a breaded chicken breast enclosing herbed butter. Indeed, it is now found on Ukrainian restaurant menus. It is almost never prepared at home in Ukraine or Russia. Some claim that it was first introduced by Nicholas Appert, the same Frenchman who perfected canning in the nineteenth century. The story continues that it was sold under the name chicken Kiev in New York City in the early twentieth century to appeal to the Russians there—an unlikely scenario, since the émigrés of that era had little disposable income for restaurant cuisine. Another theory put forth by Russian culinary historian V. V. Pokhlebkin is that it was invented in Moscow in 1912 for a private merchants' club at the European Hotel. Somehow, in 1947 the dish resurfaced for a group of Ukrainian diplomats and eventually spread to all restaurants through the Soviet travel agency Intourist. "Vkusnye rasskazy Vil'yama Pokhlebkina: Strelyayushchie kotlety," [The Delicious Stories of Vil'yama Pokhlebkin: Exploding Cutlets] *Ogonek* no. 17, 28 April 1997, 27.

16. Ukraine Industrial, "Population of Ukraine," http://www.ukrindustrial. com/en/ukraine/people.php.

17. Allrefer Reference, "Georgians," http://reference.allrefer.com/country-guide-study-/soviet-union/soviet-union103.html and Joshua Project, "Peoples Listing: Georgian," http://www.joshuaproject.net/peoples.php.

18. Elizabeth E. Bacon, *Central Asians under Russian Rule: A Study in Cultural Change* (Ithaca, NY: Cornell University Press, 1980), 25.

19. The Tatar lexical similarities of food terms among other Turkic-speaking peoples are analyzed in a detailed linguistic work published shortly after the demise of the Soviet Union. T. Kh. Khayrutdinova, *Nazvaniya Pishchi v Tatarskom Yazyke* [Food Terms in the Tatar Language] (Kazan: Yakuba of the Ministry of Information and Printing of the Republic of Tatarstan, 1993).

20. Among the many authors who wrote about their travels in Crimea are Gilbert Romme (1786), P. Pallas (1790–1801), O. M. von Engelhardt & Johann Parrot (1815), R. Lill (1825), Robert Lyall (1825), Xavier Hommaire De Hell (1847), Florence Nightingale (1854–1856), Clive Phillips-Wolley (1854–1918), and J. Buchan Telfer (1876). K. Kugelgen (1772–1832) made numerous paintings of the Crimean landscapes during his travel in 1803–1806. In 1897, Y. Ivanov wrote a book comparing the Crimean resorts with those in the Riviera (Italy).

21. NationMaster, "Koreans," http://www.nationmaster.com/encyclopedia/Korean.

22. Andrei Lankov, "Korea's Other National Dish," *Korea Times* 16 August 2004.

23. Russia trails only the United States and Germany for total number of billionaires, edging out Japan in 2004. See Paul Klebnikov, "Rising Tide," *Forbes*, 15 March 2004, 91. Trinidad and Tobago have a per capita gross domestic product of $10,025.27 per person, Russia $9,749.09 per person. NationMaster, "Economy: Top 100 GDP (per capita)," http://www.nationmaster.com/graph-T/eco_gdp_cap.

24. Rosbalt, "First Results."

25. Eve Conant, "Ghosts of the Heartland," *Newsweek*, 14 July 2003, 43.

26. James W. Mavor, *An Economic History of Russia* (London: Jm Dent & Sons, 1914), 418.

27. Belknap, *Russianness*, 60.

28. Simon Harrison, "Cultural Difference as Denied Resemblance: Reconsidering Nationalism and Ethnicity," *Society for the Comparative Study of Society and History* 45, no. 2 (2003): 350.

29. VCIOM—The All-Russian Public Opinion Research Center, "Novy obshchestvenny zapros srednego Klassa," [New Public Demand of the Middle Class] http://www.wciom.ru.

30. The Economic Research Service of the U.S. Department of Agriculture estimates that Russia's family food budget is 34.35 percent, the United Kingdom 16.37 percent, while the United States spends only 9.73 percent of its budget on food. "International Food Consumption Patterns," http://www.ers.usda.gov/Data/InternationalFoodDemand/.

31. Arable and permanent cropland: 1,268,200 square kilometers; Area (land): 16,995,800 square kilometers. NationMaster, "Russia: Geography," http://www.nationmaster.com/country/rs/Geography.

32. *Vremya MN*, "Russian Official Outlines Plans for First Farms Census in 80 Years," 10 June 2003.

33. *Vremya MN*, "Russian Official Outlines Plans."

34. Nationmaster, "Agriculture: Top 100 Meat Production," http://www.nationmaster.com/graph-T/agr_mea_pro.

35. D.K. Zelenin, *Vostochnoslavyanskaya etnografiya* [Ethnography of the Eastern Slavs] (Moscow: Eastern Literature, 1991).

36. For an excellent review of culinary and symbolic merits of the Russian stove, see the article by Snejana Tempest, "Stovelore in Russian Folklife," in *Food in Russian History and Culture*, ed. Musya Glants and Joyce Toomre (Bloomington: Indiana University Press, 1997).

37. Eugene V. Logunov, "A History of Salt Production in Russia," *Science Tribune* (January 1997), http://www.tribunes.com/tribune/sel/logu.htm.

38. M.N. Tikhomirov, *Drevnerusskie goroda* [Cities of Ancient Rus'], 2d ed. (Moscow: Politicheskaia literatura, 1956). Other examples are Sol'-Iletsk, Soligalich, Sol' Velikaia, Soligorski, Solikamsk, Usolye, and Usolye-Sibirskoye.

39. Sergius Stepniak, *The Russian Peasantry, Their Agrarian Condition, Social Life, and Religion* (London: George Routledge, 1905), 236.

40. R.E.F. Smith and David Christian, *Bread and Salt: A Social and Economic History of Food and Drink in Russia* (Cambridge: Cambridge University Press, 1984), 9.

41. George Vernadsky, *A History of Russia* (New Haven, CT: Yale University Press, 1969), 109.

42. Smith and Christian, *Bread and Salt*, 7, 21.

43. N.N. Voronin, *Istoriya kul'tury drevnei rusi* [Cultural History of the Ancient Rus'] (Moscow: USSR Academy of Sciences Press, 1948), 268.

44. Samuel Hazard Cross and Olgerd P. Sherbowitz-Wetzor, trans. and eds., *The Russian Primary Chronicle: The Laurentian Text*, no. 60 (Cambridge, MA: Medieval Academy of America, 1953), 214–15.

45. For a compelling analysis of culinary terms in Kievan Rus', see the article by Horace Lunt, "Food in the Rus' Primary Chronicle," in *Food in Russian History and Culture*, ed. Musya Glants and Joyce Toomre (Bloomington: Indiana University Press, 1997).

46. Vernadsky, *A History of Russia*, 307; Smith and Christian, *Bread and Salt*, 10.

47. Smith and Christian, *Bread and Salt*, 75–78.

48. Vernadsky, *A History of Russia*, 308.

49. Smith and Christian, *Bread and Salt*, 97.

50. Cross and Sherbowitz-Wetzor, *The Russian Primary Chronicle*, 121.

51. M.W. Thompson, *Novgorod the Great* (New York: Evelyn, Adams and MacKay, 1967), 22; Vernadsky, *A History of Russia*, 307.

52. Smith and Christian, *Bread and Salt*, 9.

53. James H. Billington, *The Icon and the Axe: An Interpretative History of Russian Culture* (New York: Vintage Books, 1970), 148.

54. Voronin, *Istoriya kul'tury drevnei rusi*, 269.

55. Carolyn Johnston Pouncy, ed. and trans., *The Domostroi: Rules for Russian Households in the Time of Ivan the Terrible* (Ithaca, NY: Cornell University Press, 1994).

56. Smith and Christian, *Bread and Salt*, 120.

57. Anthony Glenn Cross, *Anglo-Russica: Aspects of Cultural Relations between Great Britain and Russia in the Eighteenth and Early Nineteenth Centuries* (Oxford: Berg, 1993), 95.

58. Vladimir Illyich Lenin, *Collected Works*, vol. 26 (Moscow: Progress Publishers, 1972), 386–87.

59. Enlightening and highly recommended historical accounts of communal dining (Borrero) and Soviet culinary arts (Rothstein) are found in Glants and Toomre, *Food in Russian History and Culture*.

60. Kelly and Shepherd, *Constructing Russian Culture*, 293.

61. Joseph Stalin, frontispiece to *Book of Delicious and Healthy Food*, by USSR Ministry of Food Industry (Moscow: Pichshepromizdat, 1952), iii.

62. PRNewswire, "The United States and Russia Join Hands—The Largest Tourism Initiative the World Has Ever Seen," *News Wire Report*, 30 March 2004.

# 2
# Central Asia Historical Overview

The newly independent states of Uzbekistan, Turkmenistan, Tajikistan, Kazakstan, and Kyrgyzstan cover a territory about twice the size of Western Europe. They are situated east of the Caspian Sea, west of China, south of Russia, and north of Afghanistan and Iran. Central Asia is generally regarded as a vast, imprecise zone, simultaneously connecting and dividing the continents of Europe and Asia. For centuries, "barbarian" nomads menaced the sedentary civilizations[1] on their periphery, both in myth and in fact. This region is more easily defined as a cultural area than a unified territory with indelible geographic or political boundaries. For the purposes of this book, Central Asia includes the five Soviet successor states as well as the Xinjiang Autonomous Region in northwest China. Depending on context, Turkey, Azerbaijan, southern Siberia, Mongolia, Iran, Afghanistan, Pakistan, northern India, and even Tibet are sometimes lumped into the Central Asian cultural domain.

In the minds of many, Central Asia merely comprises the residual Eurasian territory—the murky middle—not claimed by Europe, the Middle East, India, and China. Some of the defining characteristics of Central Asia are its Islamic heritage, ethnic diversity, disparate geography, colonial experience, and deliberate national attempts to forge or recover its ethnic identity. Turkic and Iranian peoples are the dominant cultural groups of the region. Over time, outside contact gradually modified the indigenous cultures in their lifestyle, language, dress, beliefs, and aesthetics. As an element of culture, food, even if it does not last long on the plate, certainly does display regional influences. For Central Asian non-nomadic (sedentary) society, the vibrant culture of Iran was the primary creative inspiration, with later Arabic and Chinese contributions. Most recently, 150 years of Russian control in the Soviet area and 50 years of intensive Chinese subjugation of Xinjiang have considerably altered the foodways. The varied Central Asian cuisine also forms the foundation of cookery in modern-day Turkey, which is fond of claiming rank alongside France and China as the world's top three finest national cuisines.

The geography of the region did not favor the formation of mighty states in Central Asia. Instead, the mountain, steppe, and desert divided people into two lifestyles—scattered settlements in river valleys and along oases on the one hand, and nomadic pastoralists on the other. The swath of territory along the Silk Road—the network of exchange routes linking Asia and Europe—forms the heart of Central Asia, more specifically Uzbekistan, with its fabled cities of Samarqand and Bukhara. Transoxiana was the name of this portion of Central Asia, roughly corresponding to modern-day Uzbekistan and southwest Kazakstan. It is the dry, yet fertile region between the Amu Darya (Greek "Oxus") and Syr Darya (Greek "Jaxartes") Rivers. After the Arab conquest of this area, it became known as Mā-warā-'n-nahr, or "the Land beyond the River." Merchants, ambassadors, and pilgrims plied the routes in search of profit, alliance, and salvation. Man's eternal quest for the exotic was partially sated by the foodstuffs, spices, medicinal herbs, aromatics, precious metals, textiles, and jewels that flowed east and west. Chinese silk, the most valued of these long-distance luxuries, first reached Rome at the time of Christ. The Silk Road remained a viable trade highway until the age of exploration in the fifteenth century A.D., when sea routes made overland options less profitable.

## COMMONALITIES OF CENTRAL ASIAN CUISINE

Food studies in Central Asia traverse geographical and cultural boundaries, follow the diffusion of foodstuffs, and examine the influences and contributions of Chinese, Iranian, Arabic, Indian, Mongol, Ottoman, and Russian cultures, as well as the culinary impact of nomadic and sedentary civilizations. Central Asian cuisine is as elusive as identifying the boundaries of the area itself. From Xian (the starting point for the Silk Road in China) to Istanbul on the threshold of Europe, the variety of dishes gradually diverges from one region to the next. Yet, the similarities are more striking than the differences. Hospitality—symbolized in the *dastarkhan*

*Dastarkhan* on floor, Bukhara, Uzbekistan.

(Turkic word for "tablecloth," or "great spread")—is foremost among the common culinary cultural traits. More like a bountiful holiday table setting, *dastarkhan* refers to the prolific assortment of prepared dishes laid out for an honored guest. Uzbeks say "*mehmon otanda ulug*" (the guest is greater than the father) and they take it quite literally. The guest is given the best and the most, sometimes even to the detriment of the host's financial well-being.

The region as a cultural crossroads enhanced the richness and assortment of the cuisine and vice versa. Numerous groups and cultures borrowed from and contributed to the dastarkhan. During Soviet times, migrations of Tatars, Koreans, Uighurs, Dungans, Slavs, and Germans to the region added further cultural impact. The result is a plentiful combination of dishes, customs, and presentation styles where one can scarcely disentangle the contributions of the rulers and the ruled. The ancient Eastern hospitality, the ritual of the dastarkhan, flatbread, lamb, and cumin unite this area and its immense collection of traditions and produce, as well as set Central Asian cuisine apart from Chinese, Indian, and European fare.

## PEOPLE

Central Eurasia has been home to countless ethnic groups and kingdoms throughout the ages. While the new nations of Central Asia attempt to draw ethnic and cultural distinctions between themselves and their close neighbors, the region is a fascinating mix of Mongol, Turkic, and Iranian ancestry. As the Turkic tribes that predominantly made up the conquering Mongol armies settled and migrated southward, the result was the formation of a society composed more or less of Mongol stock with a Turkicization of speech and Iranization of culture. Today, Central Asia is home to almost 80 million people. Turkic ethnic groups dominate post-Soviet Central Asian demographics, accounting for almost 65 percent of the population. Tajiks of Iranian extraction, Russians, and others make up the remaining ethnic groups. In Chinese Turkestan, also called Xinjiang, Muslims (a mix of Turks, Hui Chinese, and Tajiks) make up about 60 percent of the population.[2]

Of all the Central Asian political units, Uzbekistan remains among the most distinctive in dress, language, culture, traditions, and customs. This contributes to a well-defined concept of identity in the post-Soviet world, due in part to the enormous Uzbek population and centuries of sedentary life. The Turkmen, Kazak, and Kyrgyz nomads were forcibly settled and collectivized by the Soviets—their culture, in essence, confined to unfamiliar apartment walls. Tajiks struggle with disarray and instability after years of civil war in the 1990s. The Uighurs of China also possess a long and noble history of civilization, but their numbers and culture are rapidly dissolving in the face of state-sponsored immigration of Han Chinese to the region. Uzbeks, as heirs to the Silk Road civilizations and the beneficiaries of virtual economic self-sufficiency, have developed a tremendously strong sense of self. Given the cultural demise of the other groups, the history of sedentary Central Asia, perhaps, is still best reflected in Uzbekistan.

### Ethnicity and Demographics

Determining exact numbers for ethnic groups in Central Asia is a very slippery exercise. Each of the new republics is prone to embellish the percentages of ethnic groups in favor of its ruling majority. For example, Uzbekistan generally undercounts its Tajik population, and Kazakstan overstates the Kazak population in relation to the Russian one. There are also serious discrepancies even among reputable demographic sources.[3] The People's Republic of China realizes the sensitive and volatile nature of the politics and security in Xinjiang, and, therefore, population figures ultimately end up as simple estimates. China wants to portray a nation of overwhelming Han Chinese population and interests. A large number of migratory inhabitants, a relatively low population density, and the social ramifications of "choosing" an ethnicity on the census forms also contribute to the demographic confusion.

Since the Soviet-made borders of the countries are fairly arbitrary, it may be useful to look at raw numbers to comprehend the main ethnic groups in Central Asia. In order of percentages, beginning with the highest, the groups with significant representation include Uzbeks, Russians, Kazaks, Uighurs, Chinese, Tajiks, Turkmen, and Kyrgyz. The national language of each country corresponds to the major ethnic group, often referred to as the "titular" nationality. Two notable exceptions are Kazakstan and Xinjiang. Kazak and Russian languages have official status in Kazakstan. Though Uighurs are among the five main official nationalities in China, the state language for all of China is Mandarin Chinese. Tajikistan is an excellent example of the dangers of drawing correlations between the name of a Central Asian country and its ethnic or linguistic makeup. Tajiks make up about 65 percent of their country, yet sizable numbers of Tajiks live in Uzbekistan, Kyrgyzstan, Xinjiang, and Afghanistan. In fact, more Tajiks live in Afghanistan than in all of Tajikistan.[4]

Xinjiang (Chinese term meaning "new frontier") is an enormous territory, covering over one-sixth of the total area of China. It is mainly a desert basin ringed by high mountains. About 95 percent of the population lives along the base of the sheltering mountain ranges in settlements near highly irrigated oases, which make up less than 4 percent of the total area of Chinese Central Asia. The Xinjiang autonomous (in name only) region counts 49 nationalities within its borders, out of a total of 56 different groups within all of China. This fact illustrates the intensive resettlement of the area with non-Turkic peoples. The major groups in Xinjiang, aside from the Han Chinese, with an affinity to other Central Asian cultural groups are Uighurs, Kazaks, Hui, Kyrgyz, Mongol, Tajik, Uzbek, Russians, and Tatars. The Hui Chinese, also called Dungans, are culturally Chinese yet profess the Muslim faith. They are the mixed descendants of Arab, Mongol, or Turkic settlers in China during the Mongol Yuan dynasty (1279–1368).

## Population Dislocations

Central Asia has experienced massive migrations from the earliest times. In the modern era, there were several population turnovers specifically at the hands of both the Russian and Chinese empires, and then again with the twentieth-century Communists. The Tien Shan and Pamir mountain ranges form the border between Central Asia and China. Throughout human history, this mountainous region was more of a unifying force for the highland nomadic herders than an impassable division of territories. Nomads moved back and forth between the areas in search of pasturage and trade. The routes of the Silk Road wended through the prodigious mountain passages from China into present-day Kyrgyzstan, Uzbekistan, and Pakistan. From the eighth to the twelfth centuries, various Uighur kingdoms were able to rule most of Central Asia across this mountainous barrier in the name of Islam. Moreover, for several hundred years, the Uighur Turkic language was the lingua franca of Central Asia.

The local populations during the nineteenth and twentieth centuries suffered tremendous upheavals. Slavs began unprecedented ethnic migration into Central Asia for more than a hundred years under the Russian Empire. One million Slavic peasants relocated in the late nineteenth century after the abolition of serfdom. Especially lucrative were the farming areas of northern Kazakstan as well as the Russian military fortresses and parallel European-style settlements created alongside major urban areas. Across the border, Chinese forces attacked Eastern Turkestan in 1876 to quell Muslim uprisings. After this invasion, tens of thousands of Uighurs, Kazaks, and Dungans fled the Manchu dynasty into Russian Central Asia. Barely three decades later, the Russian Revolution of 1917 sent thousands of Turks and White Russians back across the border into China.

Central Asia became the ideal destination for exile during the Soviet period. Russians generally considered all Turkic people as Tatars and had no qualms about tossing entire groups into the great void of Inner Asia. In the mid-twentieth century, Stalin initiated the mass deportations of various nationalities, including Germans, Koreans, Chechens, Karachais, Meskhetian Turks, and Crimean Tatars to Central Asia. Moreover, during World War II, thousands of Slavs were evacuated from the path of advancing German armies to Central Asia. Still more Slavs poured in to assist in the building of Communism, not to mention ensuring local cooperation with Moscow. The population of Kazakstan, for example, which totaled 5 million inhabitants at the turn of the twentieth century, reached more than 15 million by the mid-twentieth century.[5] In 1949, the Chinese Communists caused the final migration flood of Uighurs, Kazaks, and Dungans to Soviet Central Asia by defeating the Nationalist Chinese government. With independence in 1991, many Bukharan Jews have immigrated to Israel and the United States, Germans and Koreans have returned home en masse, and Slavs have attempted to start a new life in Russia or Ukraine. Many Slavs, however, with no memory of or roots left in mother Russia, realized that they are unable to subsist or function in the new Russian Federation and have returned to Central Asia. The continuing instability in Tajikistan has caused many Tajiks to flee to Russia, Uzbekistan, and Kyrgyzstan to seek a more peaceful existence. Today, the Chinese–Central Asian border is relatively stable, and the main movement is in the form of trucks and buses. Trade and familial contacts have also resumed. The ancient mountain highways are again open, bringing people, goods, and ideas from one side of the border to the other.

## Central Asian Identities

Before the Russian contact in the eighteenth century, settled Central Asians usually identified themselves first as Muslim, then as Turk or Tajik, and finally associated themselves with a specific locality or tribe. The society was ethnically heterogeneous yet culturally homogeneous, with the main distinction being one of lifestyle—nomadic or settled. Russians referred to all Central Asians as *musul'mane,* or "Muslims." City dwellers were often called *Sarts,* a Sanskrit designation for merchants or urban residents, and the nomad was variously dubbed as Kyrgyz, Turk, or Tatar. Russia treated the entire area as a monolithic territory and officially renamed it the Turkestan Military District. It was the Soviets, and especially the twisted mind of Stalin, who came up with the idea of separate Central Asian nationalities. New republics with borders drawn to ensure no ethnic monopolies were created for the Kazaks, Kyrgyz, Tajiks, Turkmen, and Uzbeks. Until 1936, their status and boundaries changed several times, especially in the Ferghana Valley. Substantial Uzbek populations remained in Kyrgyzstan and Tajikistan, and the Uzbek Republic received the predominantly Tajik cities of Bukhara and Samarqand.

### Azeris

Azerbaijan is often the odd man out in the Caucasus. Though Azeris are a Turkic people, and it is only natural for their dishes to have Turkic names, their food is more similar to Iranian cookery than Turkish or Central Asian cuisine. The region was controlled by Iran from the sixth through the fourth centuries B.C. and most recently from the sixteenth through the eighteenth centuries A.D. Azeris are still a divided people, located within the nations of Iran and Azerbaijan. Nationalists and expatriates tend to inflate the numbers, while Iranian officials downplay this significant minority on their soil. Fifteen million Azeris in Iran, however, is a conservative and believable estimate.[6] Most Azeris live in the two Iranian provinces of East and West Azarbaijan. There are another 1 million Azeris in the countries of the former USSR.[7]

### Kazaks

The Kazaks trace their heritage to the fifteenth century, when they broke from Khan Özbek after the disintegration of the Golden Horde. They have Mongoloid features but linguistically belong to the Turkic family. Kazaks are moderate adherents of Islam. Contacts with Islam came mainly in the form of wandering Sufi Muslim dervishes, known for their extreme poverty and austerity. The Kazak nomadic herdsmen have gradually assimilated the Russian culture over the past two hundred years, becoming the unfortunate buffer between Slavic and Iranian cultures. In 1936 they were given their own Kazak Autonomous Soviet Socialist Republic, forming the geographic and political basis for Kazakhstan. Their language and culture were on the verge of extinction in Soviet times when the Kazak population dipped below 40 percent of the total. Since independence in 1991, however, Kazakhstan has made diligent efforts to promote Kazak language and culture while not alienating or provoking the "native" Russian-speaking populations. In 1997, the country moved its capital from the Russian-built Almaty to Astana, located in the geographic center of Kazakhstan.

### Kyrgyz

Kazaks and Kyrgyz share many customs and traits. From 1918 to 1936, the Kyrgyz Autonomous Soviet Socialist Republic actually included the territories of both modern-day Kyrgyzstan and Kazakhstan. The Kyrgyz essentially were the mountain pastoralists, while the Kazaks ruled the steppe and plain. With Siberian forbearers, the Kyrgyz are among the oldest recorded groups in Central Asia. Chinese sources mention them already in the second century B.C. From the tenth to the fifteenth century, they worked their way south to the mountainous region of Kyrgyzstan to maintain their nomadic lifestyle. Kyrgyzstan is one of the most beautiful territories in Asia, with alpine lakes, mountain flowers, and vast tracts of untouched wilderness.

### Tajiks

Tajiks have inhabited the rugged Central Asian area for thousands of years and today are found in Tajikistan, Afghanistan, Uzbekistan, and Iran. They trace their history directly to the great Persian empires and civilizations. The Iranian Samanid dynasty controlled Transoxiana from about 900 A.D. with Bukhara, a jewel of the Iranian kingdom, as the capital. Together with Samarqand, the splendid cities were the cultural centers of the empire, where arts and literature flourished. No grand Iranian cities on such a scale were established in present-day Tajikistan. Samarqand and Bukhara are essentially Tajik cities, though politically part of Uzbekistan. Tajikistan was a satellite republic of Uzbekistan from 1924 to 1929 until it, too, became a full Soviet Socialist Republic. Aside from the European settlers and the Hui Chinese migrants in Central Asia, Tajiks are the most distinct indigenous cultural group in the region. They speak an Indo-European tongue similar to Farsi in Iran. Their name may have derived from the ancient Persian word *Tazi,* for "Arabs," which in time was applied to all Muslims. The lowland Tajiks are subsistence farmers and Sunni Muslims, living in small villages. Ninety percent of their country is mountainous. Pamir Tajiks live in isolated high-altitude valleys, speak several different Persian dialects, and practice Ismailism, a breakaway sect of Shi'a Islam.

### Turkmen

These desert-based nomads descended, according to legend, from the Oghuz Turks, one of the four major branches of Turks in the tenth century. The Muslim state of Khwarazm was formed by Oghuz nomads in the twelfth century with Khiva as its capital city. In the wake of both the Mongol and Seljuk Turk invasions, the Turkmen migrated south toward Persia over the next five centuries and settled in present-day Turkmenistan. These horse herders lived in the oases on the desert's edge. Turkmen are best known for their horses, but they are also well known for their carpets. The carpets are called "Bukharan rugs," after the name of the city where merchants sold and traded Turkmen products in the bazaars; many world-famous designs are based on Turkmen tribal names: Tekke, Yomud, Ersari, Salor, Saryk, Chodor, and so forth.

### Uighurs

Like the Kyrgyz, Uighurs also look to southern Siberia as their original homeland. By the eighth century, they had settled in the oases ringing the Taklamakan Desert and flourished thanks to trade along the Silk Road. Situated at the crossroads of East and West, Uighurs facilitated trade and the diffusion of culture. Following stints with Shamanism, Manichaeism,[8] and Buddhism, Uighurs embraced Islam in the tenth century. Today, the Chinese overlords marginalize them, but Uighurs receive little world sympathy in comparison to their Tibetan neighbors, who share the same cultural repression. The turbulent history of Xinjiang continues, with Chinese migrants and laborers, particularly from Sichuan, flooding the region since the 1960s and dropping the Turkic Uighur population from roughly 75 percent to less than 50 percent. Uighurs still maintain a daily routine similar to that of the Middle Ages; live mainly in urban settlements; and work as merchants, tradesmen, and farmers. By observing Islam and preserving their traditional lifestyle, Uighurs reject the atheism of Chinese Communism as well as the goal of modernization.

### Uzbeks

Uzbeks have had a settled civilization for centuries, although there also exist Uzbek seminomads. It may be more accurate to describe Uzbeks as a cultural group rather than an ethnic group. They claim ties to the Mongol Chaghatay Khanate who mixed with the sedentary Turkic tribes during the fourteenth and fifteenth centuries, although Uzbeks generally have less of a Mongol appearance than do Kazaks and Kyrgyz. Uzbeks share with Iranians a common religion and culture and their Turkic dialects are heavily Iranized. Between the deserts and mountains, in the oases and fertile valleys, they cultivated grain and domesticated livestock. The resulting abundance of produce allowed them to express their strong tradition of hospitality, which in turn enriched their cuisine. Until the late nineteenth century, Uzbeks generally referred to themselves as either Turks or Persians. In 1924, the Soviets encouraged an official identity and a literary language, and the Uzbeks claimed their name based on the fourteenth-century ruler Ozbeg Khan.

### Dungans/Hui Chinese

In the People's Republic of China proper, 10 million Hui Chinese share cultural and physical attributes with the dominant Han Chinese, yet the Hui are officially recognized as a national minority. The only major distinction between the two groups, however, is that the Hui practice Islam. In China, the primary food-related occupations of the Hui include restaurateur, innkeeper, shepherd, farmer, butcher, and tea trader. At the twilight of the Qing dynasty in the late nineteenth century, there were several Hui uprisings and tens of thousands fled across the border into Russian Central Asia. Called "Dungans" there, the Hui population is fewer than 100,000 in Kyrgyzstan and Kazakstan today. Though small in number, they have a tremendous culinary influence in Central Asia, where Dungans have largely become farmers, famous for their hospitality, ceremonies, and banquets. Settling in a region of nomadic peoples, they have changed eating habits with the introduction of new foodstuffs. One Chinese food product that has become a Central Asian staple is flat chives (*Allium tuberosum*), or *jusai* in Turkic and *jiu cai* in Chinese. Dungans are now a permanent fixture as market vendors and, in the post-Soviet period, as restaurateurs.

## ECONOMY

Central Asia was industrialized and modernized as an integral part of the USSR. Therefore, its infrastructure, trade routes, and distribution system passed through Moscow. Each Soviet republic specialized in certain aspects of industry and agriculture to meet the larger needs of the country. Central Asians produced fruits and vegetables but shipped them to other republics to be processed. They imported machinery, textiles, and consumer items produced in the Baltics or Russia. Central Asia became a major agricultural power under the Soviets with particular dependence on the growing of cotton. The result is depleted water tables, soil salinization, degradation of the terrain and vegetation, an ever-greater demand for irrigation, and a disappearing basin once known as the Aral Sea. In short, cotton production created an unmitigated environmental disaster.

Since 1991, the region has been slow to recover from the shock of economic independence from other Soviet republics. Most of the Central Asian countries now have a healthy balance of trade with Iran, Turkey, and China, in addition to the old standby trading partners of Russia and Ukraine. Kazakstan has enjoyed tremendous growth and prosperity in the energy sector with its oil fields in the west. Turkmenistan has enough natural gas reserves to allow it to recede into authoritarian oblivion under its current president Saparmurat Niyazov, or Turkmenbashi, "Father of All Turkmen." Uzbekistan has modest mineral deposits; Tajikistan and Kyrgyzstan still rely on individual garden plots to feed their nations, while Turkmenistan can import and subsidize many of its staples to placate the sparsely populated nation. The region is counting on its mineral wealth and raw materials to carry each nation to the near future. Development programs for tourism abound in attempts to revive the wonder of the Silk Road. But until new transportation routes open, the service sector improves, and the region becomes more tranquil and stable, attracting more than the current handful of adventure travelers will remain a pipe dream.

### Social Structure

The nomadic and sedentary lifestyles strongly determine the pattern of interaction between individuals or groups in Central Asia. In general, there is less social stratification within a nomadic society than in a settled context. For both groups, however, kinship and clan-based allegiances play a major role in politics and social structure. The elder males of the communities wield power, and their counsel and consent are necessary for any serious initiatives. Affiliation with a clan, tribe, or horde is the single most essential element of identity for the nomadic populations. The clans within each ethnic group maintain a resilient sense of unity. In the large urban areas, there is decreased significance on tribal affiliation, though it can still be crucial.

### Sedentary Lifestyle

The river valleys and oases of Central Asia have been settled as rural villages and market towns for millennia. Uzbeks and Uighurs are densely concentrated in permanent settlements along the fertile valleys. Lifestyle, material culture, religion, arts, and economy in the oases were heavily influenced by Iran and later by the Islamic culture. Their economy was based on agriculture, crafts, and trade. Street vendors sold pilaf, *samsa* (baked savory pastries), and confections. Cookshops also prepared main dishes or catered special events for merchants and courtiers. Other professions included butchers, bakers, and tanners. In larger settlements a weekly bazaar was held and seasonal markets appeared for trading livestock. The townsfolk tended gardens and cultivated nut trees, grapes, melons, and vegetables. Though the Soviets

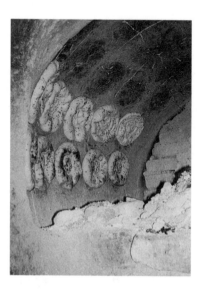

Tandoor oven with flatbread, Samarqand, Uzbekistan.

have replaced most traditional Uzbek homes with ghastly high-rise apartments, Uighurs in China still occupy the traditional Turkic square mud-brick or wooden homes. Family houses are generally spacious and comfortable with sparse furnishings. Traditional houses have an open courtyard, shaded by grapevines and fruit trees, where families gather for companionship and relief from the sun's rays. Much cooking is done on a brazier, and wealthier houses have their own tandoor oven (*tandir*) in the courtyard. The flat rooftops may be used for drying fruit, seeds, and grain. The fields contain wheat, rice, vegetables, and melons, and the orchards bloom with grapes, apricots, peaches, quince, pears, and plums.

Uzbeks and Uighurs, as the traditional settled Turks, generally reside in villages, towns, and cities. The majority of Kazaks, Kyrgyz, and Turkmen sustained a nomadic lifestyle until Stalin's collectivization, beginning in the 1930s, thrust them into makeshift settlements near communal farms and eventually into block apartments.[9] Persian-speaking Tajiks are primarily a rural population with the main exceptions being the grand ancient cities of Samarqand and Bukhara. Tajikistan is the least urbanized of all the former Soviet republics. Civil war, ethnic tensions, and social unrest have plagued the country since independence, creating an extremely poor standard of living, especially in the rural areas.

In the urban areas, for Uzbeks and Tajiks alike, the city neighborhood (*mahalla*) defines social interactions. These ancient urban divisions contained between 30 and 60 households and often specialized in specific trades such as metalworking or woodworking, music, or food production. The social composition of the mahalla is also subject to its location; hence, the membership may also include diverse representations in class, profession, or religion. Traditionally, each neighborhood had its own mosque and teahouse (*chaikhana*). The mahalla was a source of social services for the residents, where members could call on each other to assist in time of need, to organize wedding parties and funerals, and to celebrate communally. In times when raids were frequent, each mahalla was walled off and gated for protection, compartmentalizing an urban area into multiple defensive positions. In Soviet-built cities, the mahalla consists of apartment complexes with many single-family dwellings.

In China, ethnic groups in autonomous areas for the most part lead separate lives from the Han Chinese. The Han usually work as urban-based administrators and professionals or else they serve in the military or as laborers. A massive number of Han Chinese have settled in Xinjiang, and ethnic tensions sometimes result in violence. Condemnation of religious observances during the cultural revolution, Han ethnocentrism, and

Kazak woman making *qurt*, Xinjiang.

lack of sensitivity to minority cultures have led to local resentment and occasional civil unrest.

### Nomadic Lifestyle

Nomads live by and for their livestock herd to ensure self-sufficiency. Trade for the nomads emphasizes the acquisition of goods they did not produce, not the accumulation of wealth. They depend on their animals for transport, milk, wool, leather, and meat. Kazaks, Kyrgyz, and Turkmen privilege horse breeding, although sheep generally compose a greater percentage of the herd. Almost all Central Asian nomadic groups keep sheep and goats as well. Cattle and camels are also herded, even though most cattle could barely survive the winters without fodder. The main source of protein in the nomadic diet is milk products, especially *kumiss*, yogurt, *ayran* (yogurt mixed with water), and *qurt* (or *qurut*; air-dried cheese). Qurt travels well and sustains the nomads in the winter months. Crushed and rehydrated with water, qurt also serves as a fortifying drink.

Summer and fall generally mean a time of plenty for the nomads, and they slaughter any animal not deemed fit to survive the winter. What is not consumed immediately may be smoked or dried, like jerky. Fat is rendered and stored for use throughout the winter. Many foreigners complain that they do not like the taste of mutton. In fact, what they disapprove of is the taste of mutton fat. Science has shown that were it possible to remove all the fat from the muscles of mutton and beef, the flavor of the two meats would be almost indistinguishable. Horse meat is most commonly served in the form of sausage. Camel meat is much tougher than beef and requires hours of low and slow heat to ensure a tender dish. In the northern regions and the mountains, the two-humped Bactrian camel is well suited to the environment. The single-humped dromedary is found in the hot southern deserts, though the flesh is almost identical in taste to the Bactrian type. Also, the higher elevations are home to other edible animals, including yaks, Marco Polo sheep, marmots, ibex, and *jeran*.[10]

When slaughtering an animal, every effort is made to use all the flesh and edible internal organs. To varying extents, Central Asians follow Islamic *halal*, an Arabic word meaning "lawful" or "permitted." The concept of halal applies to everything in life, but it is most familiar in the West in terms of food allowed for devout Muslims. According to the Koran, specifically excluded from consumption are pork and its by-products, animals improperly slaughtered or dead before slaughtering, animals killed in the name of anyone other than Allah, and, of course, alcohol and intoxicants, carnivorous animals, birds of prey and land animals without external ears, blood and blood by-products, or foods contaminated with any of the above products.

Some Kazaks and Kyrgyz, like the Mongols, utilize the yurt, a cylindrical felt tent, as their main dwelling. A yurt can last for two to three decades and an attempt is made to decorate it brightly with felt rugs and carpets. The hearth or stove is situated in the center of the yurt, with a flap on the roof for ventilation. Similar to an American Indian tepee, the yurt may be disassembled for transport on a pack animal to move with the herd. In the winter, the nomads settle in the lowlands. They follow the spring and summer pasturage ever higher in the mountains before retreating again in the fall. Most of the herd is used for exchange value rather than direct consumption. Therefore, the diet consists largely of milk products, flatbread, noodles, mutton, and some simple herbs and greens. Wool, meat, or whole animals are exchanged for flour, rice, oil, and consumer goods. Some lowland families now engage in both herding and minor cultivation of grain and vegetables.

## GEOGRAPHY AND AGRICULTURE

Central Asia, including Xinjiang, is a massive territory (2,100,000 square miles), more than half the size of the United States (3,536,290 square miles). Far from any moderating influence of oceans, the main geographic features of the region are steppe, desert, mountains, and a thin forest belt in northern Kazakstan. The bulk of territory in Uzbekistan (two-thirds), Xinjiang (two-thirds), and Turkmenistan (four-fifths) is mostly desert and semiarid plains. Kazakstan, too, is primarily arid steppe and semidesert. Considerable seismic activity in the region also adds to its geographically hostile reputation as lifeless desert and steppe. Kyrgyzstan and Tajikistan are mountainous regions forming the "Rooftop of the World." Towering ranges from 16,000 to 26,000 feet radiating out from the Pamirs form the border separating Central Asia from India and China. As expected from a continental climate, the temperatures may vary to the extremes. Each of these environments affects the economy, society, lifestyle, and certainly the foodways of its inhabitants. People generally occupy the steppe as well as the lowland areas between desert and mountain.

The northernmost wooded periphery of Central Asia bordering Russia is situated on line with Edmonton, Canada, whereas the southernmost border in Turkmenistan does not even reach the same latitude as Los Angeles. The sedentary population of Central Asia dwells in a string of oases running east-west along the ancient trade routes. The dwindling nomadic population is found both in the steppe and the mountainous regions. Rainfall is minimal throughout, and residents rely on wells and melting mountain snow for water. Uzbeks make a distinction between *aq su,* or "white water," and *qara su,* "black water." The former is fresh flowing mountain streams, and the latter is found in wells or poplar-lined irrigation canals, called *ariq* in Uzebek.

### Agriculture

Inhabitants of Central Asia have cultivated the oases' fields in the shadow of the mountains for millennia with attentive and elaborate irrigation schemes. They also engaged in dry farming on mountain slopes. Walnuts, pistachios, and almonds grow at higher altitudes in the east. The main economic activities of the settled populations along the Silk Road were cultivation, crafts, and trade. It has become a truism that the history of any region is reflected in its food. For ages the crossroads for caravan routes, cultures, and civilizations, the oases of Central Asia assimilated various influences and contributions from the great cooking traditions of their neighbors—Chinese, Persian, and Turkic. As a result of the continual trade and the similarity of products and ingredients throughout the area, the culinary arts expanded and flourished. In keeping with human nature to resist major change, chefs of the court and home cooks could experiment with familiar products, making only incremental modifications over time instead of attempting dramatically new dishes.

Cultivators grew rice (*shali*) in those few areas with ample water resources. Alexander the Great found that the Bactrian civilization had already cultivated rice in the fourth century B.C. in heavily irrigated fields, despite persistent culinary myths that he was the one who introduced pilaf to Central Asia.[11] Seminomads on the fringes of these settlements, forced from their pasturage by stronger groups, formed a transitional zone between the sown and the steppe. The Ferghana Valley is fairly representative of the settled oasis culture in Central Asia. It is divided among the countries of Uzbekistan, Kyrgyzstan, and Tajikistan and has the highest population density in the region, as well as the most fertile territory. The main agricultural activities are cotton culture, sericulture, horticulture, vineyards, and production of meat and milk. City dwellers prefer mutton and beef but also eat fair amounts of chicken and on occasion consume horse sausage and goat. Clarified butter is the preferred cooking medium, but they usually settle for vegetable oil or rendered animal fat. Nomads and urbanites are united in their reverence for flatbreads and the ubiquitous *shashlyk* made from fat-tailed sheep.

Cotton, collectivization, and corn are the lasting residual effects of Russian influence on the region. With interrupted access to American cotton during the U.S. Civil War, Russia turned to its new territories in the south in attempts to raise "white gold" by the late nineteenth century. Several decades later, Soviet centralized agriculture policy consigned the region to essentially a single-crop economy—cotton monoculture. More social upheaval followed with the Soviet regime's policy of farm collectivization, which virtually destroyed the traditional nomadic lifestyle and culture. The final strike was Khrushchev's Virgin Lands campaign of 1954, inspired in part by a visit to U.S. cornfields. The plan was to irrigate the steppe and desert and raise corn for food and fodder. The result was more Slavic administrators and laborers pouring into Kazakstan, and another Soviet agricultural disappointment. The area was susceptible to droughts, and Khrushchev's reorganization of collective farms into larger units created resistance and chaos in the countryside.

In broad terms, the traditional nomads concentrate on herding, whereas the settled Turks tend their fields, gardens, and orchards. Cotton production dominates agriculture in the south and grain dominates in the north. Agriculture employs 20–30 percent of the workforce and accounts for about 25–30 percent of the region's gross domestic product.[12] Cereals, fruits, vegetables, nuts, and animal husbandry make up the major categories of Central Asian agriculture. Despite the harsh climatic conditions, Central Asia is home to a number of familiar foodstuffs to North Americans. Some items that were first cultivated in or are native to the region include garlic, wheat, carrots, green onions, dill, tarragon, melons, quinces, apricots, pomegranates, asafoetida, and nigella (*sedona*).[13] The intense sun imparts a special sweetness to tomatoes, grapes, melons, and other produce. The continental climate, however, makes it too cold for steady yields on olive and citrus trees.

### Grains, Vegetables, and Fruits

Grains that are grown in significant quantities are wheat, rice, millet, and barley. Rice and wheat, in the form of flatbread and noodles, are the main starchy staples. Millet is brewed into a beerlike drink called *boza* in Kazakstan and Kyrgyzstan. Alfalfa, oats, barley, and sorghum are grown mainly for fodder. Chickpeas (*nokhat*) and mung beans (*mosh*) are the standard legumes found in soups and rice dishes. As the Slavic population increased during the nineteenth and twentieth centuries, vodka distilleries were also built, utilizing local grain for the production of alcohol. Hemp (*bäng*), poppy for opium production, and tobacco (both for chewing and smoking), are understandably less publicized Central Asian commercial crops. The seeds of hemp, flax, cotton, sesame, and sunflower are processed for vegetable oil. Sesame (*kunjut*) is also the main component of Central Asian halva (*hälwa*), a confection made from flour, sugar, milk, and nuts.

Onions, turnips, tomatoes, radishes, peas, cucumbers, and red peppers are all commonly grown vegetables. *Turp*, a large green radish about the size of a rutabaga, is eaten fresh, primarily as a salad or side dish. A special type of yellow carrot (*säbzi turisida*) used in pilafs is actually a parsnip, although it has almost the identical shape and taste of orange carrots.

Noodler,    Khotan,    Xiniiang,
China.

In Uzbek, carrots are called *säbzi*, derived from the Persian word *sebz*, for "green." In both the Urdu and Hindi languages of South Asia, *sabji* refers to all vegetables. Russians introduced the potato and the beet into the local field and diet in the twentieth century. Central Asian pumpkins (actually Old World squash) are used in many soups, stews, and fillings for dumplings and samsa. They have a flavor more akin to acorn squash rather than large, sweet orange American pumpkins. Gourds are made into containers by drying the hard-rinded shell of a bottle gourd.

Hundreds of varieties make melons the principal fruit export, famous throughout the region for their unique flavor. The other main fruits are peaches, cherries, apples, plums, and figs. Fruit, fresh or dried, is eaten throughout the day as between-meal snacks. Grapes, too, are generally eaten fresh since Islam discourages the production of wine. Russians introduced new varietals for wine production in the nineteenth century, and there are still over a hundred wine producers in Central Asia, fermenting wine mostly for local consumption. Seedless dried grapes (*kishmish*) are exported throughout the former Soviet Union. Russians have adopted their word for "raisin" or "sultana," *izyum*, from the Central Asian word *uzum*, meaning "grape."

## HISTORY

### Early Eurasian Nomads and Civilizations

Nomadic herdsmen had domesticated the horse as early as 4000 B.C., but the steppe was unable to support a high population density, major urban centers, or a centralized state without substantial and stable agricultural production. Nomads lived in portable yurts and subsisted mostly on milk products, supplemented with minor game and plant food. A lack of both water resources and wood for fuel greatly influenced Central Asian cookery. Poplar trees and the desert *saxaul* (*Haloxylon ammondendron*), somewhere between a small tree and a large shrub, are essential for firewood and cooking fuel; as is dried animal dung. Poplars are also used for woodworking and construction. The tandoor oven was developed to maximize heat in relation to wood fuel, and the ceramic walls create intense heat for quick cooking of flatbreads, samsa, and meats. Most of the cuisine, however, is derived from single-cauldron cookery in the form of soups, stews, and steamed dumplings.

Iranian nomads were among the first people to settle in Central Asia sometime in the first millennium B.C. The towns of Bukhara and Samarqand appeared as centers of administration and culture as early as the fifth century B.C. By the time Alexander the Great conquered the region in 328 B.C., Samarqand was already the cosmopolitan, fortified capital of the Sogdian Empire. The urban areas of Central Asia became seats for pottery making, glassblowing, metalworking, and fabric weaving by the fifth century A.D. Archaeological artifacts show that most cooking and serving vessels were mostly ceramic.[14] These oasis cities grew wealthy, thanks to the Silk Road trade, and eventually became part of an influential and powerful Persian province. Central Asian culture and cuisine exchanged products and methods with India, Byzantium, and China. The wealth of oasis cities attracted nomadic invasions from the northern steppes on occasion and also led to persistent interest from the Persian and Chinese empires for trade or conquest.

### Arrival of Islam

Islam became the main faith in Central Asia starting in the eighth century A.D. Mā-warā-'n-nahr—the principal trading zone along the Silk Road—became a center of culture, art, education, and spirituality. Bukhara and Samarqand reached their heights of brilliance in the eighth and ninth centuries under the Abbasid Caliphate. The cities grew into powerful states and crucial trading centers, attracting the finest artisans and architects. Rulers erected magnificent palaces, azure-domed mosques, madrassas, mausoleums, and public gardens.

The region also produced some of the greatest historians, scientists, and geographers in the history of Islamic culture, especially in the intellectually flourishing period between the eighth and fourteenth century A.D. Such luminaries as al-Biruni, al-Farabi, al-Kashgari, al-Khawarizmi, and ibn Sina (Avicenna) enormously augmented mankind's body of knowledge. However, their contributions have largely been overlooked, forgotten, or underappreciated in the West. The dynasty of Timurids (fourteenth through the sixteenth centuries) continued the refinement of architecture, science, and arts in Central Asia.

Cultural inspiration came not only from the West with Islam but also from China. Tea is perhaps the greatest culinary gift to Central Asia from the East. Though mass consumption of the drink appeared only in the modern era, tea was first introduced to Central Asia, Tibet, and Mongolia from China during the Tang dynasty in the seventh century. The dynasty exerted its influence from Afghanistan to Korea, and tea and teahouses gradually spread throughout the region. Bricks of tea were transported through Central Asia along the Silk Road to India and Turkey, and eventually into Russia by at least the seventeenth century. Of the three basic categories of tea, green tea (*Camellia sinensis*) by far is the preference in Central Asia; Russians in the urban areas enjoy black tea, and oolong tea is conspicuously absent. The green tea is generally nonfermented, caffeinated, and yellow in color. Chinese sources point out that early Arab, Tocharian, Uighur, and Bactrian traders made a beeline for the teahouses in Chang'an (present-day Xi'an), the capital of the Tang dynasty and terminus of the Silk Road.[15]

Iran had a refined court cuisine beginning twenty-five hundred years ago. The cultural golden age of Iran, from the eighth through the tenth centuries A.D., resulted in extraordinary scientific, technological, and commercial achievements, as well as sophisticated dishes made with food products from the Mediterranean to China. The Islamic applied arts of the tenth century introduced new forms of elaborate glazed tableware to the region. Large, ornate dishes, bowls, and cups were festively painted inside and out.[16] Glass mugs, goblets, jugs, and bowls became widespread. Also, vessels and dishes were cast or embossed in gold, silver, and copper.

The Turkic contributions to food in this period, such as dumplings (*manti*), kebabs, wheat porridge (*sumalak*), and the milk products of yogurt, ayran, and kumiss are mentioned in Mahmud al-Kashgari's *Divanü Lügat-it Türk*, an eleventh-century Turkish-Arabic dictionary.[17] He refers to pit cooking, grilling, and baking with earthenware pots. The Central Asian Turks had numerous grain-based foods, a reflection of their sedentary lifestyle, including the flatbreads *yufka*, *chorek*, and *ekmek*; *katmer* (a pastry); *tutmac* (noodle soup); and halva. The Mongol invasions in the thirteenth century and the ensuing destruction were a profound cultural setback for the region. Fortunately for the world's culinary heritage, the Ottoman Empire continued and refined many Iranian and Turkic dishes in its court cuisine from the thirteenth to the twentieth century, hinting at the grandeur of Inner Asian cookery.

Timur, or Tamerlane, led the last great Central Asian Empire in the fourteenth century. By 1390, he had conquered Baghdad, the Volga region, and Delhi. Babur, a descendant of Timur, founded the Mughal Empire in 1526, which covered much of southwest Asia and almost all of India. The empire was famous for its cultural achievements—specifically architecture, music, literature, art, and cuisine. The blending of Persian and Indian culinary elements in a courtly setting distinguishes Mughal cooking from other cuisines of the subcontinent. Delicately spiced dishes with nutmeg, mace, and cinnamon; rich yogurt and crushed-nut sauces;

exquisite rice dishes; and rose-scented desserts are just a hint of the royal gastronomic offerings. The Mughal Empire lingered on until the mid-nineteenth century, when the British Empire subjugated the entire Indian continent. Much of contemporary Indian restaurant food throughout the world features some elements of Mughal cuisine with yogurt, grilled tandoori meats, spices, nuts, and sweet desserts. By the nineteenth century, Central Asia would again be thrust on the world stage as an imperial battleground.

### Russian Rule

During the push to colonize Siberia beginning in the late sixteenth century, Russia established a string of fortresses along the Eurasian steppe. It took about a century for the Russian Empire to completely absorb the territory of Central Asia, though the active campaign lasted only 20 years. The territory of present-day Kazakstan was already well under Russian administrative control through a series of "protection" agreements by the mid-nineteenth century. The decisive battles for southern fringe occurred during the 1860s through the 1880s.[18] English lieutenant Arthur Connally coined the term *Great Game* to refer to the imperial intrigues and rivalry that followed Russia's conquest of Central Asia. In short, England feared Russian economic or military incursions on Britain's Indian Empire, and Russia was wary of British ascendancy in the area. Immortalized in Rudyard Kipling's novel *Kim*, the term *Great Game* is frequently revived, often unsuitably, in current literature on the region.

It was Kipling as well who wrote the oft-quoted, "Oh, East is East and West is West, and never the twain shall meet," often applied to the region both then and today through colonial eyes. The other part of the text (usually omitted) continues, "But there is neither East nor West, Border, nor Breed, nor Birth, When two strong men stand face to face, tho' they come from the ends of the earth!"[19] This second statement sums up the intercultural world of Eurasia, underscoring the fact that in spite of borders, boundaries, and nationalities, there is no clear demarcation of culture between East and West. Central Asia and Russia both exhibit the phenomenon of shifting or imperceptible cultural boundaries between East and West.

Russification and Sovietization of foodways unquestionably impoverished Central Asian culinary culture by altering lifestyles and traditions. The initial Russian experience in Central Asia yielded tremendous social and economic change for the nomads in the eighteenth and nineteenth centuries. For them, Russian subjugation meant decreased pasturage, craftsmanship, and specialization, which resulted in a greater dependence on consumer goods. The foreign concept of land ownership reduced the nomads from free-spirit herdsmen to petty laborers on the fringes of town, taking on an urban diet. Hundreds of thousands of nomads also fled to China or Afghanistan. Kazaks, overall, experienced a much greater cultural blow from the Russian conquest than did the settled Turks for two principal reasons. First, the Kazaks acted as an enormous buffer between Russia and the settled Turks; second, Russian culture (like that of the Turks) was both urban and agricultural, and, therefore, clashed most directly with the nomadic lifestyle and traditions.

For the Turks, the change was primarily economic, whereas the culinary changes were more superficial. Most Uzbek peasants before the 1917 Bolshevik Revolution subsisted on gruel, meatless stew, and flatbread. The tsarist armies and administrators brought, among other things, cabbage, radishes, beets, pork, Russian-style restaurants, and vodka. Many New World foods also followed the Russians: tomatoes, potatoes, chilies, and squash. Some indigenous merchants emulated European ways and adopted Russian foodstuffs. However, Russians generally built European square-grid towns adjacent to existing Uzbek cities. Thus the nonintrusive imperial policy in the cultural realm, coupled with the physical separation of the two communities, meant that the locals in the oasis cities were able to maintain their traditional diet to a large degree.

The Great October Revolution of 1917 accelerated the economic and cultural changes down south as well. The Soviets spent the first decade simply trying to reassert Russian rule in the region. In the 1920s, Central Asian republics were assigned their own distinct ethnic profiles, languages, and histories. This titular nationality, ordained by Stalin in his role as commissar for nationalities, was further bolstered by political structures and territorial integrity. Each Central Asian republic was given a parliament, prime minister, and local and regional government—all the trappings of political nationality. Both subject to, and a part of, Soviet rule, Central Asians should not be viewed merely as innocent victims of Communist oppression. To be fair, Russians are not solely to blame for implementing social experiments across the empire. Central Asians also played an active part in creating Soviet culture and determining its role in society. With no indigenous working class, Soviets recruited untold numbers of poor, desperate, or simply opportunistic local cadre to promote and enforce the party line.

Whereas the Russian Empire built separate cities and virtually ignored the indigenous population, the Soviet regime actively destroyed nomadism, religion, and patriarchy. During the decade of collectivization beginning in the late 1920s, it is estimated that almost a million Kazaks perished. Agriculture, irrigation, urbanization, and modernization were intensified. Russians devalued horse breeding and emphasized cattle and pig farming. Authorities halted transborder migration and trade. The Communist Party suppressed tribal networks. For the sedentary population, changes tended to be greater in the cities than in the rural villages.

The Khanate of Bukhara, in existence from the sixteenth to the twentieth century, was patterned on Iranian and Mongol forms of government that preceded it. The khan enjoyed absolute authority, an extravagant lifestyle, and no enduring dissent. He was often an extreme despot. The Soviets continued this style of privileged and totalitarian command. Obviously, under Communist rule the royal cuisine disappeared and the overall variety of food was streamlined because of shortages caused by collectivization and centralized planning in Moscow. On the positive side, sanitation improved, as did the quality control of foodstuffs. As bread and grain became staples even among the nomads, a large portion of the lower classes began to have more balanced diets. Apartments were outfitted with gas and electric ranges. In other dramatic changes, the potato became universal in the twentieth century. Once considered an exclusive dish containing the luxury items of rice and meat, pilaf was consumed more frequently by the urban population, and formerly nomadic groups also came to think of the dish as their own. With the proliferation of cotton, cottonseed oil was consumed as a display of national pride, whereas in earlier times, only the poor used it.

The Islamic prohibition against alcohol was "scientifically" refuted by Marxist doctrine. The Communists convincingly argued that religion, "the opiate of the masses," was used for social control and exploitation, so many Central Asians traded in a spiritual opiate for a liquid one. Indeed, Central Asians were famous for their wine making and drinking in pre-Islamic times, and, perhaps, secret imbibing merely became public again. Shots of vodka flowed as freely in the desert as they did above the frozen canals of St. Petersburg. Central Asians learned European culture in public schools and European cooking methods in culinary schools. Institutional feeding in state cafeterias, cafés, and restaurants required standardization, a feat accomplished with the publication and distribution of a single nationwide manual for culinary preparation. The cuisine in this manual, *Directory of Recipes and Culinary Production*, was mainly Russian, and generations of Central Asians gradually began to prepare and eat European cuisine on a regular basis alongside their traditional cuisine.

## New Culinary Identities

When the USSR collapsed in 1991, independence was in essence foisted upon the Central Asian states. There were no serious grassroots uprisings advocating revolutionary movements in either 1917 or again in 1991. The new states with their present boundaries and ethnic identity are clearly a legacy of the Soviet Union. The elite of Central Asia have adopted a top-down policy of state building, especially in terms of defining the national identity. Central Asia leaders point to the civil war in Tajikistan (1991–97) to justify political repression and clamp down on all forms of opposition. The states are still in a process of stabilizing their authority in wake of the enormous economic and social problems made clear with independence. The existing state ideologies, organizing principles, and institutions in Central Asia are not strong enough to support a functioning democracy.

Today all of the governments in Central Asia are authoritarian regimes. Turkmenistan and Tajikistan form the extremes, with an egomaniacal ruler in the former and random criminal and political violence in the latter. Since independence in 1991, Niyazov retains unconditional control over Turkmenistan, and opposition is not tolerated. His likeness appears on every unit of currency and is plentiful on posters, banners, and statues. Since 1991, Tajikistan has had three separate governments and waged a five-year civil war. Although a peace pact has been signed between President Emomali Rahmonov and opposition parties, there is little real progress for representative participation in the Tajik government.

The situation is more stable in the other countries of Central Asia, but that equates neither to democracy nor to reform. Uzbekistan, Kazakstan, and Kyrgyzstan harass opposition groups, curb basic human rights, and make little effort to integrate into the global community. Using the threat of Islamic fundamentalism as a pretext, all three countries have been under direct executive rule by their respective presidents since 1991. It appears that their terms of presidential service are set for life. Xinjiang has experienced regular bouts of Chinese-Turkic violence for centuries. Though three time zones away from Beijing, Xinjiang runs according to the same figurative and literal timepiece on the rigid hand of the Communists.

In typical Soviet fashion, the present-day leaders of Central Asia try to support or create national culture in the process of nation building. A country's history needs a museum; its literature demands libraries; its music requires a national stage; and its cuisine naturally needs to find expression in restaurants and cookbooks. Tremendous financial burdens and social and economic turmoil followed independence in 1991. Nevertheless, among the first post-Soviet books to be published were cookbooks, as well as the mandatory rewritten Central Asian histories and rediscovered classics of literature. It was not unusual for a Central Asian "national" cookbook to lift word for word a potato salad recipe from a Kazak cookbook, for example, and insert it into a Tajik one. Whereas the Soviet-style cookbooks were usually written only in Russian, the new cookbooks are presented in the native tongue, some even with English and German translations. Although the recipes may be imprecise or outright fabrications at times, these cookbooks are among the only written records of the culinary offerings of the region.

Soviet cultural policy fluctuated between two extremes: suppression and promotion, building (*stroika*) and rebuilding (*perestroika*). This oscillating cultural policy of the USSR was based on the Marxist-Leninist notion of "social construction," where culture is something to be produced, invented, constructed, and reconstructed.[20] In the aftermath of the purges of the 1930s and again in 1951–52, Central Asian leaders displayed their loyalty and conformity by eradicating nationalism, local favoritism, and archaic customs such as religion. A period of national and cultural perestroika immediately followed Stalin's death.

One specific example from Uzbekistan illustrates how the policy affected culture and the publishing industry. In 1956, twelve hundred delegates to the Congress of Intelligentsia of Uzbekistan affirmed that Central Asia is one of the most ancient centers of development of human culture. The First Secretary of the Community Party urged the delegates to take the lead in developing the nation's culture. Cultural nationalists naturally brought language issues to the fore and advocated the use of the Uzbek language in administrative and social-cultural spheres. History books were rewritten, literature flourished, and, not surprisingly, the first Uzbek cookbook appeared.

Karim Makhmudov, a philosophy professor, cultural nationalist, and avid cook, wrote the first book on Uzbek "national" cuisine in 1958. His one-page preface mentions neither the USSR nor the Communist Party, a standard fixture in all Soviet publications. Instead he pays tribute to ibn Sina (Avicenna), an eleventh-century Iranian philosopher and physician whom the Uzbeks claim as their own. Makhmudov does his part to reclaim and revive traditional dishes and methods of cooking lost with industrialization, urbanization, and Sovietization. In his role as cultural nationalist, Makhmudov searches for origins and essences of identity and culture in the remote past to construct a long and continuous history of the Uzbek people and nation. By the end of the Soviet era, his works on tea, noodles, bread, and food traditions were published in the Uzbek language, since his earlier works were written only in Russian. When the USSR fell, the Uzbeks had already succeeded in creating a culinary cultural legacy, defining themselves through their national dishes, and leaving a written record for future generations.

Beginning in the 1960s, foreign travel to Central Asia increased under the auspices of Intourist, the Soviet national travel agency. Hotel restaurants gilded with Asian art and motifs catered to visitors easily bedazzled in an isolated and mysterious land. They served Russian cuisine and a sampling of the regional Central Asian cuisine. This very public display of national culinary culture (though at the time they were Soviet republics), however, reinforced the locals' sense of identity and uniqueness in the international arena. Cultural nationalists worked to preserve or create national heritage through the revival of their language, religion, and arts, and in this instance, prepared the basis for political nationalism in Central Asia. The local elites certainly recognized the power of food and identity. They fully understood the idea that cuisine exists as a normative art, with both descriptive and prescriptive standards.[21] The other Central Asian republics, following Uzbekistan's lead, introduced their own national cookbooks in the 1970s. Two more spurts of cookbook publications occurred again in the late 1980s under Gorbachev and then, obviously, after independence in the 1990s. Cookbooks, hence, played a role in further refining the ideology of their respective national cuisines.

Soviet cookbooks differed dramatically from their Western counterparts. First of all, they are not actual guides to cooking, but a collection of recipes usually cobbled together by a hotel chef to prove that a republic had a repertoire of dishes in the national cuisine. The cookbooks include gross assumptions and omissions, knowing that the homemaker can compensate for the defects. Secondly, like all published material in the USSR, cookbooks followed strict guidelines with a set ideological strategy. These books ostensibly promoted Moscow's nationalities policy—"nationalist in form, socialist in content." Furthermore, they served to boast the diversity of culture within the Soviet brotherhood of nations, while harmlessly appeasing nascent nationalist sentiments in response to increasing Russification. After all, allowing a people to flaunt a national cuisine is infinitely less threatening than giving a national language prominence over Russian. The general goal of a national cookbook (i.e., Uzbek, Tajik, Kazak) was to consciously shape a culinary culture in an effort to create national unity as part of the national myth. By accentuating differences and removing foreign elements in a portrayed cuisine, a cookbook was designed to sharpen the cultural boundaries. In essence, if one eats Uzbek food, one is an Uzbek. A secondary motivation was to present their culinary culture to the outside world. Additionally, ethnic cookbooks (Uighur, Dungan, Tatar, etc.) also strove to preserve traditions and heritage in the face of the dominant national identity.

### Globalization

Food and drink in Central Asia today are being overlaid and transformed by the global processes of markets, transportation, and communications. The embellishment of a national cuisine mirrors the resurgence of national theater, music, literature, art, and other elements of culture that are currently the target of spontaneous or directed revival in the newly independent Central Asian states. As cooking is the most ephemeral of arts, it stands to reason that it may be overrun by global influences. Despite the pork sections in most markets and the addition of vodka and beets to the diet, in general Central Asians staunchly maintain their allegiance to traditional dishes and hospitality.

The cuisines of Central Asia are also dynamic and open to outside influences. Turkish doner kebabs, Milky Way ice-cream bars, Coca-Cola, Chinese beer, and Uncle Ben's rice are all changing today's eating habits in the region. Any sense of culinary inertness has given way to gastronomic experimentation. The same can be said for Central Asian culture in the larger context. Considering the region's history of borrowing, adopting, and contributing elements of culture, the foodways and culinary arts of Central Asia are bound to flourish if their esteemed traditions of hospitality keep pace with the introduction of new foodstuffs. In the short time since independence, Central Asians have fostered a new national consciousness, developed a distinct identity, and cooked up increasingly distinct culinary boundaries through the savvy use of national cuisine.

## NOTES

1. The term *sedentary* refers to settled and agricultural, as opposed to nomadic cultures. Sedentary and nomadic distinctions are highly relevant to the history of Central Asia.

2. Nationmaster.com, "Asia," http://www.nationmaster.com/region/ASI.

3. CIA *World Fact Book*, U.S. Census Bureau International Data Base, United Nations, and the World Bank all have figures that can vary in the millions from group to group.

4. Nationmaster.com, "Asia: Tajikistan: People," http://www.nationmaster.com/country/ti/People.

5. Local Government and Public Service Reform Initiative, *Reform on the Silk Road*, Local Government Brief (Budapest, Hungary, 2001), 11.

6. CIA, *The World Factbook—Iran*, http://www.cia.gov/cia/publications/fact book/geos/ir.html.

7. Joshua Project, "Azerbaijan People," http://www.joshuaproject.net/peoples. php?rop3=100675.

8. Manichaeism was one of the major ancient religions founded in Iran in the third century A.D. Its central tenet was a theology of dualism, the struggle between good and evil. Manichaeism spread to the west (Africa and Europe) for a thousand years, but it flourished mainly in Central Asia and further east in northern India, western China, and Tibet.

9. From 1926 to 1959, the urban population increased fourfold in Kazakstan and Turkmenistan, threefold in Kyrgyzstan and Tajikistan, and by 50 percent in Uzbekistan. Edward Allworth, ed., *Central Asia, 130 Years of Russian Dominance, A Historical Overview* (Durham, NC: Duke University Press, 1994), 97.

10. The high-altitude marmot is a stocky, fatty rodent consumed by humans on occasion. The jeran is the Persian goitered gazelle, *Gazella subgutturosa subgutturosa*. Both the ibex and gazelle are specifically mentioned in Deuteronomy 12:15 as "clean" animals according to the dietary laws for the Chosen of God.

11. Elizabeth E. Bacon, *Central Asians under Russian Rule: A Study in Cultural Change* (Ithaca, NY: Cornell University Press, 1980), 3.

12. Nationmaster.com, "Uzbekistan Agriculture," http://www.nationmaster.com/country/uz/Agriculture.

13. See Alice Arndt's 1999 fact-filled *Seasoning Savvy: How to Cook with Herbs, Spices, and Other Flavorings* (New York: Hayworth Press, 1999) and Susie Ward's *The Gourmet Atlas: The History, Origin, and Migrations of Food of the World* (New York: Macmillan, 1997).

14. Uzbek Institute of Archaeology, *Culture and Art of Ancient Uzbekistan*, vol. 1 (Moscow: Vneshtorgizdat, 1991), 47.

15. Edward H. Schafer, *The Golden Peaches of Samarkand: A Study of T'ang Exotics* (Berkeley: University of California Press, 1963), 20.

16. Uzbek Institute of Archaeology, *Culture and Art of Ancient Uzbekistan*, 52.

17. Mahmud Kashgari, Türk Siveleri (*Divanü Lügat-it Türk*) [Encyclopedia of the Turkish Language], trans. Robert Dankoff, 3 vols. (Duxburg, MA: Basildigi yer Harvard Universities: Basimevi, 1982–85). Another eleventh-century source is Yusuf Khass-Hajib and Fikri Silahdaroglu, trans., *Kutadgu Bilig* [The Book of Knowledge] (Ankara: T.C. Kültur Bakanligi, 1996), covering Oghuz eating habits, feasts, and table service rather than dishes. For information about the food

and customs of the fourteenth-century Oghuz Turks, an additional source is The Book of Dede Korkut [*Stories of Dede Korkut*], ed. and trans. Geoffrey L. Lewis (Hammondsworth: Penguin, 1974).

18. In 1864 Russian armies conquered Qoqand and Chimkent, Tashkent in 1865, Samarqand in 1868, Khiva in 1873, Goek-Tepe in Turmenistan in 1881, Merv in 1884, and halted only after taking the Tajik oasis of Panjdeh near the British-Afghan border in 1885.

19. Rudyard Kipling, *Ballad of East and West* (New York: M. F. Mansfield and A. Wessels, 1899).

20. For a detailed look at the fluctuating Soviet policy in the cultural history of indigenous people (Nivkhi of Shakalin) of the Russian Far East, see Bruce Grant, *In the Soviet House of Culture: A Century of Perestroikas* (Princeton, NJ: Princeton University Press, 1995).

21. Carole Counihan, *Food and Culture: A Reader* (New York: Routledge, 1997).

# 3

# Major Foods and Ingredients

## RUSSIA

Russia is the largest country in the world yet ranks only fourth in arable and permanent cropland.[1] The foods generally associated with Russia include hearty breads; fresh, smoked, and cured sausages; and winter vegetables such as cabbage, beets, and potatoes. Although the beverage that immediately comes to mind with Russia is vodka, a diminutive form of the word *voda* (water), the national drink is actually tea. Russia has a closer proximity to the North Pole than the equator and the growing season is obviously shortened, but the cuisine is not solely based on the limited indigenous plants and animals of the forest and steppe. The foods and ingredients that have become standard Russian fare are the result of many divergent factors: the range of climatic conditions in this continental-sized country; the culinary contributions of numerous ethnic groups; the Slavic peasant diet that developed over the centuries; the region acting as a commercial and cultural crossroads east and west, north and south; and the dramatic expansion of the Russian Empire since the seventeenth century. Russians today without difficulty consider all the following foods to be part of their cuisine: Baltic herring and rye breads, Pacific salmon, Siberian ferns and pine nuts, Asian dumplings, Korean pickled vegetables, Central Asian pilaf, shish kebab from the Caucasus, Romanian *brynza* (feta cheese), Bulgarian peppers, and eggplant from the Middle East. Thanks precisely to this assortment and range of ingredients, dishes, and preparation styles, Russian food is abundant and varied, and as a result, inadequately understood by the outside world.

## Colorful Markets

One of the most fascinating and rewarding cultural experiences in the former Soviet Union is a leisurely visit to a local produce market. Even towns with only a few thousand residents set up a weekly, if not a daily, market for foodstuffs, clothing, and personal effects. A typical food market includes garden items grown by locals; commercial products hawked by middlemen; and the bright fruits, vegetables, and nuts usually controlled by merchants from Central Asia and the Caucasus. Elderly ladies (*babushki*), often adorned in multicolored scarves, sell their greens (parsley, dill, green onions, and cilantro); the industrial vendor retails his hothouse tomatoes and cucumbers; and everyone else offers what he or she can grow, acquire, or make.

Throughout the seasons, the markets present an amazing variety of foodstuffs. Starting with the unprocessed or bulk section, the pantry traditionally contains a selection of grains and flours; pulses and dried beans; vegetable oils sold in reused plastic bottles; walnuts, almonds, and pistachios; macaroni and vermicelli for soups; rice; and dried apricots, raisins, and dates. The vegetables, in order of quantities sold, include potatoes,

Uzbek grapes at market, Andijon.

cabbage, carrots, tomatoes, cucumbers, beets, turnips, and radishes. Besides apples, pears, and berries, most fruits come from the southern regions or are imported. Though rarely perfect in shape, marked with minor external blemishes, and small in size, most of the fruits and vegetables have a vibrant and distinctive taste, one that is slowly fading from Western memory. Pickled garlic, peppers, and cucumbers are almost always locally produced and homemade. Most markets have a Korean food section with prepared dishes of spicy pickled vegetables and fish.

In the dairy products section, vendors tempt the passerby to taste their homemade specialty. Sour cream, fresh cheese (*tvorog*), cheeses, yogurt, and kefir are displayed in glass bottles or buckets and sold by volume. Extraordinary honeys—liquid honey, creamed honey, combed honey, and even walnuts or almonds preserved in honey—are often found in this section.

The meat market is not for the squeamish. Whole heads of cattle, pigs, and sheep are mounted next to their quartered flesh. Men with hatchets and axes hack sides of beef on well-worn tree stumps that serve as cutting blocks. Whole plucked chickens, hares, and game (on occasion) dangle from the pipes or girders above. Dogs, cats, and flies are continually shooed from the fresh carcasses. As primitive as it sounds, meat sterilely packaged in Styrofoam and plastic wrap cannot compare with the taste of freshly slaughtered beef, mutton, and pork. If the stench and the proximity of death become overwhelming, a quick stroll down the aisle reveals the prepared meats: smoked and cured hams and pork, rows of sausages and salamis, roasted chickens, and cured pork fat (*salo*). There are many rivers, lakes, and seas in Russia; therefore, fresh fish is often found at the market. It is also available smoked, dried, canned, and frozen. The fish section certainly includes caviar, black and red.

Delectable fresh or prepared products from the remnants of the Russian Empire still permeate the country's markets. Yet the foodstuffs available in the markets provide only a hint of a country's cuisine. It is how those ingredients are prepared and during which occasions they are served that distinguishes the cookery of one region from another.

### Elusive Categorization of Russian Cuisine

The pitiable international reputation of Russian cuisine is usually based on deleterious experiences with Soviet commercial cookery, which suffered decades of deprivation and demise under a centralized economy. Restaurants in the former USSR rarely did justice to the flavorful domestic cookery found within its expansive territory. Over the past century, even the handful of decent and even fine Russian restaurants in Paris and New York could not challenge the connections of Russian food with cabbage, sausage, and vodka. Discussions of national cuisines usually focus on haute cuisine, the ornate and skillful manner of preparing food, often based on classical French ideals of the eighteenth century. It is the cuisine of the court, of the nobility, of the wealthy. For those who can afford it, haute cuisine is inextricably related to gastronomy, the art and practice of choosing, preparing, and consuming fine food and drink. *Cuisine,* on the other hand, defined as a certain set of cooking traditions, is simply the French word for "kitchen." As in many European languages, *cuisine* in Russian is also the same word for "kitchen" (*kukhnya*). When associating certain foods with an entire nation, stereotypes are unavoidable. Yet products are ever changing, aesthetics evolve, and cuisine rarely heeds national boundaries, especially in an era of globalization. Gastronomy in Russia essentially vanished with Soviet power, but cuisine was never vanquished. Under Communism, Russian cuisine did not disappear; it was merely impeded at home by the lack of products. There was insignificant opportunity for Russian culinary expression globally as opposed to other "national" cuisines, which showcased their culinary treasures through cookbooks and restaurants.

To have any chance of understanding a country's cuisine on the most basic level, pigeonholing is inevitable. One approach is to identify the *cultural superfoods* of a nation, an attempt to describe the meaning of foods within their cultural context. It has been noted that "even when material characteristics frame food preferences, *culture* makes such eating habits respected, and in this way turns them into traditions."[2] Certain foods take on such symbolic overtones that they come to represent the cuisine as a whole. They may be humble, everyday foods. The Brits have roast beef, Americans have hamburgers, and Russians have caviar—or cabbage, depending on perspective. Most so-called descriptions of ethnic or national cuisines end up being a list of representational foods that are rarely eaten on a daily basis, but those that are predictable, clichéd, and mythologized.

One food historian in the 1980s attempted to classify cuisines through "flavor principles," or flavor profiles, whereby "definitive combinations of flavorings ... produce distinctive tastes which are unique and characteristic."[3] This structural approach to cuisine divides the world into food regions and defines the main flavor elements. Mexican cuisine is reduced to only two primary flavor profiles: lime–chile and tomato–chile. According to this typology, Russian food is simply "sour cream–dill, or paprika or allspice or caraway," a mere subcategory of Northern and Eastern European cuisine. Central Asian cuisine is defined as "cinnamon–fruit–nut," obviously a reference to Iran and not the entire region. These generalizations, while interesting, do more to simplify cooking approaches than to achieve an understanding and appreciation of a culinary culture.

A more practical, yet labor-intensive method for describing cuisine is proposed by a leading sociologist. He discards national boundaries and focuses on foods in a cultural context. A researcher is thereby forced to examine in great detail the range of foods in a given area and search for origins, similarities, and contrasts with adjacent areas. This results in organizing culinary cultures that, of course, generally defy geographical borders.[4] Many countries not only have several culinary cultures within their borders, but they also overlap and share a culinary culture with other nations. This is certainly the case in Russia, China, and India, for example, where the size and diversity of the country have produced a "nation of nations." Therefore, the term *culinary culture* is a much more flexible concept when classifying regional foods. The main elements of a culinary culture are products, techniques and tools, and most significantly, its cultural context. Russian cuisine (as for most cuisines) is not exclusive, easily defined, or static. It is as dynamic as life itself.

### Food Production

Geography, religion, and tradition are the major influences on the Russian diet. Look into Russia's larder, and although most foodstuffs may be familiar, there will be plenty that is unusual, if not downright mysterious, to foreigners. Ferns and wild mushrooms vie for attention next to the potato and tomato. The variety of grains, vegetables, fruits, meats, fish, and dairy products used by Russian cooks is dazzling, even during the lean decades of the twentieth century.

The early Slavs (before the ninth century A.D.) were subsistence agriculturalists and relied heavily on wild or natural foods from the forest. Their fields and herds provided them with food and clothing.[5] "Gifts of the forest" (*dary lesa*) is mainly a reference to mushrooms, although it may also include nuts and berries (currants, wild strawberries, gooseberries, raspberries, blackberries, lingonberries, among others), as well as game such as rabbits, squirrels, and deer. The diet consisted chiefly of millet, rye, and milk. The principal task each autumn was preserving food for the long winter months by means of pickling, drying, smoking, and freezing. Slavic communities in the wooded central European plain were small and scattered.

Long-distance trade with the Vikings from the north and the Byzantine Greeks from the south was not well established until the tenth century. This trade gave Slavs access to the bounty of Asia and the Middle East. By the eighteenth century, however, Russia was becoming a power in Europe, and new foodstuffs and dishes entered the cuisine. This was also the time that New World foods—potatoes, tomatoes, peppers, chocolate, among others—began to diffuse throughout Eurasia. The later European culinary influence in the Russian noble houses transformed local ingredients and peasant dishes into haute cuisine, forming the primary characteristics of Russian national cuisine today.

## Catalog of Common Foods

### Grains

Grains, specifically rye, buckwheat, barley, oats, millet, and wheat, are the main staples. Cereals (seeds of cultivated grasses) are of central importance to Russia, so much so that they in many ways define the national cuisine. They form the basis for the delectable breads, filling gruels, savory pies, pancakes (bliny), dumplings, and the beloved fermented beverages. In general, cereals are resilient and easily cultivated, a requirement for survival in the northern regions. Russia maintains the top spot worldwide for both production and consumption of rye, oats, and barley, though barley is used primarily for beer brewing and livestock feed.[6] Maize and rice have only recently entered the Russian table. Maize was mainly livestock feed until sweet corn appeared consistently in the 1990s. Rice, of course, has a longer Russian connection through Central Asia. Cereals are used whole in gruels, hulled and crushed (groats) in porridge and soups, or ground into flours for baked goods and fried or boiled doughs. Rye was the preferred grain for breads of the north, found in the famous Baltic and Russian black breads. Farther south, on the fertile steppes of southern Russian and Ukraine, the Scythians were among the first to cultivate wheat. The Greek historian Herodotus claimed that Russian wheat, exported by the Greek colonies on the Crimean peninsula, sustained the builders of the Parthenon in Athens in the fifth century B.C.[7] Starting in the thirteenth century and lasting almost continuously until the 1917 Russian Revolution, merchants from Genoa and Venice established trading posts on the northern coast of the Black Sea to supply wheat to the whole of Europe. In the late nineteenth century, hard durum wheat from southern Russia, stamped "Taganrog"—reflecting the name of the Russian port on the Sea of Azov—yielded the most prized semolina flour for pasta making in Italy and the United States.[8]

### Baked Goods

Bread forms the basis of the Russian diet, symbolizing sustenance and hospitality. Russians consume an amazing two pounds of bread per person a day. It is the ubiquitous delight of every meal. The very word *hospitality* (*khlebosol'stvo*) derives from the roots *khleb* (bread) and *sol'* (salt), which were traditionally presented to guests as a sign of welcome, warmth, and generosity. In almost endless varieties, most tables are graced with slices of both white wheat bread and dark rye or black bread. *Bulka* is a small roll or loaf, from which arises the word for "bakery," *bulochnaya*. In cosmopolitan urban environments, the word *baton* means "single loaf of white bread," entering the vocabulary with numerous other French terms in the eighteenth century. Though *bâton* in French refers to white bread smaller than a baguette, in Russia, a baton is larger, or what is known in America as French bread. Among the most popular dark breads are *Borodinskiy*, a rye-type made with whole coriander seeds, and *Rizhskiy*, a sourdough rye named for Riga, the capital of Latvia. Although most breads today are made in factories or large-scale bakeries, there are infinite variations and everyone has his or her own opinion on what is truly authentic Russian black bread. Breads and baked goods may be salty or sweet, made from rich or lean doughs, leavened or unleavened, and seasoned with any number of spices, nuts, or fruit, such as caraway seeds and raisins. Although Russians never developed the wide assortment of pastries and sweet treats as in other parts of Europe, their extraordinary breads more than compensate for that particular deficiency.

Other popular baked goods are *sushka, bublik, krendel'*, and *kulich*. A sushka is sort of a cross between a cracker and a bagel—a boiled and baked dough, ring-shaped like a small bracelet. Dozens of them are strung together on a thread and draped over the samovar, the ubiquitous tea urn, as the ever-present accompaniment to tea. This barely sweetened treat is often given to teething babies. Sushki are made plain, with vanilla sugar, or with poppy seeds. A larger, softer version of the sushka is the bublik, a white bread dough covered with poppy seeds. Krendel' is similar to a large, soft pretzel and can be either sweet, with raisins and nuts, or else savory. A sign shaped like a large golden krendel' is often hung over Russian bakeries even to this day, a tradition from European bakers' guilds in the Middle Ages. Easter bread, or kulich, is the towering airy cake served during the holy week of Easter, made from rich dough that often includes raisins and other fruits. Other typical cakes and pastries include *pryaniki* (soft ginger honey cookies), tortes (European layer cakes), *rum baba* of presumed Polish origin (fruit yeast cakes soaked in rum), *khvorost* (deep-fried twisted pastry strips dusted with powdered sugar), and assorted tea cakes and cookies.

### Porridge

Russians have a saying, "*Shchi da kasha—pishcha nasha*" (Cabbage soup and gruel, that's our food). Kasha, or boiled buckwheat groats, is a Russian cultural superfood, and it is difficult to overrate the symbolic importance of a food that has nourished a people for more than a thousand years. Kasha was most likely eaten before bread baking had been perfected. The process of preparation has changed little over time. It can be boiled with milk or water, prepared sweet or savory, or served for breakfast or as a side dish. Smaller groats are often used to make a more liquid kasha with only milk. Buckwheat kasha can be prepared with almost anything mixed in—eggs, pork, pork fat, liver, onions, mushrooms, fruits, cheese, and so forth. In Russia, particularly in the Urals and in Karelia in the far north, kasha is still an important part of the daily diet. The buckwheat varieties originated in parts of Siberia and China. As the largest consumer of buckwheat worldwide, Russia is also the number-one producer of the crop. Today kasha can refer to almost any porridge made from any groats, such as cream of wheat, rice pudding, hot oatmeal, or even less common barley or millet porridge.

### Pies

Pies (*pirogi*) in Russia come in a dizzying array of preparations and presentations. The dough can be leavened or not, salty or sweet. Pies can be round, square, triangular, open, closed, large, small, or fully enclosed like the classic salmon *kulebyaka* (*coulibiac*), for example. Pirogi are usually 9–10-inch-round filled savory pies, made with a yeast dough or sometimes a short crust. They usually signify a special occasion or are a part of holiday fare. Meat, fish, or berries are common fillings. Their boiled cousins in Poland are actually dumplings, although they have almost the same name as Russian pies, *pierogi*. The terms *pirogi* and *pierogi,* with identical pronunciation, illustrate the point that making definitive conclusions about dishes based on etymology can quickly become a speculative or misleading affair. Some contend that the Slavic word *pirog* actually derives from the Turkic *borek* (also a savory pastry); others point to the Russian root *pir*, meaning "feast." Smaller, individual-sized pies are called *pirozhki*. Pirozhki are a baked or fried yeast dough with any number of fillings. They may be served with soup or eaten as a snack or appetizer. Some of the more common contents are meat, mushrooms, buckwheat, potatoes, liver, cheese, eggs, and cabbage.

### Pancakes

*Bliny*, among the few Russian foods known internationally, are small pancakes a little larger in size than a compact disc (5–6 inches in diameter). They are a traditional dish in the Spring Equinox folk festival, Maslenitsa, perhaps symbolizing the sun with their round shape. The yeast batter is what makes the taste and texture distinctive. Piled high with a pad of butter between the pancake layers, bliny provoke a festive reaction. Though traditionally made with buckwheat flour, wheat-flour bliny are now more common. Bliny are found on almost every Russian restaurant menu, with fillings of black and red caviar, fruit jams, or simply sour cream and sugar. The Jewish *blintz* is also a derivative of bliny. It has been suggested that the root *blin-* is a corruption of *mlin*, whence comes the word *mel'nitsa*, a mill where grain is ground into flour. *Blinchiki*, however, are paper-thin crepes made with little flour and served as a dessert or as a tea accompaniment. *Olad'i* are another type of pancake, smaller than bliny but much thicker and sweeter, panfried in generous amounts of butter or oil.

### Pasta and Rice

Macaroni and vermicelli are made from wheat flour and are commonly added to soups. *Makarony* is the long, tubular pasta, similar to Italian *bucatini*, sometimes reaching lengths of up to one meter. Buttered macaroni is a common side dish served with any meal. The popular *makarony poflotski* (literally "pasta of the fleet," because it is filling and easy to make—a bachelor's specialty) incorporates boiled macaroni and seasoned ground beef, fried together in a pan. *Makarony* can sometimes mean "spaghetti" or "pasta" generically in Russian. *Lapsha* is an all-encompassing term for "noodle" but specifically refers to homemade flat noodles, similar to linguine and fettuccini. The most famous noodle dishes from the region are *pelmeni* and *vareniki*. Both are filled dumplings that are boiled. Pelmeni are associated with Siberia; one Russian ethnographer has attributed the etymology to a Finno-Ugric word from the Udmurt and Komi languages where the combination *pelnian* means "ear-shaped bread." Although that may be true, the Chinese word *mein*—meaning "wheat flour," but also generally referring to dough and noodles (as in *chow mein, lo mein, ramen,* etc.)—could have made its way into the Russian Far East and been adopted by the northern tribes. Many Turkic noodle dishes also have the same *men/man* root—*laghman, manti, manpar,* and so on. Ethnic or national claims to the origin of this dish aside, pelmeni are considered as Russian as fur hats and vodka. Vareniki are Ukrainian, from the Slavic root "to boil" (*varit'*). They are similar to pelmeni, yet vareniki are usually larger and often half-mooned or triangular-shaped. During the summer vareniki are filled with cherries, plums, or berries. They can also be made with potatoes, mushrooms, soft cheese, cabbage, and meat. Pelmeni and savory vareniki are generally topped with melted butter or sour cream, but vinegar, mustard, and ketchup are also possibilities.

Rice in Russia became common in the nineteenth century, mainly through the pilaf dishes adopted from the territories of Central Asia and the Caucasus that were absorbed by the empire. The American cookbook author and teacher Fannie Farmer, in her 1918 edition of the classic *Boston Cooking-School Cook Book,* includes a recipe for Russian pilaf, "substituting cold cooked lamb in place of chicken."[9] Her Turkish pilaf, however, contains chicken, when lamb was the meat of choice among the Turks and other nomads of the region, and chicken was the Slavic preference. This confusion only underscores the difficulty of identifying the origins of dishes and the unreliability of the concept of authenticity every time a recipe is passed down, either orally or written.

### Vegetables

Russians have a hearty appetite for vegetables, usually served in soups or separately as a pickled dish. Cooked vegetables are also a main component of many salads. Eating uncooked vegetables such as broccoli, cauliflower, or mushrooms is unusual. The exception is fresh salad made of sliced cucumbers and tomatoes. Turnips, cabbages, radishes, and cucumbers are considered traditional Russian vegetables. Not surprisingly given its climate, Russia is the third-largest producer of roots and tubers.[10] Carrots, onions, and garlic provide the flavors for many savory dishes. One salad that incorporates almost all the customary Russian vegetables is *vinegret.* Stemming from the French word *vinaigrette,* a seasoned oil-and-vinegar emulsion, the salad vinegret contains potatoes, pickled cabbage or cucumbers, beets, carrots, and onions dressed with oil and vinegar. This dish has secured an ongoing place at the table during any special occasion.

Nowadays the potato reigns on the table as the caloric king. Peasants adopted the "earth apple" by coercion from Tsar Peter the Great, and the potato overtook turnip cultivation only in the nineteenth century. Potatoes, after bread, sustain the population. The most common and preferred method of preparation is peeled boiled potatoes, garnished with butter, dill, and sour cream. Fried potatoes, similar to home fries, are also widespread. They become exceptionally enticing when fried with bacon and mushrooms. Potatoes are also served mashed or pureed. French fries are now the rage in restaurants. Baked potatoes are curiously uncommon (except at campfires) given the preeminence of the Russian stove, which gave rise to such an amazing variety of breads. Potatoes are particularly suited to the low, long heat of a Russian stove. Potatoes are also frequently found in salads such as *Oliv'ye*, named for the nineteenth-century French chef Olivier, who owned the Hermitage restaurant in Moscow in the 1860s. Oliv'ye is the famous cold Russian salad of boiled and diced potatoes and carrots, onions, peas, pickles, and chicken, mixed with mayonnaise. The original recipe calls for roast game instead of chicken, but the chef's name and his dish are still found throughout the world.

Russia and cabbage are inextricably bound, and rightfully so. No self-respecting Russian can survive long without fermented or sour cabbage (*kvashenaya kapusta*). Russian cookbooks from the nineteenth century on refer to sour cabbage as kislaya kapusta, though kvashenaya is currently more frequently encountered today. The two terms are roughly synonymous, despite some attempts to identify distinct differences. Recipes and methods for making kislaya and kvashenaya so overlap, there is no single ingredient or method that distinguishes one from the other. Homemade Russian sauerkraut contains only salt, no vinegar for tartness, and it is not served as a hot side dish. Every cook has his or her own secret, like adding carrots or certain spices, but the method is straightforward and natural. Hard white cabbage is best suited for kvashenaya kapusta. The cabbage, preferably after the first frost when it hardens, is scrubbed, rinsed, shredded, and then salted. It is worked and pressed to release the natural juices. This is the fundamental difference between wet-salting in a brine solution and dry-salting, where the liquid comes from within the preserved product itself. The cabbage is placed in an open container, pressed down with a weight, and left out for a few days to naturally ferment (ideally at 70–75 degrees Fahrenheit), converting the sugars to tart lactic acid. Traditionally, it is held in wooden barrels, but glass containers are frequently used in modern homes. Naturally occurring bacteria, yeast, or other small organisms break down the sugar in the cabbage into alcohol and carbon dioxide—a process similar to the making of wine, cheese, yogurt, and so forth. Once the cabbage reaches the desired level of tang, it is refrigerated and ready for consumption.

Cabbage is an extremely versatile vegetable, great in soups, stews, salads, stuffings, and side dishes. A sulfurous scent of cooked cabbage seems to permanently saturate most modern apartment blocks in Russia. Cabbage soup (*shchi*) rates among the most popular national dishes. It was most likely made even before the consolidation of Kievan Rus' in the tenth century. At one time *shchi* was the all-encompassing term for "soup," and Russian proverbs are full of references to it. One example is "A good wife not only speaks well, but makes shchi well." *Tushyonaya kapusta* is braised cabbage, usually with meat, onion, and tomato, cooked for several hours. Cabbage rolls, called *golubtsy* in Russian and *holubtsy* in Ukrainian, are another well-known dish in which seasoned ground meat and rice are wrapped in young cabbage leaves, sometimes baked in tomato sauce, and garnished with sour cream. When meat is scarce, they can be made simply with rice or buckwheat filling.

Cucumbers, especially the pickled variety, also have a special place in the Russian culinary psyche. Again, like cabbage, Russian pickled cucumbers are pickled in brine (salt solution) and not vinegar. Fresh and pickled cucumbers are added to many hot and cold dishes. Some salads contain both. The quintessential Russian soup is *rassol'nik,* made from a broth spiked with pickle brine (*rassol*) and the following ingredients: cabbage, potatoes, carrots, parsley root and celeriac, meat or poultry, and more pickle slices. Touted as a hangover cure, it was found on the tables of nobility as early as the eighteenth century.

Culinary lore credits Mongol invader Genghis Khan bringing pickled cabbage and cucumbers to Russia, but there is no definitive proof that sauerkraut moved from east to west through Russia—in a beeline from China to Germany. Lacto-fermentation of vegetables seems to be a universal phenomenon. Wild cabbage crops were found growing along the Mediterranean and Atlantic coasts of Europe, and they were probably domesticated about two thousand years ago. The ancient Greeks and Romans ate salted cabbage. Roman texts praise sauerkraut for both its taste and medicinal properties. Pickled vegetables could also have been introduced to Russia by any number of earlier steppe people of Asia, who migrated westward across the expansive plains for centuries before the

Mongols arrived in the thirteenth century. And it is also possible that the early Slavs figured out the process all by themselves with a little help from local microorganisms.

Whereas potatoes, cabbages, and cucumbers are essential components of the Russian table, mushrooms create magic in the meal. Mushrooms, or *griby*, are neither plants nor animals, but Russians would swear they have a soul. Many civilizations, including the Slavs, have relied on mushrooms for medicinal purposes, and mushroom hunting in Russia remains a national obsession. Considering the expanse of forest and the assortment of mushrooms, it is no wonder that many a lazy day can pass in search of the perfect mushroom patch. Some people have equated the mushroom quest to fishing—an exercise in patience, care, and luck, whereas others compare it with shopping and the heady rush of finding the perfect bargain. Great mystery surrounds these fungi, in no small part because some are poisonous, deadly, or hallucinogenic. Most, however, are edible, although Russians are very particular about their culinary mushrooms. *Mukhomor*, literally "a fly exterminator," is known in the West as "fly agaric," a common toadstool that is highly poisonous and hallucinogenic. Tasteless or inedible mushrooms are called *poganki*, meaning "vile" or "filthy," arising from the Latin word *pagani*, meaning country people or peasants, only later used to refer to "non-Christians." *Borovik* is any edible mushroom of the boletus family. White mushrooms (cep or white boletes) are the most highly prized in almost all of Russia, although pickled *gruzdi*, or "milk agarics," are generally preferred in the Urals and Siberia. Other favorites are the orange-cap boletus (*podosinoviki*; literally, "from under an aspen tree"), the brown mushroom (*podberyozoviki*; literally, "from under a birch tree"; *boletus scaber*), *maslyata* (or "buttery ones"), saffron milk caps (*ryzhiki*, "little redheads"), chanterelles (*lisichki*, "small foxes"), coral milky caps (*volnushki*), and morels (*smorchki*).

Every autumn, preferably a few days after a good rain, Russians flock to the woods in search of the mushroom families *Agaricaceae* and *Boletaceae*. Mushrooms begin to decay as soon as they are picked, so they are often dried, brined, or pickled in vinegar. But the aroma of freshly picked mushrooms fried with onions in butter creates such anticipation for the meal. Mushrooms are also incorporated into fillings and stuffings, soups, and vegetable dishes. Even a mushroom stock or sauce can transform an ordinary dish into haute cuisine.

Turnip (*repa*), rutabaga (*bryukva*), and red beet (*svyokla*) form the rearguard of traditional Russian vegetables. Turnips are less common on the current Russian table but are still part of the national consciousness through folk sayings ("More commmon than stewed turnips") and folk-tales (*The Enormous Turnip*). Often pureed or cooked together with meat dishes, turnips were the staple crop of northern Russia until well into the eighteenth century. Beets were better known in the area of Ukraine, although they are now firmly established as part of the Russian culinary repertoire. The most famous dish from beets is indisputably borscht. Another common dish is the Georgian salad of boiled and diced beets mixed with garlic, walnuts, and mayonnaise. Sugar beets, sometimes confused with red beets, are the primary source for granular sugar in Russia. Beetroot sugar is generally coarser and more translucent than cane sugar because of the way it is processed. Although chemically identical to cane sugar, earnest cooks swear there is a difference between the two for baking and making marmalade.

Countless other vegetables are grown on private plots or at the dacha. Tomatoes, squash, zucchini, radishes, bell peppers, peas, green beans, cauliflower, and leafy greens add color and zest to the Russian table. Many vegetables, especially eggplant, are made into spreads or a "caviar," which is a cooked mixture of vegetables with tomatoes, onions, garlic, oil, and vinegar that preserves well. During the twentieth century under Communism, most agriculture was nationalized on state and collective farms. In addition to potatoes, Soviet farms grew beets, carrots, cabbages, cucumbers, tomatoes, and onions. A large number of hothouses made it possible to supply cucumbers and tomatoes to the markets of major cities throughout the year. Private plots accounted for roughly 40 percent of the vegetable harvest in the USSR, and even today much of the population grows produce for their consumption.[11] The harvests of the individual plots played a vital role in keeping the nation's diet varied as well as keeping alive a taste and appreciation for adeptly grown and freshly picked food.

### Fish and Seafood

Fish dominated the table of the Eastern Slavs due to its abundance and to religious prohibitions of meat, milk products, and eggs. Since the conversion of Kievan Rus' to Orthodox Christianity in the tenth century, Russians began to strictly adhere to meatless days of fasting (*post*), holy days, and festivals that covered just over half of the year in an Orthodox calendar. The Soviets accelerated the trend of fish consumption beginning in the 1970s with the creation of a massive fishing fleet that contain processing facilities aboard the larger ocean-based vessels. Russia remains a leading fish producer.

Caviar is a fish product (more specifically the fish eggs) most often associated with Russia. The familiar dark or black caviar comes from three particular species of sturgeon: *beluga, osetra,* and *sevruga.* Beluga roe is considered the most regal, ranging in color from slate to dark gray. Golden to dark brown osetra caviar with its characteristic nutty flavor is also highly prized. Light gray sevruga eggs are generally smaller with a distinctively salty taste. One type of roe rarely seen outside Russia is pressed caviar (*payusnaya ikra*). It was a preservation method for caviar before the advent of refrigeration. Today, damaged, immature, or overripe eggs are still pressed into blocks, resulting in a robust, salty, and significant fishy taste. The larger, bright red-orange caviar is roe harvested from the Siberian salmon (*keta*). It is considerably less expensive than black caviar. Recently, trout roe has become a popular addition to the caviar line in Russia. It is a medium-grained roe similar in color and taste to salmon caviar.

All these types of caviar are served with bread and butter, on deviled eggs, wrapped in bliny, or incorporated into a sauce. In more affluent households caviar is served as zakuski. Purists prefer the finer caviar served chilled on white bread, though butter is certainly not frowned upon. A sterling silver mother-of-pearl caviar spoon is also an appreciated accessory. For an elegant presentation, small, light puff pastries (*vol-au-vents*) are filled with caviar and garnished with piped butter rosettes.

The elite and venerated reputation of caviar also conceals a darker side. Until recently, the state control over Russian harvesting of roe and a U.S. trade embargo with Iran held caviar production more or less in check. Caspian sturgeon have now become an endangered species due to overfishing, unscrupulous poachers, and caviar smugglers. Yet both the caviar and the fish remain available and popular in the former Soviet Union. The sturgeon fish is still served in many restaurants, especially in the southern coastal areas. The firm, white flesh lends itself well to grilling, especially served as kebabs.

Fish is most commonly served as a smoked, cured, or salted appetizer. Salted Baltic herring (*sel'd'* or *selyodka*), by far the most abundant and popular, is found in many cold salads or served plain with oil and onions. Boiled potatoes are a perfect complement. Salted herring is sometimes soaked in milk before usage to remove excess salt. A mixed platter of cold smoked fish (*rybnoe assorti*) served as zakuski may include thin slices of eel, mackerel, sturgeon, whitefish, turbot (*paltus*), shad, and salmon. Salmon (*losos'*) comes in four main varieties in order of value: Atlantic (*syomga*), Siberian or chum (keta), sockeye (*nerka*) and humpback or pink salmon (*gorbusha*).

Herring, black bread, and potatoes.

Other familiar fish are prepared by panfrying, broiling, or baking, such as salmon trout (*forel'*), carp (*sazan*), perch (*sudak* and *okun'*), cod (*navaga* and *nalim*), flounder such as *limanda* or *kambala,* northern pike (*shchuka*), and catfish (*som*). *Ukha* is a traditional Russian soup made from almost any freshwater white fish, potatoes, onions, and carrots. Like many other Russian dishes, recipes for ukha call for the soup to be topped with fresh dill and parsley and served with a shot of vodka. Boiled crayfish (*raki*), similar in taste and appearance (though miniature) to lobster, also find their way into salads or are served whole to peel and eat with a foamy glass of beer. Anchovy species such as *khamsa* (*barabul'ka* or *sultanka* in Russian) are highly regarded, and the Black Sea anchovies (*kil'ka*) are plentiful, often canned in oil or tomato sauce. Another zakuski treat is rich cod liver (*pechen' treski*) canned in oil. Canned crab legs, imitation crab sticks, and shrimp are familiar seafood, mainly served in cold salads. Mussels, oysters, and other seafood are primarily found along the coastal regions.

A family of freshwater fish, abundant in rivers, lakes, canals, and reservoirs, the roach fish (*vobla*) is perhaps the most humble yet emblematic Russian fish. Salted and dried, it is sold in every market. Paired with beer, it is analogous to the American combination of nuts and beer. Nothing promises a better evening than several whole dried vobla laid out on a newspaper tablecloth. The head is ripped off, the side skin removed with great effort, and the little meat that remains runs along either side of the spine. The lucky diner gets the fish with dried roe. As a final part of the ritual, the air sac is burned with a match flame and consumed with glee.

### Meats and Poultry

It is difficult to exaggerate the importance of meat in the Russian diet. Whether as an entrée or an appetizer, or simply a frankfurter or a sausage, no meal is considered fully satisfying without some form of meat on the plate. Russia is among the world's leading producers, consumers, and importers of meat.[12] Beef, pork, poultry, and mutton—in order of preference and consumption—constitute the primary protein types. Soviet agriculture policy addressed animal husbandry in the late 1950s, which soon led to a modest increase in the production and consumption of meat, milk, and eggs. Even though Russia ranks sixth worldwide in meat production, it still produces seven times less meat than the United States.[13] Meat also dominates the average food-budget share for Russians, eating up almost 70 percent of the total food expenditures.[14]

Shish kebab (*shashlyk*) is the ideal method for preparing any meat or poultry in Russia. Marinated meat threaded onto metal skewers is slowly grilled, roasted, and smoked over the gentle heat of charcoal embers. Mention shashlyk (grilled skewered meat) to people in the former Soviet Union, and they will undoubtedly give credit for its existence and perfection to the people of the Caucasus, although each country has its own name for it. Shashlyk is the national dish of Georgia (called *mtsvadi*), Armenia (*khorovats*), and Azerbaijan (*kebab*). Even Russian dictionaries define shashlyk as a Caucasian food. Yet the words *shashlyk* and *kebab* clearly have Turkic roots. *Kebab* is the dominant term in Central Asia for this dish and most likely derived from the Arabic word *kabāb*, meaning "cooked meat in small pieces." *Shish* means "skewer" in many Turkic languages, and the suffix *-lik* is used to form abstract nouns or adjectives, roughly meaning "pertain-

Pork *shashlyk*.

ing to." As a matter of fact, the very word *shish kebab* is a combination of Turkic and Iranian words, underscoring the difficultly of assigning culinary heritage based entirely on etymology.[15] Obviously, grilled meat is a simple and ancient dish of nomads or herdsmen, among the first combinations of flesh and flames. So, regardless of its origins, which are hopelessly lost to antiquity, the significant factor remains that both Russians and Caucasians concede that the dish belongs to the Caucasus.

In addition to shashlyk, beef is generally prepared as fried or baked individual cuts, as part of soups and stews, or as mincemeat for meatballs or various fillings. *Zharkoe* is roasted meat, potato, and vegetable stew traditionally baked in small earthenware pots for hours in the Russian hearth. Sautéed ground beef patties, *kotlety*, are perhaps the most common meat dish. Ground beef is cut with breadcrumbs and diced onions and panfried. *Frikadelki*, from the German *fricadelles*, are small meatballs simmered in broth. Ground meat mixed with onions also creates the common fillings for pirozhki, dumplings, golubtsy, and *chebureki* (Crimean Tatar fried meat pies).

Jellied meats still maintain popularity in Russia as well as in Europe. *Zalivnoe*, from the verb zalit'(to pour in, cover with liquid), is made from fish, meat, or poultry. A gelatinous stock poured into a bowl and allowed to cool forms a translucent congealed stock around the meat and vegetables. A brother to zalivnoe, *kholodets* is simply a dish of boiled pig knuckles served in aspic, a clarified jellied meat stock. Both are served as an appetizer with mustard or horseradish. A common picnic, hiking, or camping food is *tushonka*. Stemming from the word *tushit'* (to braise or stew), tushonka is the canned beef ration found in hiking knapsacks and bachelor pads.

Internationally, Russia is probably best known for its sausages. Although the brunt of foreign jokes and derision, Russian *kolbasa* can rival the finest Italian salami and German wurst in quality. Sausage is generally made from both pork and beef. Rows of fresh sausages, liverwurst, frankfurters, and links fill store display cases. The most prevalent is the cured sausage—smoked, dried, or both. If the saying "The flavor is in the fat" is indeed true, then Moscow (*Moskovskaya*) sausage is the tastiest, because it contains more fat than meat. Ham (*vetchina*) is the most common cured pork product. Among the most flavorful, however, is *buzhenina*, salted and smoked pork loin. The Ukrainian love for pork has made its way into Russia in the form of salo, cured pork backfat. According to Armenian literary sources, salo is mentioned as a food of the Khazars of southern Russia already in the seventh century. A high-energy food, this salted and smoked pork fat is perfect on black bread as a pick-me-up to start the day in the fields, to work around shots of vodka, or to invigorate the body after the sauna.

Russian chicken dishes are as scrawny as the birds on a Soviet collective farm, so most of the preferred dishes are borrowed from their neighbors. Chicken is a major Russian import, especially since the demise of the Soviet Union. Affectionately called "Bush legs" in reference to President George H. W. Bush, American companies began to flood the Russian market with frozen chicken in the early 1990s. Poultry is used in soups, salads, and pilafs. Chicken Kiev, which takes its name from the capital of Ukraine, is a pounded chicken breast, bone attached, wrapped around a frozen seasoned butter log, breaded, and deep-fried. The sign of a properly prepared *kotleta po-kievski* is for butter to shoot out when a knife pierces the crust. *Tabaka* is a Georgian dish of whole butterflied chicken, pressed down with a weight to ensure even cooking, and panfried or roasted. It is served with a plum sauce, *tkemali*. *Chakhokhbili* is the Georgian equivalent of *coq au vin*, a seasoned chicken dish braised in red wine, with the addition of fresh herbs and tomato sauce.

### Dairy Products

The amount of milk and milk products Russians consume is surpassed only by the quantity of bread they eat, whether they are city dwellers or country folk. Where the cow is sacred in India, it is part of the family in Russia.[16] Cattle provide some of the products most dear to Russians—milk, cream, fermented drinks, cheese, butter, yogurt, sour cream, and ice cream. After sunflower oil, dairy products are the largest segment of Russian agricultural exports, specifically condensed milk and cream, yogurt, butter and milk fats, sour milk, cheese, and curds.[17]

Fresh milk is a rural treat, though it lasts only for a couple of days unprocessed. Fortunately, nature has its own ways of providing milk derivatives, and humans throughout the centuries have devised ingenious and tasty methods for preserving dairy products. If milk is allowed to settle overnight, the milk solids rise to the top forming cream (*slivki*). Sour cream (*smetana*) is cream that has begun to naturally ferment, creating the quintessential Russian addition for perfecting any dish. From the verb *smetat'*, literally "to remove" the cream from the milk, smetana is as Russian as soy sauce is Asian. Some variations approximate *crème fraîche,* or "clabber cream." Smetana is the symbolic icon of health and home; most Russians also believe that it improves the flavor of any dish—sweet, sour, spicy, or salty.

Somewhere between buttermilk and yogurt lies *prostokvasha*, where bacterial cultures act on warm milk to produce a thick, subtly tart and sweet drink. It has the reputed positive effects of aiding digestion, and therefore it is given to young and old alike. Other fermented yogurt-type drinks with active cultures are kefir and *ryazhenka*. Kefir is from the Caucasus, where numerous people regularly reach one hundred years of age with much of the credit for longevity and health going to the daily consumption of kefir and wine. The sediment of kefir is used to start the fermentation of the next batch. Kefir should be slightly carbonated, foamy, and served chilled. Most kefir today is commercially produced. Ryazhenka is also a common breakfast drink made by baking sour milk to a golden brown color. Sour milk and its offshoots virtually disappeared in the West with pasteurization. Sterilized milk spoils without souring, since any natural bacteria and microorganisms are destroyed in the industrial processing.

Gently heating prostokvasha produces tvorog, the fresh or unripened cheese of choice in Russia, similar to quark. Thicker than cottage cheese and with varying degrees of sweetness, homemade *tvorog* is sold in every market. Two dishes most often associated with this cheese are *syrniki* and *vareniki*. Syrniki, from the word "cheese" (*syr*), are tvorog pancakes. Fried in plenty of butter, syrniki are topped with smetana and sugar or jam, incorporating three dairy products in one dish. But full dairy dishes are not unusual; another example is tvorog-filled vareniki (boiled dumplings) served with butter and sour cream. *Vatrushka* is roughly equivalent to a cheese Danish or the Czech and Polish *kolačky/kolache*, a round pastry filled with a sweetened tvorog filling. But the favorite Russian cheese dish is simply a mixture of tvorog and cream, milk, or kefir, topped with sugar, usually eaten for breakfast.

Russians generally love cheese, although it was not plentiful in the Soviet era. The most common variety was *plaveny syr*, literally "soft cheese," but a more accurate meaning would be "processed cheese." The consumption of processed cheese for decades distorted the traditional Russian appreciation of cheese. Hard and soft cheeses were a rarity. Well-known semihard cheeses are Swiss and Dutch, and the most common semisoft cheese is *Rossiyskiy* (literally "Russian"), similar to Danish Havarti with a porous and smooth texture. *Brynza* is a popular salted cheese of Swiss origin (town of Brienz) made from sheep's milk, but made in the Romanian fashion. Homemade varieties most closely resemble a type of feta cheese. Brynza is often part of the hors d'oeuvres (*zakuski*) and eaten with bread or crackers.

### Fats and Oils

An overinformed public, confused about the true value of fats and oils, often unjustifiably relegates them to the role of pariahs. Yet fat is an essential source of energy and it also helps to absorb vitamins A, D, E, and K. The main fats in the Russian diet are butter, sunflower oil, and rendered animal fats. A common critique of Russian cuisine is that it is too greasy. Fatty dishes, however, are a sign of luxury, containing not only the necessary calories to supplement a sparse diet, but also adding flavor and palatability. No wonder the Russians say "One cannot spoil kasha with too much butter."

Russians make butter from the milk solids in cream and soured cream. *Maslo,* or butter, comes from the verb *mazat'* (to spread, oil, or grease). To prolong its shelf life, butter was clarified (melted) and stored throughout the winter as ghee. In nineteenth-century cookbooks, recipes called for either Russian butter (*toplyonoe;* same as ghee) or *Chukhonskoe maslo,* solid butter made from sour cream.[18] Butter is used as a spread, a frying medium, and a condiment. Sunflower (*Podsolnechnoe maslo*) is the oil of choice for frying and salads. Though native to North America, sunflowers were adopted by Russians who began to commercially produce the crop in the nineteenth century. The Russian Orthodox Church forbade other fats during Lent, and therefore Russia became the world's leading producer of sunflower oil. Finally, as all gourmands know, many of the famous classic French and European dishes, such as *cassoulet,* begin with rendered pork fat or bacon. This tradition continues in Russia, and pork fat or bacon is often used in soups and stews and fried vegetables, such as eggplants, potatoes, or bell peppers.

### Fruits

Fruit production is highly restricted in northerly climes. Therefore, apples, pears, and forest berries are the most common fruits in Russia. Many other fruits are brought in from the southern regions, particularly peaches, cherries, plums, and melons. Watermelons from Astrakhan on the Volga River delta near the Caspian Sea compete with those from Central Asia and the Caucasus in Russian markets. The best melons, however, are imported from Central Asia, along with grapes, dried apricots, and raisins. During the 1970s, bananas and oranges began to be imported in bulk from brotherly Socialist governments in Latin America and Africa. Today the Russian fruit import market exceeds 1 billion dollars.[19] Citrus fruits mainly come from Morocco, Egypt, and Turkey. Until recently, there was no separate word for lime in Russian, since limes were not imported until the 1990s. Now exotic fruits from all over the world are available in the major metropolitan areas.

Berries and cherries are the quintessential fruits of Russia. The sour cherry (*vishnya*) and the black cherry (*chereshnya*) are the most common varieties. The bountiful assortment of berries is similar to that of Scandinavia, Canada, and the northern United States. Popular varieties include the raspberry (*malina*), the gooseberry (*kryzhovnik*), the cranberry (*klyukva*), the berry known variously as the lingonberry, bilberry, huckleberry, and whortleberry (*brusnika*; *Vaccinium myrtillus*), the blueberry (*chernika*), the rowanberry or ashberry (*ryabina*), and currants—red, black, and white (*smorodina*). The delicious strawberry (*klubnika*) and the wild strawberry (*zemlyanika*) are a special treat. The berries can be eaten raw as well as frozen or dried for later use. But more often than not they are made into rich preserves, jams, and jellies used in desserts and to sweeten tea.

### Sweeteners, Condiments, and Seasonings

The customary knock against Russian food is its apparent blandness, attested by the general avoidance of pungent and hot spices by Russians. Yet an extremely flavorful cuisine derives from the Slavic combination of sour, sweet, and salty tastes with freshly picked produce. Sweeteners traditionally include honey, jams, jellies, and dried or preserved fruits. Beet sugar and fructose within fruit juices are incorporated into many dishes. Honey is largely fructose and glucose; sugar is pure sucrose. Both honey and sugar are used in preservation of other foods because they stall or prevent the growth of bacteria, yeast, and mold. Sugar bonds with water, which is essential for microbial growth. Honey has demonstrated antibacterial activity, and the moisture content is generally too low for yeasts to survive. A common preserved dessert candy is *marmelad*, fruit jelly slices coated with sugar.

The most common condiments are mayonnaise, sour cream, butter, vinegar, horseradish, mustard, ketchup, and a couple of Georgian spicy sauces. Mayonnaise is found in every sort of Russian salad, sometimes mixed with sour cream. A bitter root, horseradish (*khren*) is first grated and mixed with vinegar. Homemade versions at the market are found as either white or red, the latter made with beet juice for additional color and flavor. Horseradish, native to eastern Europe, is usually eaten with fish and cold or jellied meats. It is also incorporated into a cream sauce for classic dishes like roasted pork or poached sturgeon. Despite the Russians' love of this condiment, *khren*, in Russian (at least its adjectival form *khrenovy*), can also mean "lousy" or "awful," or describes a person in a foul mood or condition. Mustard (*gorchitsa*) is also a traditional Russian condiment, served with roasts and pork dishes as well as cold cuts and beef tongue. It is extremely hot and spicy, although some milder varieties are not uncommon. Finally, *tkemali* and *adjika* have been readily adopted in Russia from Georgia. Tkemali is a plum sauce served with grilled meats or added to other dishes for flavoring. Adjika is a spicy tomato and garlic sauce used in much the same way as tkemali.

The primary herbs in Russian cuisine are parsley and dill (*pertrushka* and *ukrop*). They are found on almost every table in a variety of guises: as a dish of whole stalks, an ingredient in most salads, an added flavor for soups and stews, and a garnish for these same dishes. Bay leaves and sweet paprika are often added to soups and stews. In making many Central Asian or Caucasian dishes, cilantro (fresh coriander) is essential. Seasonings are minimal; usually only salt and black or red (paprika) pepper are used in cooking and also found in shakers on the dining tables. Anise, allspice, cloves, cinnamon, and nutmeg are sparingly applied to some pastries and baked goods. With a traditional dearth of lemons, many Russian recipes call for citric acid, extracted from acidic fruits. The acid imparts sour warmth to borscht, jams, and drinks.

### Beverages

In marketing terms, Russia and vodka are inextricable. In reality, however, tea retains the title of the Russian national drink. Beer is the trendy and affordable beverage of choice of the younger generations, while traditional drinks such as *kvas, kisel', sbiten'*, and mead (*myod*) still hold an important, if not purely symbolic or nostalgic, place in Russian culinary thought and action.

Tea, or *chai* (from the Chinese character *cha*), is consumed at breakfast, lunch, and dinner. It is served in the afternoon and as a late-night drink. Russian tea, with lemon and sugar cubes, is served piping hot in porcelain cups with saucers or in glasses with metal holders. It is usually strong and well sweetened with sugar, or perhaps jam and honey. It is hardly an exaggeration to claim that everyone drinks tea. Even children learn from an early age to enjoy it, no doubt because it is often served with chocolate, candy, wafers, cookies, or other pastries. Although the traditional tea pot, the samovar, is less prominent in small urban apartments, tea drinking has not lost its significance. At the workplace, employees frequently break for tea. At a reception, if a full meal is not served, tea and appetizers or sweets are more than sufficient to create a jovial atmosphere. Tea arrived in Russia in the seventeenth century and was firmly entrenched by the nineteenth century. As the tea craze was sweeping Europe, especially Holland and England, tea became the ideal Russian drink—strong, inviting, and nourishing—to counter the unforgiving environment. Russia attempted to grow tea in Crimea in 1814 but was successful only in the semitropical climate of Georgia in 1847. From there, it has had limited success in other regions of the Caucasus. Coffee, too, had its admirers, especially among the Balts and Crimean Tatars, but fresh coffee beans practically vanished with the 1917 revolution. Later generations were raised on instant coffee in the Soviet period, a preference that has persisted for many in the older generation. Coffee, in all its Italian varieties, has now found favor with the younger crowd.

Mention vodka and Russia pops to mind. The converse is also true. It may be the most familiar Russian word in the English language. Originally consumed for medicinal purposes, vodka mixed with salt, pepper, or honey is still found in folk remedies. The Russian state has maintained a monopoly on vodka beginning in the seventeenth century that filled the government coffers with plentiful and steady tax revenues. Vodka fueled the indomitable Russian army, bestowed merriment to royal and peasant occasions alike, and in a peculiar way obscured, as well as added to, the misery of the Russian historical experience of the last two centuries. Vodka is served with meals as part of a celebratory event. Toasts to health, the host, success, and family are mandatory. Vodka is invariably imbibed straight, usually in two-to-four-ounce portions. Russians rarely drink cocktails and never drink alcoholic beverages without food. An appetizer immediately follows each drink, even if it is a humble pickle, or a piece of salami, or bread.

Since the breakup of the Soviet Union, beer has overtaken vodka in terms of sheer quantities consumed. This is due in large part because it is less expensive than vodka, it is marketed profusely, and, for the younger generations, it establishes a type of illusory kinship with greater Europe. While beer was also consumed in great quantities in early imperial Russia (until it cut into vodka revenues), kvas continued to be freely produced and sold by street vendors. This traditional drink, known in Kievan Rus' by the tenth century, has a texture similar to beer, but it is sweeter and has almost no alcohol. It was made at home with water, bread, malt, and flour. Today kvas is still very popular as a drink with meals or as a midday refresher, much like soft drinks in the United States. But it is difficult for kvas to compete with ubiquitous western soft drinks.

Honey was used in kvas, sbiten', and, of course, mead. Sbiten'—a hot drink made from honey, treacle (sugar byproduct similar to molasses), and spices (cinnamon, cloves, mint, hops, etc.)—competed with tea and coffee throughout the nineteenth century. It is served with cookies and cakes. Mead (or *myod*, the same word for "honey" in Russian) is an ancient fermented drink of honey, water, and spices. Roman writers mention that mead was a favorite Scythian drink, although it became widespread in Russia much later. Homemade wine is produced from apples, pears, quinces, cherries, and practically every berry. *Nastoyka* is a wine or liqueur made by steeping roots and herbs without distilling. Samogon, literally "self-brewed," refers to moonshine and comes in as many varieties as there are home distillers. Samogon was strongly revived in Russia during the antialcohol campaigns of Gorbachev in the mid-1980s, with the unintended consequence of nationwide sugar shortages, since sugar is the main component in the production of alcohol.

Two traditional Russian drinks are *kompot* and kisel'. Kisel' is a thick, starchy drink made of cooked, strained fruit with pectin for consistency. Kompot (compote) is made by boiling fresh or dried fruits and sugar in water. *Limonad* is lemonade but also used generically to include any soft drink. Mineral water, both noncarbonated and carbonated, is available from several dozen sources and manufacturers, particularly from Siberia and the Caucasus.

## CENTRAL ASIA

It is tempting to view Central Asia as a uniform geographic area. Indeed satellite photographs of the region reveal a continuous brown swath between the forest greenery of Siberia to the north and the countries of China and India to the south. Beginning in Mongolia and stretching to the Black Sea, this well-worn patch of high plateau shouldered recurrent migrants and conquerors, nomads, and splendid civilizations. On the ground, however, this seemingly uniform patch ranges to the extremes: fertile steppes of northern Kazakstan, imposing alpine mountains of Tajikistan and Kyrgyzstan, the oases and deserts of Uzbekistan and Turkmenistan, and fertile mountain valleys interspersed throughout. Much of the arable land is reserved for pasturage to feed the sheep and goats, a nomadic custom for centuries. Since the Russians introduced the "white gold" of cotton and massive irrigation projects in the nineteenth century, it has been difficult to forgo the profits of cotton export in favor of growing more fruits and vegetables. The land is exhausted and highly saline; water sources are becoming scarce. Despite the bleakness of first appearances, Central Asia produces some of the world's sweetest sun-drenched melons, tomatoes, grapes, and apricots. Combined with the meat and milk products of the pastoralists, a picture of Central Asian cuisine begins to take form. Regardless of the geographic diversity, Central Asian cuisine possesses more inherent similarities than the cookery of Russia can claim.

The rich, mildly seasoned, and celebratory qualities of Central Asian cookery reflect the nomadic, eastern, and Islamic customs of the region. The high courtly style of Persian cuisine, famous for its perfumed rice dishes and fatty-tailed sheep, heavily influenced the regal cities of Samarqand, Bukhara, and Merv. Central Asian cuisine also incorporates the distinguished cooking methods of China with its reliance on woks and steaming. Grilled meats, yogurt, and stuffed vegetables are similar to those found in the Middle East. Rice pilaf, shashlyk, noodle dishes, flat breads, and halva are among the most recognizable dishes. Dishes that may seem unusual to the Westerner include green turnip salads, pumpkin or mung bean stews, horse sausage, and hearty kebabs of liver and sheep fat. The Russians introduced beets, potatoes, and vodka, and the modern era brings pizza, beer, and ice-cream sandwiches.

## Regional Distinctions

As part of the process of nation building, the five new Central Asian states that emerged from the demise of the USSR consciously strive to draw cultural distinctions among themselves. Russians referred to most inhabitants as Turkomen or Tatars, making a distinction only for city dwellers, who were called Sarts. These settled inhabitants generally derived their identity first as a Muslim and second as a native of a town or region. The European notion of ethnicity and nation had yet to take root in Central Asia. In terms of culinary cultures, it is possible to divide the region into multiple categories: nomadic or urban; highland or lowland; and Mongol, Turkic, or Iranian. Kazakstan, Kyrgyzstan, and Turkmenistan represent the subsistence nomadic diet based on meat and dairy products. The settled Turks—Uzbeks and Uighurs (from western China)—form another Central Asian tradition. Their core cuisine includes pilafs, kebabs, noodles, stews, tandoori breads, and savory pastries. The Eastern philosophy of harmony and balance permeates the cuisine, underlying the preventative and medicinal qualities of food. The third culinary group is Iranian, encompassing Tajikistan and southern Uzbekistan, extending into parts of northern Pakistan and India. Rice dishes, stewed vegetables, extensive spices, and lavish sweets mark this cuisine. Despite attempts at classification and definition of all the varied features or regional variations, the uniformity of lifestyle, customs, and history produces a singular identifiable culinary culture.

## Food Production

After a century of Soviet development of an infrastructure to support cotton production and to supply the rest of the USSR with fruits and vegetables, agriculture in Central Asia has struggled to transform since independence. State control of agriculture persists, and, like in Russia, a sizable percentage of produce comes from private plots and gardens. The governments generally manage production, marketing, and pricing of food commodities. Problems with transportation and distribution of fresh crops continue in the post-Soviet period. During the height of the season, local markets cannot sell the huge quantities of fruit and vegetables quickly enough; therefore, a large portion of the harvest goes to spoilage. Food-processing companies attempt to preserve the remainder of the crop by increasing the production of juices, jams, tomato paste, and canned vegetables.

Uzbekistan and Turkmenistan are 80 percent desert; Kyrgyzstan and Tajikistan are dominated by mountain ranges; and Kazakstan, the largest of the five countries, is mountainous in the south and three-quarters desert or semidesert, with fertile steppe under heavy cultivation in the north. The arable and permanent cropland in these countries ranges from 4 to 11 percent of the total size of each country.[20] For all the natural obstacles to agriculture, Uzbekistan trails only the United States in cotton exports and enjoys a mild climate and a bountiful growing season. It also contains the region's two major rivers, the Amu Darya and Syr Darya, indispensable for irrigation. The primary agricultural products of Uzbekistan and Tajikistan, after cotton, are grains, fruits, and vegetables. Kyrgyzstan produces impressive livestock from its alpine pastures. Orchard crops, livestock, grain, and honey occupy the main sectors of food production in Turkmenistan. Kazakstan supplies the region with grain, rice, meat and poultry, dairy products, alcoholic and nonalcoholic beverages, vegetable oil and fats, and sugar.

## Catalog of Common Foods

### Grains

Grains form the dietary basis for most Central Asians. The most common use of grain is in the form of wheat flour for breads. Rice and noodles

Bread seller, Kashgar, China.

are the other starchy mainstays. Kazakstan is a major producer of wheat, but all five countries grow wheat, oats, corn, barley, and rice to some extent. Flatbread (*non*) is present at every meal. Non was traditionally made at home, although now it is increasingly sold at markets or communal bakeries. The standard non is simply a mixture of wheat flour, water, yeast, and salt. The dough ferments and proofs overnight, then it is baked in a tandoor before dawn. European-style dark and white wheat-bread loaves have become common in urban areas through Russian influence.

Though nothing compares to the flavor and texture of non baked in a tandoor, flatbreads can also be made in a regular oven, in a pan, or on a griddle over an open flame. Special varieties of non resemble a cross between a calzone and a pizza; the dough is cut with onions, pumpkin, pieces of sheep's tail fat or meat, and then baked. *Katlama* is flaky, fried flatbread cooked on a skillet or in a *qazan* (woklike pan). This rich dough is made by repeatedly folding in oil or butter, much like the process for puff pastry. Katlama is very similar to the Indian *parathas* in appearance and taste.

Rice was first cultivated in south Asia thousands of years ago and eventually made its way to Central Asia by the third through the second centuries B.C., via the Silk Road. Rice pilaf (*palov*) is the flagship of Central Asian cookery. In its most basic form, it is a dish with rice, meat, onions, and carrots. However, it has a much greater cultural significance. Palov is intimately bound to hospitality, community, and identity. Palov provides nourishment as well as a glimpse into the Central Asian psyche. Ideally, the master chef (*oshpaz*) cooks palov in a qazan over an open flame. Palov is sold on the street, served in restaurants, and served as the traditional meal whenever entertaining special guests. It is therefore understandable that visitors mistakenly conclude that pilaf is the only Central Asian dish. This also illustrates the inherent problem in describing a "national" cuisine: foreigners have a tendency to say "they always do it that way," perhaps based only on a single experience, while the locals say "we never do it that way," based only on their family or community experiences.

From the earliest times, a paste of flour and water has formed the basis for many meals. Turkic nomads have added dough to their dishes for centuries. *Sutli atala* is an Uzbek milk soup thickened with flour, while a similar dish in Tajikistan is called *atolai kochi*. *Manpar* are small bits of pinched dough, or sometimes small square noodles, in a meat soup. The varieties of noodles and filled dumplings make Central Asian cuisine especially diverse. *Laghman* is a thick noodle dish served with a soup or dry with meat, peppers, tomatoes, and onions. Kazak *beshbarmak*, literally "five fingers" since it is traditionally eaten by hand, are large square noodles topped with thin slices of boiled meat. Among the most distinctive noodle dishes is *noryn*, very thinly sliced flat noodles with horse sausage. Uighurs, many of whom emigrated from China in the late nineteenth century and again in the mid-twentieth century, are the masters of hand-pulled noodles. They can transform a ball of dough into laghman in minutes. *Chuchvara* in Uzbek, or *tushbera* in Tajik, are the Central Asian version of pelmeni, filled with meat and onions. A special spring treat is *koq chuchvara*, a filling made with any mixture of greens available: sorrel, spinach, mint, cilantro, dill, basil, thyme, parsley, celeriac, garlic, green onion, arugula, shepherd's purse, and topped with yogurt. *Hunon* is a steamed noodle roulade stuffed with meat, potatoes, or pumpkin. The dough is thinly rolled out, and the filling is spread on top. Then the edge is rolled up like a jellyroll and coiled onto a steamer. The favorite dumpling dish, however, is *manti* (*mandoo* in Korean), served as a main course. They are usually filled with mutton and onions, although sometimes they are made with pumpkin and served with a sauce of tomatoes, potatoes, and diced mutton. In Kazak they are called *hoshan* and fried in butter after steaming. Adding to the confusion, manti in Turkey are small, triangular boiled dumplings, that go by the same name as their larger steamed Central Asian relatives.

The savory meat pastries in Central Asia are similar to those found in Russia, which is not surprising since many have the same source and the same name. A Kazan Tatar dish, *belishi* (Russian *belyashi*), is a fried dough with mincemeat and onion filling similar to chebureki, eaten throughout the former Soviet Union. Central Asians also use the tandoor to make triangular or round *samsa* (Uzbek) or *sambusa* (Tajik) with the standard mutton-and-onion filling. A near kin of the Indian *samosa*, samsa are

Tandoor oven with *samsa*, Bukhara, Uzbekistan.

made with both rich and lean doughs. The lean-dough samsa are every-day fare, while the spiraled-top rich doughs are made with fat or butter to produce a flaky pastry with a texture reminiscent of the Greek *spanoko-pita*. Potato, pumpkin, fresh cheese, greens, or chickpeas (Tajik) are other possible fillings for either manti or samsa.

### Dairy Products

The Central Asians remain true to their pastoral heritage as manifested in their sizable livestock herds. The principal products from cattle, sheep, and goats are dairy products, leather, meat, and wool. Central Asia is re-nowned for the vibrancy of its fermented dairy products. The region can claim *kumiss*, fermented mare's milk, among its most well known con-tributions to world cuisine. Few tales of the Mongol Empire are as often repeated as that of the magnificent silver-tree fountain from which kumiss and other drinks poured from four heads of a beast, variously attributed as lions or dragons.[21] Central Asia uses the natural fermentation cycle of milk, just like in Russia, to achieve a wide variety of dairy products. Fresh milk sours by the process of naturally occurring yeasts and bacteria in the air, and thus becomes yogurt. Some yogurt is made with naturally occurring bacteria, while other yogurts are made by adding a bacterial culture to fresh cow, ewe, goat, or even camel milk. *Katyk* is made from heating milk and then allowing it to sour naturally. Both yogurt and katyk are served as an appetizer and used frequently as a garnish in soups and stews. *Ayran* is a salty mix of yogurt and water, especially refreshing in the summer. Ayran is found in Turkey, too, and is essentially the same as the Indian salt *lassi*. *Kaymak* is made from heating fresh milk and leaving it to cool overnight. The higher-fat cream layer skimmed from the top of raw milk results in a product comparable to *crème fraîche*. The milk solids are removed and eaten with flatbread and honey for breakfast. Yogurt may be drained to make *suzma*, similar to tvorog or fresh cheese. Suzma is eaten plain, served as a garnish to a main course, made into salads when mixed with herbs and spices, or added to soups. Some Central Asians use sour milk products in their batters and doughs, much like buttermilk, to give a distinctive sour flavor profile.

Quite unlike anything in the United States are the milk drinks from mares and camels. Kumiss is sold from the roadside throughout the highlands in the summer, but it does not compare to the kumiss obtained directly from the herders in remote mountain regions. Kumiss is made in a specially prepared sheepskin flask (*chinach*), which has been smoke-dried to impart a distinctive flavor to the milk. The milk is churned on occasion with a stick called *bishkek*, now the name of the Kyrgyz capital city. Once the mare's milk ferments, a portion of the fermented milk may be added to fresh milk to start the next batch. The end result should be fizzy and mildly alcoholic, creating a taste that one rarely forgets, no matter the reaction to the first sip. In Turkmenistan and Kazakstan, where camels are more plentiful, fermented camel's milk is called *chal* and *shubat*, respectively. The creamy froth of chal is *agaran*, a dromedary version of the vaunted Devonshire clotted cream.

*Panir* is the general term for Central Asian cheese that is set with rennet from the sheep's stomach. Salted sun-dried cheese is enjoyed from Mongolia to Macedonia—variously referred to as *kurt*, *kurtob*, *kurut*, *chake*, *qurut*, *keş* (in Turkey), *mizithra* (in Greece), and so on. It can be made from boiled milk from a cow, ewe, goat, or mare. These small, white cheese balls are ideal travel food for the nomad or warrior, although today they are eaten as a snack with beer or crumbled into salads and soups.

### Meats

Archaeological and scientific evidence indicates that the domestication of sheep and goats probably began in southwestern Asia eight to nine thousand years ago. Contrary to common assumptions, meat was a rare treat in the traditional nomadic lifestyle. A herdsman's pride, as well as his wealth, largely depended on the number of livestock owned by the family or clan. Therefore, sheep were slaughtered mostly during grand festivals or holidays. Much of the meat consumed came from the older sections of the herd. Today, meat is part of most meals. The primary source of protein in Central Asia comes from mutton, beef, poultry, and eggs. Goat and camel are less common. Pork is usually raised and eaten by Slavs, Koreans, and Germans who live in the area.

Mutton is the most important meat, and unless otherwise specified, almost all recipes and menus that list meat denote mutton. Throughout Central Asia fat-tailed sheep are esteemed for their meat, fat, milk, and wool. These sheep get their name from the large amounts of fat that they store in their rumps. While their wool can be used for weaving carpets or kilims, the sheep are also kept for their milk-producing ability. But the fat itself is most cherished, sometimes costing more than the meat from the same animal. It is rendered for oil, added to fillings for flavor and moisture, used for roulades instead of meat, and eaten grilled with liver. In a premodern subsistence world, high-calorie, fatty treats were few and far between. In most any recipe, beef can substitute for mutton, but there is no replacement for sheep fat. It gives the cuisine of Central Asia its most distinctive and luxurious characteristic. Rendered fat, since it is so expensive, is usually mixed with vegetable oil. Sheep fat is also the source for a familiar sticking point—external protests by cholesterol-conscious do-gooders that the food is too greasy. Excess, however, occurs only with regular daily consumption, which is beyond the reach of the majority of Central Asians.

Meat is most commonly served as kebabs made from beef, mutton, liver, mincemeat, and chicken. It is also found in pilaf, soups (*shorpo, shurva, sorpa*), stews (*kovorma*), and salads. Horse meat and horse sausage are consumed mainly in Kyrgyzstan and Kazakstan. *Chuchuk* or *kazy*, sausage made from horse meat, is considered a delicacy. Central Asians still enjoy

*Shashlyk*, Qarshi, Uzbekistan.

animal offal, internal organs such as the heart, liver, lungs, brains, and tongue. When an animal is slaughtered, almost every portion of the beast is utilized in some fashion. *Hassip* is a steamed sausage of rice and offal made into links within animal casings.

### Vegetables

In regard to state vegetable production, all five Central Asian countries grow huge quantities of tomatoes and potatoes. Both are New World foods introduced to Central Asia as commercial crops in the nineteenth century with the arrival of the Russians. Kyrgyzstan harvests and processes sugar beets, and Turkmenistan claims almond and even olive groves. The vegetables from private plots and small farmers are among the freshest and most succulent in the world. Almost all produce is locally grown, and the bazaars have a tremendous selection of fruits, vegetables, and nuts. The chief vegetables are tomatoes, peppers, onions, cucumbers, and eggplant. Some kinds of vegetables that are virtually unknown outside Central Asia include green radishes (*turp*), yellow carrots (actually a type of turnip), and dozens of pumpkin and squash varieties. Pumpkin is found in stews, samsa, and manti. Vegetables most often are grilled or stewed. A salad made from fresh tomato, onion, and hot pepper (*achik-chichuk*) is enjoyed throughout the warm months, and turp salad accompanies the main dish in the winter. Among the legumes, chickpeas and mung beans are the most prevalent. One succulent dish, *dimlama*, is made with layers of mutton and vegetables, slowly braised in a tightly sealed pot. Meat and fat go on the bottom of the pot, layered with onions, carrots, potatoes, cabbage, garlic, and even beets—whatever the imagination and market offer. *Dolma* is a Turkic word meaning "stuffed." While the most common association of dolma is with grape leaves, practically any vegetable—cabbage, peppers, tomatoes—may serve as a container or wrap for a filling.

### Fruits

The superiority of Central Asian fruit has been hailed over the ages. In the seventh century the Kingdom of Samarqand in present-day Uzbekistan sent a gift of golden fruit (perhaps apples) to the Chinese emperor of the Tang dynasty. Early travelers to Central Asia, Western China, and Iran never failed to mention the selection of luscious melons. Grapes, apples, quinces, and melons compose the largest fruit crops of the region. The spring is eagerly awaited for all the new plants, herbs, vegetables, and fruits that begin to appear. The fresh, young grape leaves are stuffed with a rice-and-meat mixture in a fashion almost identical to that found in Middle East cuisine. Although the Russians attempted to produce wine from the massive grape harvests of the region in the early twentieth century, the fruit is still primarily enjoyed fresh or dried as raisins. In fact, almost every fruit, if not eaten fresh, may be cooked in pilafs and stews; dried; or converted into preserves, jams, and drinks. Apricots, strawberries, cherries, figs, and peaches are other fruits that appear in the early warm months. Toward the end of the summer, the fruit orchards bloom with apples, quinces, persimmons, and pears. The final growing season produces the legendary melons, as well as pomegranates, lemons, and mandarins. Pomegranate seeds are mixed in salads, and one effortless dish combines only onions and pomegranate seeds. Citrons, similar to lemons, are native to Central Asia and have a thick, aromatic rind. The rind and the pulp are usually preserved in sugar or salt. The peel may be used as a seasoning, and the juice is indispensable for acidity and vitamin C. Sun-drying fruit also preserves the foodstuffs for travel or to last through the winter months. After drying, melon slices may be braided into long ropes. Dried apricots, figs, dates, and raisins are eaten as a snack or with green tea, and sometimes they are added to pilafs and stews. Fruits and nuts from Central Asia are still widely exported throughout the NIS.

Spice market, Namangan, Uzbekistan.

### Seasoning and Oils

Central Asian cuisine is characteristically mild, but piquant sauces, garlicky relishes, and even whole peppers are added for punch in some regions, especially in the Ferghana Valley—the fertile region shared by Uzbekistan, Tajikistan, and Kyrgyzstan. Rendered sheep fat is the general cooking oil, often mixed with cottonseed oil. Cottonseed oil has a strong and distinctive taste, and Central Asians bring it to the smoking point before adding the food, in the belief that the heat purifies the oil and seasons the wok. Vegetable oils are becoming more popular, although olive oil and butter are not traditional cooking fats.

In addition to the flavor provided by the cottonseed oil and rendered animal fat, the secondary seasoning comes from black cumin, red and black pepper, barberries, coriander, and sesame seeds. The Uzbek cumin (*zera*) is smaller, darker, and more pungent than the seeds found in the West. Barberries are an acidic fruit, gathered in the autumn, from an ornamental shrub. They contain vitamin C and, used in moderation, impart a tartness to any pilaf or stew. Cilantro (*kinza*) and parsley are the primary herbs, although dill, celeriac, and a pungent basil are broadly available. The Central Asians share with Russians a fondness for seasoning with wine vinegar (in salads and marinades) and garnishing dishes with fermented milk products and fresh herbs.

### Beverages

Green tea (*koq choy*) reigns as the main beverage in Central Asia. It is the drink of hospitality, of leisure, and of health. Countless cups are consumed throughout the day. Green tea is served at every meal, and it is always the right time for a cup of tea. Central Asians prefer to drink it straight, but sugar is customarily offered to guests. While not as elaborate as a Japanese tea ceremony, there still exist certain rituals when taking tea in Central Asia. One custom, called *shapirish* in Uzbek, is to pour a cup of tea and return it back to the teapot two times. The tea figuratively goes from mud (*loy*) to tea (*choy*) to wine (*moy*). Another is to pour only half a cup or less, as a show of respect, since a full cup may cool before it is finished. Black tea, too, is served in Slavic areas.

Mineral waters are common to the mountainous regions and several are bottled. In Kyrgyzstan, *bozo* is a wheat and millet-fermented winter drink containing a trace of alcohol, and *maksym* is a thick, wheat-based summertime drink. Fermented millet beer is found throughout the world: Turkey (*boza*), West Africa (*pito*), Nepal (*thongba*) and Tibet (*chang*).

Fruit juice is *sharbat*, a Farsi word that made its way to Europe to describe a frozen dessert made from fruit juice (sherbet). Kompot and kisel' in the Russian tradition have also become common beverages.

### Sweets and Desserts

Dessert in general is another European borrowing. Sweet dishes are, however, part of teatime. An addictive mixture of walnuts and raisins is a frequent offering with tea. Endless varieties of halva, fruits, and confections—including sugar-coated almonds and crystallized sugar (*novvot*)— also make an appearance at teatime. Dried fruit is combined with honey, walnuts, pistachios, or almonds into many dessert recipes. Cakes and pastries, however, are a Russian addition. Central Asians have several other sweetened-dough recipes. In Uzbekistan, *chakchak* is fried dough fingers coated with honey, and *urama* is fried spiraled strips of dough dusted with powdered sugar. *Boorsok* are unsweetened triangular pieces of leavened dough deep-fried and served with tea in Kyrgyzstan.

## NOTES

1. Russia has 126,820 hectares of arable and permanent cropland, behind the United States (179,000), India (169,700) and China (135,557). NationMaster. com, "Map & Graph: Agriculture: Top 100 Arable and Permanent cropland," http://www.nationmaster.com/graph-T/agr_ara_and_per_cro.

2. Barbara Santich, *Looking for Flavour* (Kent Town, South Australia: Wakefield Press, 1996), 69.

3. Elisabeth Rozin, *Ethnic Cuisine: The Flavor-Principle Cookbook* (New York: Penguin Books, 1983), 12.

4. Steven Mennell, A. Murcott, and A. van Otterloo, *The Sociology of Food: Eating, Diet, and Culture* (London: Sage, 1992), 84.

5. N.M. Karamzin, *Istoriya gosudarstva Rossiyskogo* [The History of the Russian State] (Moscow: Kniga, 1988).

6. NationMaster.com, "Russia: Agriculture," http://www.nationmaster.com/country/rs/Agriculture.

7. G.R. Mack and J.C. Carter, *Crimean Chersonesos: City, Chora, Museum, and Environs* (Austin, TX: Institute of Classical Archaeology, 2003), 25.

8. Eva Agnesi, *Time for Pasta* (Rome: Museo Nazionale Paste Alimentari, 1998), 63.

9. Fannie Farmer, *Boston Cooking-School Cook Book* (Boston: Little, Brown, 1918), http://www.bartleby.com/87/0006.html.

10. After China (170,478 metric tons) and Nigeria (53,717) stands Russia (35,664). NationMaster.com, "Map & Graph: Agriculture: Top 100 Root and

Tuber Production," http://www.nationmaster.com/red/graph-T/agr_roo_and_tub_pro&int=3.

11. AllRefer.com, "Country Study & Country Guide—Soviet Union USSR," http://reference.allrefer.com/country-guide-study/soviet-union/soviet-union360.html.

12. USDA Foreign Agricultural Service's Production, Supply and Distribution (PS&D) online database, "Beef and Veal Summary Selected Countries," http://www.fas.usda.gov/psd/complete_tables/LP-table2–7.htm.

13. China is the largest producer with 53,747 metric tons, followed by the United States (35,085), while Russia ranks sixth (4,953). NationMaster.com, "Agriculture: Top 100 Meat Production," http://www.nationmaster.com/graph-T/agr_mea_pro.

14. USDA Economic Research Service, "International Food Consumption Patterns—Russia," http://www.ers.usda.gov/Data/InternationalFoodDemand/RERUN.ASP?RUNID=126850454&RSTYLE=1&VIEW=FBS&FILETYPE=None&Country=Russia&Commodity=999.

15. The word shashlyk was well known in Russia as early as the seventeenth century with the first written reference appearing in Staneinii spisok 1639–49 (a type of diplomatic report) by F. Yelchin, who spent much time in Georgia. Central Asians mainly use the word kebab/kebob for all types of skewered meat dishes, but shashlyk is also commonly heard.

16. M. S. Zimina, Entsiklopediya russkoy kukhni [Encyclopedia of Russian Cuisine] (St. Petersburg: Diamant, 1998), 125.

17. Ye. Gaidar, Russian Economy in 2000: Trends and Outlooks (Moscow: Institute for the Economy in Transition, 2001), http://www.iet.ru/trend/.

18. Chukhontsy is the pejorative Russian term for the Finno-Urgic peoples living around the area of St. Petersburg, particularly the Estonians.

19. In 2002 Russia imported 2.8 million tons of fruit. "Russian Fruit Market—Tendencies. Materials for Study Case at Eurofruit Conference at Cape Town, 2003," http://www.foa.org.ru/news/capetown/fva_sp.doc.

20. Cropland as percentage of total land—Uzbekistan, 11 percent; Kazakstan, 8 percent; Kyrgyzstan, 7 percent; Tajikistan, 6 percent; Turkmenistan, 4 percent; United States, 20 percent. NationMaster.com, "Agriculture: Top 100 Arable and Permanent Cropland," http://www.nationmaster.com/graph-T/agr_ara_and_per_cro.

21. In his 1254 depiction of the court of the Great Khan of Mongolia in Karakorum, William of Rubruck reported that the fountain was tree shaped and made of solid silver. Four lions at the base of the fountain dispensed kumiss and the top four branches flowed with wine, rice wine, mead, and distilled kumiss. These drinks represented the four major areas of the Mongol Empire—Persia, China, Russia, and Central Asia.

# 4

# Cooking

In the domestic sphere of traditional societies in Russia and Central Asia, the typical division of labor places the woman in charge of household affairs, while the man leaves the home for commercial or agricultural activity. Cooking by and large is the most time-consuming (if not the most important) responsibility of the woman of the house. In general, females are responsible for feeding the family and maintaining the domicile, and the man has free reign cooking outdoors with an open flame. In a multigenerational household, the grandmother may assume the bulk of the cooking chores and the wife and children assist in preparation. Men in both Russia and Central Asia rarely concern themselves with daily meals and are often completely lost in their own kitchen. They are responsible for procuring bread and other basic staples, but the full brunt of family care and nutrition rests with the females. This conservative division of labor remains rigidly in place in Russia and Central Asia. Until the middle of the nineteenth century a woman in Russia had no legal rights. She was the property of her husband, and her social status depended on that of her husband. In rural settings, the men planted and harvested the crops or worked outside the home to earn a wage, and the womenfolk were expected to feed the livestock, prepare and store raw products, plan the weekly menus, apportion the food among family members, and clean up after meals.

Men, on the other hand, predominate in the commercial food sector, working as street vendors, produce and meat merchants, cooks, and pro-

Mother and daughter make *pelmeni*,
Moscow.

fessional chefs. There is nothing in the male genes, however, that endows
them with some particular disposition in the culinary realm in restaurants
or cafés, despite the lingering stereotypes about the superiority of male
chefs. Generally, women in traditional societies did not engage in mar-
ketplace activity. Some men still argue that the preparation of enormous
quantities of food and the management of a staff of cooks and subordi-
nates are better suited to the masculine qualities of power and control.
Until the twentieth century, women in many societies were confined to
the home, where the number of healthy offspring often determined family
wealth. Indeed, until recently, work in a commercial kitchen required raw
physical strength and stamina. Standing all day long, working with whole
animal carcasses, withstanding the temperature extremes, and hoisting
pots and serving containers are back-breaking activities. The other crucial factor for an all-male kitchen was the woman's hierarchical position
in society. Run much like a military operation, the kitchen was not a
place where a woman could command the requisite respect to be able to
order men to perform their duties.

Even after a century of Soviet Socialist experiments promoting the
equality of the sexes, these stereotypes of "the fairer sex" remain in the
former Soviet Union. In management or positions of authority, men still
dominate in all areas of professional, administrative, and commercial activity. It will be many generations before women are regularly accepted in

leadership positions in the large-scale commercial kitchen. In the West, this transition has been alleviated with the introduction of convenient technological kitchen innovations that require less physical exertion. Specially designed equipment mechanically performs the tasks that formerly demanded significant physical strength. One example is the tilting kettle (10–200 gallons), in which huge quantities of soups, stews, and sauces may be prepared and then transferred to smaller pots or serving dishes with the assistance of an easily manageable lever.

If fire is involved, men in both Russia and Central Asia permit themselves to cook shashlyk and pilaf. These are the standard dishes for a party or picnic, and men jostle for the best results as a point of masculine pride, much like an American barbecue. Men must be accomplished with the flame before attempting to make pilaf for a group. In Uzbekistan, the quantity of food prepared at one time leaves little room for error. As ingredients are expensive, one mistake could mean wasting the equivalent of a week's worth of wages. Usually the patriarch is in charge of the pilaf when it is prepared outside or during special occasions. The matriarch prepares pilaf for everyday dining or during the winter when using the indoor kitchen. When the next generation is handed the reigns from the matriarch or patriarch, it signifies not only culinary prowess; it symbolizes a dramatic shift in family dynamics, a new position of power. The patriarch becomes a figurehead—the new leader is acknowledged as the head of the family.

How do young men and women learn to make shashlyk and pilaf if they are not allowed to make it at home? First of all, the method of preparation and the requisite ingredients and proportions are known from their earliest childhood experiences. Children watch the cook hundreds of times

Preparing family lunch, Tashkent, Uzbekistan.

before ever holding a skewer or spatula. Young people are allowed to help start a fire, chop the meat and vegetables, or pick the rocks out of the rice. For young men, picnics allow a chance to experiment. A small group may cook as a team or allow one to attempt it on his own. In Central Asia, it is fairly common for restaurants or teahouses to rent woks (*qazan*) and firewood to customers for picnics. A man becomes so thoroughly familiar with the dish throughout his life that the chances for successful cooking are great. He who is destined to lead the household must master the secrets of cooking with flame.

## RUSSIA

The kitchen is the principal domestic space for a Russian woman. A great part of her day is spent at the market looking for products, preparing the raw ingredients, cooking, and cleaning. Without the convenience of electric kitchen appliances, Russian women exert tremendous effort in basic kitchen prep work. Despite the arrival of processed foods and semiprepared dishes in the 1990s, Russians have taken to them with concern. Whether they distrust foreign products or simply prefer to cook from scratch is open to debate, but the fact is that almost all food is still made at home using only fresh ingredients. This is a time-consuming task, one that only increases as the summer draws to an end. Adding to their daily workload of meal preparation, women are also expected to

Typical kitchen, Moscow.

pickle and preserve fresh produce to last throughout the winter months. Fruits and vegetables are purchased at the height of the season to ensure the best price. Some are eaten fresh, but most are dried, pickled, or preserved.

As most people in the former Soviet Union live in apartments, the kitchen occupies a very small space in terms of total square footage. In the early years after the revolution of 1917, large city houses were transformed into communal apartments, where several families would share the residence, including a kitchen and bathroom. By the 1980s, after a tremendous two-decade-long effort to house its citizens, most of the Soviet population lived in single-family apartments. The standard kitchen equipment is a sink, a gas stove, and a small refrigerator. Most of the preparatory work is done on the kitchen table since counter space is limited or nonexistent. Some wealthy families have added dishwashers if space permits, but in general, all dishes are washed by hand.

The brilliance of Russian women lies in their ability to produce delicious and healthful food with crude cookware and shoddy supplies. Designer cookware is decades away and hardly considered a status symbol. Most of the cookware is still coarse Soviet aluminum pots and pans, sometimes with an enamel glaze. Recently, poor-quality Turkish and Chinese cookware have also flooded the market. Small electric appliances are rare. Food processors, juicers, coffeemakers, mixers, and microwave ovens are unnecessary luxuries. The most indispensable kitchen tool in the Russian kitchen is the manual meat grinder. It is used to make ground beef and fillings for pies and pastries. The main cookware generally includes a large stockpot for soup, a cast-iron skillet for fried foods, a tea kettle, and perhaps a baking dish. Knives, also made of aluminum or soft steel, quickly dull, no doubt because they also function as a hammer and can opener. Spatulas and cooking utensils are either wood or aluminum. Silverware is made from crude light aluminum, and it is not unusual to find the price stamped into the metal in older pieces.[1] Daily dishware is simple, and the fine china is brought out only for special occasions.

The staples of the Russian pantry include flour, salt, sugar, and tea. Rice, macaroni, and cereal grains are common dry goods, the culinary term for all items that do not require refrigeration. As living space is always a rare commodity and refrigerators are exceedingly small, many apartment dwellers also use their balconies for food storage. With nine months of cool or cold weather a year, the balcony offers an ideal area for keeping overflow items. Freezer space is even smaller, and most families cycle through their fresh-food supplies within a week. Russians forgo putting leftovers into

Tupperware or other storage containers, instead placing the cookware or serving dish in the refrigerator.

In the rural areas the traditional family working roles are still maintained. The women tend to the vegetable garden and the smaller livestock, bring in the well water, and prepare all the meals. Russian peasant women, according to some historians, could hold their own with the men in terms of strength and endurance.[2] After cooking all day, they would then join their husbands in the fields. Today there are still entire villages without running water or electricity, making the process of food preparation even more arduous. Most houses and dachas in the countryside have a root cellar, alleviating some of the need for refrigeration. Men are assigned the tasks requiring physical labor, such as harvesting and cutting wood, and many males are still employed by nearby state farms.

## CENTRAL ASIA

Today's food production and cooking techniques differ little from those employed by the ancients. Women are responsible for all of the cooking except on those occasions when the men want to demonstrate their proficiency with the flame. Nomadic women make most of the dairy products, although the men sometimes help milk the horses. Central Asians cook over open flames in qazans (wok-shaped cauldrons) for deep-fat frying, frying, stewing, and simmering. Street vendors and home cooks still grill kebabs in braziers over glowing coals, make bread and *samsa* in tandoor ovens, and make dumplings (*manti*) in a bamboo or aluminum steamer (*qasqan*). The brazier, or grill, for cooking shashlyk is called a *mangal*. The preparation of Central Asian dishes resembles in many respects Chinese methods of cutting, cooking, and seasoning foods. All vegetables are cut according to strict traditional guidelines—shredded, diced, sliced, and so forth—depending on the dish. For the main courses, meat and vegetables are also fried before stewing (pilaf, *shavlya*—meat and rice porridge) or boiling (stock for *laghman*—noodles). Among widely used dishware are *kasa* and *piala* (a handleless teacup), round and oval serving platters, china teapots, and trays, as well as ceramic and wooden dishes.

Pilaf is found from China to North Africa and even in the New World. Mexico has a type of *sopa seca*, which is a variation of Spanish paella.[3] Though there are thousands of variations of pilaf, its most basic form is revealed in an acronymic device. The letters of *palov osh* spell out the main ingredients in Uzbek: (p)*ioz*—onion, (a)*yoz*—carrot, (l)*akhm*—meat, (o)*lio*—fat, (v)*et*—salt, (o)*b*—water, and (sh)*ali*—rice.[4] Preparation methods can also vary, but they essentially involve a combination of cooking methods—frying, stewing, and steaming. Oil should be heated just to the smoking point before adding pieces of sheep's tail fat (*kurdyuk*). While any vegetable oil will work, Central Asians prefer cottonseed oil. When kurdyuk has been transformed to a crackling (crisp piece of fat that is created when animail fat is fried), it is often shared as a special appetizer treat. Mutton is by far the favored meat for pilaf, though beef and chicken are quite common. The nominally Muslim Central Asians, of course, avoid pork. The meat is cubed and added to the qazan for a good searing. The caramelization of the meat adds yet another layer to the flavor. Then the onions and carrots are frizzled to a golden brown and water is added. When the broth becomes thick and has reduced to the proper amount (so the volume of liquid is two times more than the volume of rice), the cooks add cumin, crushed coriander seeds, salt, and black pepper. Turmeric, chickpeas, barberries, red pepper flakes, fruit (raisins, quince, apricots, apples), and paprika are common pilaf seasonings.

The master chef (*oshpaz*) cooking pilaf over an open flame in a single cauldron may sometimes serve hundreds of people on holidays or other special occasions such as weddings. The basic tools needed for pilaf are a fire, a qazan, and a spatula. A standard quantity of prepared pilaf feeds about a dozen people. For a wedding party, an oshpaz may prepare pilaf for twelve hundred guests from a single pot. Some woks are from 1.5 to 2 meters in diameter. A highly skilled oshpaz is in high demand not only for his culinary prowess but for the capital required to purchase qazans large

*Oshpaz*, pilaf master chef, Tashkent.

enough to feed hundreds. In the mid-1990s, the price of a car was almost the same as that for an oversized qazan. One dedicated chef chose to purchase the qazan instead of the car, only to make enough money from preparing huge quantities of pilaf to buy a car six months later.[5] It certainly takes years of practice to prepare a dish, at times, containing more than three hundred pounds of rice.

Flatbread (*non*) has its own category of equipment and utensils. Decorative impressions are marked in the center portion of the bread dough by a *chekich*. The chekich is a small wooden handle with nails protruding in geometric or floral shapes. By punching holes in the unbaked bread with a chekich, the center of the round loaf does not rise with the intense heat of the tandoor (*tandir*) oven. The bread may be glazed with milk, water, sugar or egg wash and finished with sesame, *nigella,* or poppy seeds before baking. The bread maker wears an elbow-length glove and places the ready dough facedown on a padded circular pillow called a *yengicha*. The yengicha is a specialized potholder that straps to the back of the gloved hand. The baker then quickly and skillfully slaps the dough vertically onto the wall of the tandoor. With much practice on the part of the baker and just the right consistency of dough, non clings to the sides and bakes in a matter of minutes. The finished non is removed from the oven with a long metal hook. The punched holes from the chekich result in a crispy middle portion with a soft, chewy outside ring.

In nomad cookery, the amount of equipment is minimal because it must be transported from location to location to follow the grazing herds. Furthermore, there is no luxury of electricity or running water. The iron qazan is the most indispensable cookware, used for cooking pilaf, soups, and even bread. If the qazan is shallow, it may be turned over a flame to create a convex cooking surface to produce flatbreads among other things. Many parts of the sheep and goat—especially the cleaned, emptied stomach—are used for holding milk products or producing cheese. The main dairy products are milk, yogurt, ayran, kumiss, butter, and qurt made from the milk of sheep, goats, yaks, and even camels. Large (up to 10 gallons), sealable aluminum storage cans are one modern convenience the nomads have adopted for storing liquids or oil.

Kazaks maintain a tradition of using beautiful dishware when possible, even though many of their customs have been Russified. Kumiss is usually served in wide bowls decorated with silver or in painted cups, and meat is served on wide platters. Tea is steeped in ornate teapots and served in beautiful cups. Unusual ingredients such as dried melon (*kuanshek*) and small intestine (*eporgem*) were regularly woven into intriguing patterns before the Russian conquest. The breads boasted floral designs, painted with berry juice. Kazak craftsmen made an assortment of wooden cups (some of them had a handle) for kumiss, ayran, and other beverages, but they were eventually replaced by porcelain teacups. A common practice of Kazaks was to serve meat on a flat, round platter made from a single large piece of wood. Bigger and deeper bowls are used to serve dairy products. Small wooden basins are used for making dough. Various wooden ladles may be decorated with silver, ivory, or carvings. Each family has wooden spoons, which are transported in felt and wooden cases. Kazaks use a variety of leather items and utensils. The largest is a horsehide sack for making kumiss and butter. It is conical in shape, with a square base narrowing to a small opening at the top, where a wooden pestle for churning is inserted. During migrations Kazaks used leather flasks made of sheep's hide, which held up to 10 liters of kumiss or ayran.

## COMMERCIAL FOOD TRAINING AND PREPARATION

As in Europe and the United States, the professional kitchen remains largely the domain of men. During the restaurant boom beginning in the mid-1990s, the higher-end restaurants and hotels in Moscow and St. Petersburg imported chefs from Europe, just as they did a hundred years earlier. Other restaurants must rely on the local talent—those trained in culinary schools based on the Soviet model of standardization, instructed by an older generation of cooks who never experienced variety, choice,

Making *samsa* in Uzbek restaurant, Tashkent.

or a market economy. The Soviet system for training in the culinary arts was essentially a combination of the European and U.S. systems. In Europe, a cook generally fulfilled a lengthy internship with a master chef and slowly worked his way up the ranks. While this is still a viable option in the United States, it is more common for chefs in the United States to be trained in a professional culinary school.

The Soviet system took youngsters as early as 15 years old and placed them in a vocational school (*tekhnikum*) for three years of training. After the eighth grade, a student has three routes for further education. The first option is simply to continue with high school until the 11th grade and then graduate. The student could also enroll in a tekhnikum or go to an *uchilishche* (for professional training in occupations such as mechanic or nurse) after the eighth grade, where he or she receives specialized training in addition to his or her high school studies. The third and most competitive path is to attend an institute or university after the 11th grade.

Teaching methods have changed over the years because of the emphasis on the hospitality industry—restaurants and hotels—rather than *obshchepit* (public cafeterias and large companies) as emphasized by the Soviets since the 1930s.[6] Communal dining dominated the Soviet culinary arts in training and trade. Most graduates of the tekhnikum were sent to work in public cafeterias or institutional feeding establishments. Women dominated this realm, while the men tended to work in hotels and restaurants.

Cooking schools in the former Soviet Union have become part of a national joke, but not because of the food or the graduates they produce. Somewhat like lawyer jokes are associated with the legal profession in the United States, mention the words *kulinarny tekhnikum* (culinary institute) and invariably someone brings up the stand-up monologues of the Russian comic Gennadiy Khazanov. He tells several stories about a naïve and dim individual who worked as a cook after completing his studies. In one of them, a cook looking for work puts an advertisement in the paper. The lonely woman searching for a lover misinterprets the abbreviations in the ad, and the rest of the parody is filled with double entendres related to food preparation and sex.

Haute cuisine to the Communists was only for the bourgeoisie, a blatant show of wealth and decadence, which the Soviets spent 70 years trying to snuff out. In the Communist era, the centralized government was so intent on standardization that its tentacles reached all the way to the food-service industry, and the influence remains to this day. In the Soviet era, the Ministry of Trade published a book entitled *Sbornik retseptur blyud i kulinarnykh izdeliy* [*Directory of Recipes and Culinary Production*] for all restaurants, cafés, cafeterias, and institutional kitchens in the USSR, and the book is still being published today in the Russian Federation. It mandates the categories of restaurants from high to low into three levels: deluxe, high, and first class. It contains more than fourteen hundred recipes for entrees, sides, sauces, and drinks, not to mention elaborate instructions for regulating portion sizes, preparation, and service for the army of cooks, managers, and accountants. McDonald's, it seems, was not the only master of standardization. This book is the sole reason why borscht tasted the same in Moscow, Tashkent, or Vladivostok. The pernicious influence of *Directory of Recipes and Culinary Production* still haunts Russian culinary education and restaurants. Generations of chefs and cooks trained from this book are still instructing and cooking for the next generation. But the pendulum for an evolving Russian cuisine is swinging swiftly and far afield in the early twenty-first century.

The restaurant industry in the former USSR is dramatically changing based on two factors: a small but exceedingly wealthy clientele willing to pay excessive amounts for quality food and service, and the appearance of long-forgotten products that were not produced or available in Soviet times. New restaurants are opening in Russia and Central Asia every day, and the vocational schools cannot provide students with the necessary experience to work with novel or exotic foodstuffs that are now part of the industry repertoire. Restaurants are desperate for cooks and chefs with foreign experience because they are familiar with classic European dishes and modern food-presentation styles. And they understand the pace of work required in a market economy. At present, some of the higher-end restaurants import chefs from Europe to work in their establishments. U.S. chefs are frequently brought in to train the franchise and chain-restaurant sector. In present-day Russia and Central Asia, the culinary schools generally follow the same curriculum as in the Soviet era, but radical changes are on the horizon. Schools are now teaching beyond the basics of the *Directory of Recipes* because the book does not include much of the seafood, vegetables, or fruits that are now readily available in the markets. The newly opening private schools train chefs in professional development classes; shorter courses than the three-year programs designed for high school–aged youths are available; and internships in Europe are highly prestigious. During the summer, students work at resorts and restaurants. Admission is competitive, mostly based on grade point average, but experience is not required to enroll. But it will be many years before the new school of Russian and Central Asian chefs shed their Soviet standardized heritage and begin the exploratory and creative process of culinary arts in a global world.

## NOTES

1. The selling price for most commercial products was stamped, painted, or permanently marked during the Soviet period, to discourage "speculation," the practice of reselling goods for a profit.

2. B. A. Shelton and D. John, "The Division of Household Labor," *Annual Review of Sociology* 22 (1996): 299–322.

3. Though the standard etymology of *paella* is attributed to a Catalan word meaning "frying pan" (*paella,* from Old French *paelle,* "frying pan," "pot," from Latin *patella,* diminutive of *patina,* "pan"), it is equally valid that the word may be related to the word *pilaf. Pilaf* (*pilau*) is spelled numerous ways in eighteenth-century cookbooks—pulao, pilaw, pillow, pellow, polloo, and so forth.

4. Karim Makhmudov, *Plovy na lyuboy vkus* [Pilafs for Any Taste] (Tashkent, Uzbekistan: Mekhnat, 1989).

5. This account was relayed to the author by Murat Rakhmanov about himself in the early 1990s in Tashkent, Uzbekistan, September 1994.

6. Informative accounts of communal dining, the conflict between the elite and the masses over food production (Borrero), and the development of Soviet culinary arts in the 1920s (Rothstein) are found in Musya Glants and Joyce Toomre, eds., *Food in Russian History and Culture* (Bloomington: Indiana University Press, 1997).

# 5

# Typical Meals

The composition and character of meals in the former Soviet Union underwent a tremendous change in the late twentieth century. The greatest symbolic change is that the traditional Russian stove and Central Asian tandoor have largely been replaced by gas or electric ranges. Transformations toward a modified market economy in the 1990s introduced new foodstuffs from Europe and Asia, opening a whole new world of cuisine for many. Imported kiwis, spinach, olives, and ice cream bars appear in local produce markets, while pizza, sushi, and hamburgers vie for attention in the new eateries. However, many people, especially the abandoned elderly, cannot afford to purchase even the meager basics of bread and sausage available under the Communist regime. Describing a standard meal in today's Eurasia, therefore, is a tricky proposition, rife with generalizations and oversimplification. What, for example, is the typical modern-day clothing or hairstyle in a given country? Any daily activity considerably depends on family influence, social status, and individual preference. In the preindustrial world, routines were determined by the seasons. Life revolved around cultivation and livestock. Planting, harvesting, and processing of the crops were the primary concern from morning until night. Daily life, and consequently the meals, followed the movement of the sun. The evening meal, once the central and most cherished event of the day, has become almost an afterthought in this period of relative stability and abundance. Scarcely restrained by darkness, distance, and climate, people can now eat whenever and whatever they want. The paradoxical result for meal patterns is simultaneous homogeneity and diversity around the world. Frozen chicken nuggets may taste the same everywhere, yet the use of ketchup or plum sauce as a condiment provides a chance for culinary variety. Still, certain characteristics of Russian and Central Asian daily meals continue to define part of their culture in the face of globalization and standardization.

## RUSSIA

The kitchen may be regarded as the unifying and defining locus of daily life in Russia. Family activity centers on the kitchen, used more frequently than any other room in the house. The majority of the population still lives in cramped Soviet-style apartments, most often in two- or three-room residences. The kitchen is generally arranged with the cupboards, stove, and refrigerator on one side, and a small collapsible table on the other. Small, square backless stools known as *taburetki* (from taboret in French) slide beneath the table to conserve space.[1] Some newer Western-style apartments have open floor plans with a kitchen opening into a living room, but this is still rare. Most apartments do not have a designated dining room. The largest room of an apartment is usually the living room. Often it is also called the dining room (*stolovaya*, from the root *stol*, meaning "table"), although it rarely contains a permanent dining table. A foldout couch, wall-length bookshelf or cupboard, and television are the customary furnishings. For formal celebrations and holidays the table is moved from the kitchen into the living room to accommodate more guests. Family meals are most often served at the crowded kitchen table. Friends, too, inevitably converge on the kitchen for an evening of tea or drink, with conversation and camaraderie lasting well into the night.

A meal in Russia is almost always a sit-down affair, even if the diners are tightly packed around the table. There are two acceptable exceptions where standing while eating occurs. Sometimes cafés or street vendors provide stand-up counters for dining, although this option is still considered substandard even when one is in a hurry. Also, during buffet-style presentations—*shvedskiy* (literally "Swedish table," or "smorgasbord") and *furshet* (a drink reception)—sitting space may be limited. For an event to be regarded as respectable, table seating is mandatory, especially when elderly guests are invited. In short, the best meal is served at a table, no matter how cramped or crowded.

The seasons still greatly determine the choices in the diet. Dairy products and vegetables are abundant in summer, while meat dishes and pick-

Russian-style reception table.

led vegetables reign in winter. Russians relate to food with enormous care and concern. Providing for the family requires thoughtful prudence, especially in the late winter and early spring when supplies run short. Conditions were particularly difficult in the Soviet period with the reduction of available goods and their unstable supply. Bread is considered a sacred foodstuff, and it is egregious to drop a piece of bread on the floor or to leave breadcrumbs on the table. Simply throwing bread away altogether is unthinkable, and making croutons (*sukhariki*) becomes the inevitable solution. As a result of centuries of hardship in Russia, it is better to eat stale bread than to be wasteful. Meat appears in greater frequency during the holidays, and, after months of sacrifice, the best food products that money can buy ensure a rich celebratory table. Russians, above all, value an abundance of food on the table. One historian remarked that even by the end of the eighteenth century, the great quantity of food offered was already one of the distinguishing characteristics of the Russian cuisine, and not only for the wealthy.[2] The quality and variety of dishes were always secondary concerns.

For everyday meals the table is informally set. The quintessential Russian lunch or dinner contains bread, soup, and hot tea. Bread is required at every meal and is placed on a plate or in a basket and covered with a cloth or paper napkin in the middle of the table. A combination of sliced black, rye, and white bread is considered indispensable. Russians consume huge quantities of bread, and is it justifiably revered in the highest degree as a sustainer of life. Such veneration is reflected in many proverbs, like "*khleb vsemu golova*" (bread takes precedence over everything). It has been calculated that Russian peasants in the eighteenth and nineteenth centuries consumed more than a pound of bread per meal.[3] Such quantities have dropped off somewhat in the modern era, but people still do not sit down to a meal without bread, even if pasta, rice, or another starch are served.

A soup tureen may sit alongside the bread basket, and its contents are ladled out into large, shallow bowls. But usually the soup is directly served from the stockpot on the stove, a mere arm's length away if everyone is sitting in a tiny kitchen. If a salad is served, it too is placed in a large serving bowl or on a platter. Salad is served during the main course and does not require a separate plate. At the end of the meal, tea is regularly offered in china cups with saucers. It is quite common for tea to be the only beverage offered at a meal, and soft drinks are still rare during mealtime.

Soup is a daily Russian dish. Soups may be served cold or hot, with a meat, fish, chicken, or vegetable base. In the days of old, everything—including the soup—was eaten with wooden spoons from a communal ceramic bowl. For that reason, a spoon has always been the main Russian utensil, appearing in Russia almost five hundred years earlier than the fork.[4] A Russian adage reveals the disparaging attitude toward the fork: "The fork is a fishing pole, but the spoon is a net" (*Vilkoyu, chto udoy, a lozhkoyu, chto nevodom*).

Because people eat in the kitchen, everyday dishes are plated at the stove or counter and placed directly on the table. Sometimes family members serve themselves, although the woman of the house generally apportions the serving size. Portions are usually generous, and seconds are anticipated by the diners and encouraged by the hostess. Despite this, Russian visitors are often shocked at the portion sizes in most American restaurants. The traditional tableware is china or ceramic, and paper or plastic plates and cups are almost never used. Even though very few Russians have dishwashers and must wash all dishes by hand, they consider disposable dishes both improper and wasteful.

Russians maintain the greatest reverence for food, especially the older generations who experienced famine, war, and rationing. The younger generations are not as prudent, in part because they view excess and waste as part and parcel of being modern, free, or rebellious. Yet in general, Russians are frugal, using every part of a vegetable or animal. The older folk generally distrust imported food products, more from a lack of experience than from any problems with the quality of the product. Sanitationobsessed Westerners are often dismayed by what they consider lack of concern for food safety in the former Soviet Union. While there are unsafe practices by U.S. standards, such as leaving a dish in the pot unrefrigerated overnight, for the most part, Russians have a great understanding and appreciation of the properties of food and its storage.

In addition to cooking and cleaning, women handle the responsibilities of child rearing, even though they usually also work outside the home. They restlessly scamper around the table serving everybody, rarely getting a chance to sit down and enjoy the fruits of their own labor. Russians, as a rule, are not very particular about table settings on an everyday basis. However, table manners receive enormous emphasis, and children are taught to eat properly from a fairly young age. This means that little children are not allowed to eat with their hands and are encouraged to use forks and knives as early as possible. Elbows should not rest on the table, and mouths should be closed when chewing. Napkins are placed only in the center of the table, not at each table setting, and should be used only for unfortunate spills or spots. Russians eat all desserts, even cakes and pastries, with teaspoons rather than forks.

Breakfast can be as modest as bread and tea, or as elaborate as the remains from the previous night's celebratory feast. Of course, the breakfast meal varies by household, with numerous options. Finishing the leftover salads, pickles, fish, and cold cuts from the night before is fairly common, particularly in working-class families. Even hot dogs make their way onto the breakfast table. But more often than not, most Russians enjoy a simple open-faced sandwich of cheese, ham, or salami with hot tea and a boiled or fried egg. Coffee, generally instant, is also popular, and serving juice in the morning has been on the rise in recent years. Consumption of fermented dairy drinks such as *kefir* (fermented milk) and *prostokvasha* (sour milk) generally correlates to the age of the individual. The older the person, the more dairy products he or she drinks for the nutritive and healing properties. Fermented dairy products are also now in vogue among the trendy crowds and the health conscious. Boiled eggs, omelets, and fried eggs are some of the more familiar offerings. Also exceedingly common, especially for the children, is some sort of hot cereal, such as *kasha*—oatmeal, rice pudding, cream of wheat, and buckwheat. Among the first choices for sweet offerings are *tvorog* (farmer's cheese) mixed with sour cream and sugar, and three types of pancakes—*syrniki* (made with tvorog), *bliny* (thin), and *olad'i* (thicker). Still, day in and day out, the overwhelming majority of Russians simply have tea and bread for breakfast, perhaps accompanied by cheese or tvorog.

Children receive both a midmorning snack and lunch at school. All schools have cafeterias, and meals are prepared on-site. The midmorning snack is usually a sweet roll with tea, and lunch typically includes meat patties (*kotlety*) or hot dogs with a starchy side dish, plus *kompot* to drink. At the workplace, a midmorning or midafternoon tea break includes sweet rolls or *buterbrody* (literally "butter-bread")—the German and Scandinavian term for open-faced sandwiches. Tea breaks are very common in most workplaces. If there is no kitchen or kitchenette, a heating coil or, more recently, an electric teapot is used to boil water for tea. Everybody contributes to the teatime with their offerings of sweets, crackers, and pastries. Ice cream is the primary snack of choice from street vendors, consumed outside even in the depths of winter.

Lunch generally occurs around noon on weekdays and may be served as late as two o'clock on the weekends. Many people eat lunch at work since numerous large companies and institutions have their own cafeterias. In some new, more prosperous offices, lunch is catered. Since women often work outside the home, few men go home for lunch even if they have an opportunity. Lunch usually consists of soup as a first course (*pervoe*); protein (meat or poultry), starch (potatoes, rice, pasta), and a salad, sometimes with kompot to drink, as the second course (*vtoroe*); and tea and dessert are the common third course (*tret'e*). Public cafeterias continued to grow in numbers after World War II when more women joined the workforce. These factory canteens have been declining in popularity since Russia's independence at the end of the twentieth century. As most cafeterias are no longer subsidized by the state, it is often cheaper for workers to eat at home, bring their own lunch, or risk questionable hygiene and food safety at the corner street vendor. Those who can afford to eat out prefer restaurants that offer a *biznes lanch*, often less expensive and a speedy alternative to the elaborate restaurant experiences of the near past.

Tea break at workplace.

Dinner is served around seven in the evening, after people have had time to come home from work. The mother, or a grandmother if she lives with the family, prepares the meal. Generally it follows the same pattern as lunch: soup, a meat dish and a starchy side, finished off with tea and something sweet for dessert. The ubiquitous bread basket adds bulk and calories to the meal. Potatoes—boiled, mashed, fried, or part of a salad—serve the same satisfying function. The usual condiments for pork, beef, or chicken are ketchup, mustard, or horseradish. Hot dogs, without a bun, are a common dish, with green peas, potatoes, macaroni, or rice served on the side.

Common salads include *vinegret* (made from potatoes, pickled cabbage, and beets in oil) or the Russian salad (Oliv'ye) of boiled and diced potatoes and carrots, peas, pickles, and chicken, mixed with mayonnaise. Beets in oil with a hint of garlic make a superb salad, side dish, or garnish. The most universal salad, however, is made from freshly shredded cabbage, perhaps with carrots or a touch of onion, dressed with oil or mayonnaise. Fermented cabbage in salt, less stringent than sauerkraut, is made at home and always ready for the table. Cabbage can also be the primary ingredient for filling savory pies (*pirogi*) or smaller baked pastries (*pirozhki*). It is the darling of the vegetable choices because of its versatility, and Russians consume more than seven times the amount of cabbage that Americans do.[5] Mushrooms, when in season, are equally adaptable, served as the main course, used for fillings or eaten pickled.

The most familiar appetizers are dill pickles and lightly brined cucumbers, but any pickled vegetable can stand in. Cheese, sardines, smoked fish, or cold cuts are the standby appetizers (*zakuski*) on a daily basis. The vegetable choices have considerably grown in recent years at the market, but most homemakers are content to make the dishes with which they are most familiar. Most of the cooks in Russia today who pass on their culinary heritage and tradition to the next generation learned their craft in lean times with a lighter larder. A full pantry was a luxury seldom experienced in the Soviet era. Only a very few courageous home cooks venture outside of their comfort zone, so even if spinach, broccoli, and asparagus are available at the market, they have yet to be embraced by the general population. This generally limits the vegetable menu to cabbage, cucumbers, tomatoes, beets, cauliflower, squash, and eggplant. While the market provides more and more novel foodstuffs, the means and ability to expand the list of culinary options at the daily table remains limited. The majority of Russians would be equally content to serve pickles; boiled potatoes with butter, sour cream, and dill; and perhaps a shot of vodka—the classic Russian dinner.

Contrary to Westerners' popular belief, based largely on portrayals in Western film and literature, average Russians rarely drink vodka, or any

Vodka and dinner.

alcohol for that matter, except as an integral part of the meal. On occasion, an everyday dinner may be accompanied by vodka or beer and, less frequently, wine. Vodka is usually not mixed with anything but enjoyed straight up from small shot glasses in 50-to-100-gram portions (approximately 2–4 ounces). The shot is always immediately followed with a bite or two of food, preferably something salty, such as a pickle.

Vodka has been a source of Russian identity, for better or worse, of both nobility and serf, elite and proletariat. Its consumption cuts across all social and economic classes. Through clever marketing and culinary cachet, this humble spirit in the West became the wine of the 1990s, the hip drink. The global production and distribution of vodka illustrate the selling power of myth and style, placing vodka far from its lowly origins as a "pernicious drink" that eventually came to play "a vital role in Russian culture, in the financing of the Russian state, and, sadly, in the destruction of families ... due to alcoholism."[6] In Russia, the vodka selection is enormous and the price is relatively inexpensive. A liter bottle (one quart) can cost as little as $2–3, yet some collector sets with fancy decanters sell for hundreds of dollars. Not surprisingly, the least expensive brands account for 70 percent of alcohol sales in Russia.[7]

The profit motives go far in explaining why alcohol producers in the West go to such lengths to create a perfect-tasting drink, only to be covered up with juice or sugary sweet mixers. One in four mixed drinks in the United States is made with vodka. Of course, the culinary elite, gas-tronomes, and trendsetters can greatly influence the taste of a society.[8] It is astonishing how quickly the West embraced the clear stout spirit in seductive containers, much like it did with bottled water. The advertising campaigns for vodka and bottled water in the West are nothing short of incongruous—the labels on the sleek bottles imply (and the advertise-ments scream) "fresh, pure, clean, natural"—while the health effects of the drinks are polar opposites. Although many in the United States can-not detect considerable taste differences between vodkas, thanks to adroit marketing strategies, a sizable number of people believe that one's level of sophistication and social standing can be distinguished by the name and myth attached to the vodka bottle.

## Russian Tea

Until recently, Russians observed a separate time for afternoon tea. Now tea is almost always reserved for the end of the meal. Still, Russians drink tea three to five times a day, and it is customarily accompanied by candies, pies, *pryaniki* (sweet and soft spice cookies), and pastries. There are many competing theories about how and when tea first arrived in Russia. Writ-ten sources note the tsars drinking tea beginning in the seventeenth cen-tury. But it was probably known and consumed by merchants and those living in the trading towns in Central Asia and Siberia much earlier. Even more contentious, however, is the origin of the *samovar,* a metal urn used in Russia to boil water for tea, literally meaning to "boil on its own."

The samovar is a large, rounded vessel with a boiler inside. Early ver-sions have a central tubing for placing hot coals and wood that extends from the base of the urn to its top. To start the fire, air is blown into the tubing—either with the mouth or by creating a vacuum by holding a boot over the tubing and squeezing the boot repeatedly. Water is poured into the enclosed reservoir for boiling. A true coal samovar is a noisy affair with the coals crackling and the water bubbling against the metal sides. Once the water boils, it is dispensed from the spigot at the base into a tea-pot to create a strong tea infusion (*zavarka*). The potent zavarka is poured into individual cups and then diluted with water from the samovar until the proper tea strength is reached. Since the water comes straight from the boiling samovar, sometimes people pour just a splash of tea into their saucer and drink it when it cools. Any number of baked goods and sweets can be eaten with tea. There are two more tea customs with reputed ori-gins in Russia, in addition to drinking from the saucers: adding lemon slices to the cup, and *vprikusku*—holding a sugar cube with the front teeth

Tea time, Tula, Russia.

or simply holding it in the mouth, sweetening the drink as the tea washes over the sugar.

Most locals insist that the samovar is a purely Russian invention, since it has become emblematic of Russian cuisine and hospitality. There are at least three other competing versions of its genesis. The most common hypothesis is that the samovar is an adaptation of the Mongolian hotpot used for making soups. The hotpot consists of a central cylinder for the coals or burning wood with an open metal bowl that surrounds the cylinder. The liquid boils from the internal heat source. The Russians simply enclosed the bowl to form a large vessel to hold boiling water only and added a spout at the bottom for dispensing the hot water. Another theory claims that it "moved northward into Russia with the Greek Church" from Byzantium, which indeed exerted monumental influence on Russian culture since the tenth century, especially in the religious, artistic, and administrative realms.[9] The final conjecture is that Peter the Great brought the invention from Holland. While much more research is required to convince any skeptical observer, it is curious to note that the town synonymous with samovar production is Tula, a settlement south of Moscow. Not only are samovars and weapons made there, a foundry was built in Tula by the Dutch in 1632. While historians work out the details, the Russians continue to enjoy the romance and nostalgia provided by the samovar.

Few households now own a wood-burning samovar. Electric samovars became the rage after World War II. Today, almost everybody has a simple European-style electric teapot. However, as the price of electricity goes up, people on a budget have returned to boiling water on a gas stove in a traditional kettle. Tea at the dacha is a distinctive pleasure. First, there is a greater likelihood that a traditional samovar will be used since electricity at the dacha is still not widespread. Second, tea is often consumed outdoors in the fresh air. Finally, no one is in a hurry to go anywhere, adding the final element required for a proper Russian tea-drinking ritual—pleasant, leisurely conversation.

## Dachas

Meals at the dacha are a chance for all Russians to feel as though they are returning to their rural and agricultural roots. Fresh herbs and vegetables from the garden, mushrooms and berries from the nearby woods, and grilled meat are common expectations of the appetite at the dacha. The word *dacha* is often translated as a summer or country house, but the term has an alluring and enchanted quality, especially in the culinary realm. One drab, yet precise, definition of a dacha that defies its real charm is "a house on a plot of land, whose function is not primarily economic, and that is located within reasonably easy reach of a major city, and is intended for intermittent, not permanent, residence."[10] During the 1990s, however, dachas became centers of economic activity, where owners op-

Russian dacha table setting.

Russian family eating a meal at their dacha near
Moscow.

erated more like farmers than gardeners, growing vegetables, fruit, and
berries, and even raising chickens, cows, and pigs. Dacha food production
was a matter of survival (not simply a matter of supplement as in earlier
years) for many during the difficult transition to a market economy.

Dachas have been part of the Russian landscape since the time of Peter
the Great and define a segment of the social and cultural history of Russia. Paradoxically, dachas are viewed as a sanctuary of freedom from the
fast-paced urban lifestyle and highly regimented society. They were generally granted to individuals by the restrictive Russian Empire, a practice
continued by the Soviets. While the whole point of a visit to the dacha
is to do nothing in particular, there is always work to be done, even if it is
work of one's own choosing. In addition to the maintenance of the home
and garden, much of the day may be spent preparing a meal. Children
pick the ripe tomatoes or cucumbers, the women prepare their specialties,
and the men smoke and prepare the fire. Over dinner, everyone romanti-
cizes about the freshness of the air, the vibrant taste of the food, and the
smoothness of the vodka. Hangovers, it is believed, are unlikely in such
an environment. What is probable, however, is that the meals will be the
focus of the stay, faith in the bounty of Mother Earth will be restored, and
the Slavic rural roots will be nourished.

## CENTRAL ASIA

If Russia defies generalizations for its daily diet, Central Asia poses even
more obstacles for all-inclusive descriptions. The five countries of Cen-

tral Asia have populations that exhibit a mix of urbanized, Sovietized, nomadic, Russian, Turkic, and Iranian cultures and influences. While the apartment kitchen epitomizes Russian daily meals, the open flame sets Central Asian food apart. Fire is the preferred method of cooking for the region's staples of pilaf, kebabs, samsa, and flatbreads. For the sake of simplicity, meals in Central Asia may be crudely divided into two groups—urban and rural. The meals of the city or apartment dweller have taken on many Russified elements, such as the number and timing of meals. The rural group, including the remaining nomads of Kazakstan and Kyrgyzstan, has experienced a tremendous change of lifestyle but generally maintains much of the basic foodways of its forefathers.

Three meals a day is standard for both nomads and city dwellers, with every meal including tea and flatbread (*non*). For breakfast, fresh cheese or honey may be added, but the meal is normally light. Lunch, usually a soup, may be taken at home, or a quick snack can be bought from street vendors. The largest meal is usually eaten in the evening.

As with other Muslim customs favoring the right side, most Central Asians enter their home or yurt with the right foot first and immediately remove their shoes. In Islamic thought, the right hand is associated with goodness and purity, and the left is associated with evil and pollution. According to tradition, the prophet Mohammed "commanded people to eat with their right hands and forbade them to eat with their left hands." It is also considered impolite to accept plates of food, cups of tea, and so forth, with the left hand. Men, women, and children often eat separately in strict patriarchal homes. Others may begin eating only after the eldest or the guest starts, depending on the household tradition. Despite their

Tea time, Nukus, Uzbekistan.

Muslim heritage, many Central Asians drink alcohol, although rarely during everyday meals.

The meal customarily starts with a prayer. After the prayer, diners make a passing gesture across their eyes with two hands as if they are washing their face. The men are expected to break and distribute the flatbread, taking care not to place a piece of bread upside down (the side of flatbread that clings to the tandoor wall or a sheet pan is the bottom side). Many believe that bread is God's first and most important gift to humans. Thus the food acquired a religious significance beyond the practical and frugal considerations of sustenance on the Asian plateau.

Tea is first offered to everyone who passes a threshold in Central Asia, and a whole subset of customs exists surrounding the preparation, presentation, and consumption of tea. Green tea is predominant and the drink of hospitality. Black tea is preferred in Russian regions. Green tea is generally served straight, but sugar, milk, salt, or even butter may be added depending on individual preference. An entire portion of the cuisine—samsas, bread, halva, and various fried foods—is dedicated solely to tea time.

The nomads of Central Asia live in portable felt dwellings called yurts. Felts are made of pressed sheep or goat wool; for finer pieces, camel wool is used. The nomadic evening meal, as in antiquity, is the most substantial and often consists of mutton or beef. The traditional Kyrgyz and Kazak dinner table is low and round and covered with a cloth. It is usually positioned near the center of the yurt. Diners sit around the table on decorative felts topped with long narrow mattresses or pillows for comfort. The place of honor is reserved for the elderly, guests, or the head of the family. The daughter-in-law sits near the tea urn and serves the guests. These customs are still preserved, especially in rural areas. The visitor is first served *kumiss* (mare's milk) or *ayran* (yogurt and water). Kyrgyz prefer green tea (*koq chai*) during the summer. It is served in the morning, before and after lunch, and in the evening with fresh milk. *Aktagan* is one type of Kyrgyz tea drink made with milk, butter, sour cream, and salt.

Turkmen consume large quantities of meat, cereals, grains, dairy products, legumes, and fruit. Bread makes up a significant portion of the diet, especially in the rural areas. Their traditional bread is *chorek*, a tandoori flatbread. Flatbreads can be leavened, unleavened (*petyr-gorek*), flaky (*gatlama*), or formed as large pancakes (*chapady*). Other popular baked goods are unfilled fried pies (*pishme*); pancakes (*shavoty*); various dumplings (*borek* and *deshvare*); noodles (*gaiish*); pies with fillings of meat, ground beef, and onions. Some of the more common flatbreads are *chorek-chovurma, ishlekdi, etli-nun, etli-bukhtirme*, and *kady-borek*.

Uzbeks normally have three or four meals a day—breakfast, lunch, afternoon snack, and dinner. Traditionally, freshly made green tea is served at the beginning and end of every breakfast, lunch, and dinner. Baked goods, sweets, and tea (sometimes with milk or cream) are served for breakfast. It is fairly common for the Tajiks, Turkmen, and Uzbeks to have a dining room that is devoid of furniture, with only a brightly colored wool carpet hanging on the wall. The tablecloth, or *dastarkhan*, is laid out on the floor or on low tables and everyone eats on pillows surrounding the tablecloth. For both lunch and dinner, flatbreads, sweets, and fruits are served first, with tea. Then a hot dish is served and fresh fruit follows as dessert. Desserts are generally the tea adjuncts—raisins and nuts, lightly sweetened cookies, multiple variations of halva, fruits, and confections. Pastries and layer cakes are a European addition.

The Uzbek winter diet traditionally consists of vegetables, dried fruits, and preserves to provide the necessary vitamins throughout the season. Hearty noodle or pasta-type dishes are common chilly-weather fare. Nuts (walnuts, peanuts, pistachios, and almonds) and honey are eaten separately or used in sweets and desserts. Even in the middle of winter, melons, apples, pomegranates, pumpkins, and other products of the fall harvest are available in the market almost up until the spring harvest. If the produce is carefully handled and stored (generally in conditions more than 32 degrees and less than 55 degrees Fahrenheit) under grain straw, it can last anywhere from one to eight months.[11]

Central Asian cuisine is extremely labor intensive, requiring long preparation and cooking times. Therefore, it is quite common to eat modestly throughout the week and make a special effort for when guests come over or for the Friday meal. Muslim men usually gather at a mosque to participate in community worship on Fridays, and that evening is considered a family time at home. Those Central Asians fortunate enough to have a home with a courtyard often take their morning and evening meals outside in the shade. A raised square platform or dais with a low table in the center is the main place for enjoying family meals. In the heat of summer, it is fairly common to eat bread, fruit, and tea all day to stave off hunger and have only one large meal a day. Increased contact with the outside world pushes some Central Asians to adapt their eating habits and mealtimes to conform to world patterns. Restaurant culture, European convenience foods, imported Turkish and Iranian dishes, and inexpensive Chinese cookware and equipment have all contributed to the changing foodways.

## NOTES

1. Another loan word from the French, *tabouret* is often defined as a low stool without a back or arms.

2. V. V. Pokhlebkin, *Sobranie Izbrannykh Proizvedeniy: Natsional'nye Kukhni Nashikh Narodov: Povarennaya Kniga* [Collected Works: National Cuisines of Our People: A Cookbook] (Moscow: Tsentrpoligraf, 1996), 37.

3. V. V. Pokhlebkin, *Sobranie Izbrannykh Proizvedeniy: Istoriya Vazhneyshikh Pishchevykh Produktov* [Collected Works: History of the Most Important Food Products] (Moscow: Tsentrpoligraf, 1996), 63.

4. Pokhlebkin, *Povarennaya Kniga*, 38.

5. V. Kovalev and N. Maksimov, *Traditsii, obychai i blyuda russkoy kukhni* [Traditions, Practices, and Dishes of Russian Cuisine] (Moscow: TERRA-Knizhnyi klub, 1998), 168.

6. Paul Richardson and Mikhail Ivanov, "The Little Water of Life," *Russian Life* April 1998, 8.

7. BBC News Online, "Russian Vodka Faces Flood of Beer," 20 June 2002, http://news.bbc.co.uk/1/hi/business/2055332.stm.

8. Sociologist Steven Mennell defines the social role of gastronome as theorist and propagandist about culinary taste in Steven Mennell, A. Murcott, and A. van Otterloo, *The Sociology of Food: Eating, Diet, and Culture* (London: Sage, 1992), 84.

9. Alan Davidson, *The Oxford Companion to Food* (Oxford: Oxford University Press, 1999), s.v. "Byzantium."

10. Stephen Lovell, *Summerfolk: A History of the Dacha, 1700–2000* (Ithaca, NY: Cornell University Press, 2003), 2.

11. Susan Schoneweis and Durward A. Smith, "Storing Fresh Fruits and Vegetables," Cooperative Extension, University of Nebraska Institute of Agriculture and National Resources, http://ianrpubs.unl.edu/horticulture/g1264.htm.

# 6

# Eating Out

The food of Russia and Central Asia offers bountiful choices, particularly when presented on the public stage of restaurants, cafés, and the street. Since the demise of Communist rule, a new show emerges, providing a remarkable glimpse of numerous cultures misrepresented by decades of obscurity, stereotyping, and political antagonism with the West. Throughout the twentieth century the approach to food in the former Soviet Union was greatly affected by civil strife, scarcity, and ideology. The turmoil and intentional isolationism also kept away foreign visitors and international business, removing the need for a service economy. Nowadays, diversity and transformation are prominent features of the cultural landscape that is both influenced by and accessible to the rest of the world. Nowhere is change more evident than in the increasing opportunities for dining out, including any of the multiple options for taking any meal outside the home. From white-tablecloth restaurants to cafeterias to street food, the culinary influences of Russia, the Caucasus, and Central Asia play off each other to create a dynamic restaurant scene. Eating out in Russia is a major event—fun, fascinating, and full of surprises, mostly pleasing ones.

The restaurant, defined as any commercial public-dining facility, traces its origin to eighteenth-century France. A distinction is usually made between the modern restaurant and its lowly ancestors of cook shops, inns, taverns, food stalls, and the like. What makes modern food service truly modern, however, is not simply French influence or an a la carte menu. It is the commodification and consumption of culture. Restaurants both reflect and shape culture. Many observers point to consumption as the single most important factor for creating culture in urbanized and industrialized societies.[1] Traditional products and dishes are assigned a monetary value, imbued with cultural cache, and placed in a commercial setting with the sole purpose of trying to re-create the atmosphere of a special, celebratory meal.

## RUSSIA

Russia's culinary culture has changed more in the last decade of the twentieth century than it did during the 350-year Mongol yoke.[2] Russia has experienced rapid and far-reaching cultural and commercial changes. This transformation is particularly evident in the culinary field. Once stereotyped as the land of shortages and sausage queues, Russia now presents an exceptional opportunity to explore dining out as an intersection of economics and culture, of consumption and national identity. As one of the fastest-growing segments of the Russian economy, the food-service industry initiates restaurant construction on the urban landscape, while at the same time promoting a national cuisine that reinforces a sense of Russian identity. It will be several generations before a new Russian cuisine emerges, based on a combination of imperial, peasant, and Soviet heritage, not to mention the global influences of the hospitality and travel industries. In the meantime, most newer restaurants serve what can be considered Russian food. There is less risk of business failure because the traditional ingredients are generally available, the chefs have eaten and prepared this type of food all their lives, and the customers are comfortable and familiar with the cuisine.

### Russian Dining History

By the middle of the nineteenth century, French language, culture, and cuisine (adapted to Russian ingredients) dominated aristocratic circles. Moscow and St. Petersburg began to open large, exclusive restaurants. Many French chefs eventually returned to Paris to open their own Russian restaurants, some of which are still considered to be serving the finest Russian food in the world.[3] This cross-fertilization between French and Russian culinary cultures is still a prominent factor in the debate as to what composes genuine or authentic Russian cuisine.

On the eve of the 1917 Bolshevik Revolution, commercial consumption of any kind was fairly restrained in major cities like Moscow and St.

Petersburg. The grand restaurants of Russia resembled the large dining halls found in the Victorian hotels of Europe. Fine gentlemen assembled in the bright rooms with ornate plasterwork, high ceilings with flamboyant chandeliers, and art-covered walls. However, the restaurant industry never developed on the European scale. True, it was cut short by the 1917 revolution, but the country lacked the necessary proponents to make fine dining an end in itself. "Russian intellectuals have a long and sturdy contempt for commercialism,"[4] a practice later heartily embraced by the Communists. Russian restaurant culture all but died in the early Soviet period.

### Contemporary Russian Dining

Dining out in Russia today offers the greatest variety of restaurants and menus in the country's history. During the Soviet period with a centralized economy, choice and service were not a priority. Today, upscale restaurants dominate the city nightlife and, during the short summer season, outdoor cafés line the green-shaded streets. Almost three-quarters of Russians live in urban areas, and 13 cities have populations of 1 million inhabitants or more. Moscow leads the way in both population and restaurants, followed by St. Petersburg, Nizhnyy Novgorod, Novosibirsk, and Yekaterinburg.

The types of restaurants in Russia can be roughly divided into a few sectors: exclusive restaurants and private clubs, international cuisine, fast-food chains and cafés, restaurant chains, independent middle-range restaurants, and, the latest arrivals, coffee shops and beer halls. After initial entry by European and American entrepreneurs and corporations into the market, Russian companies quickly countered to dominate Moscow's offerings. Prevailing trends include more middle-range restaurants for the ever-expanding middle class, while new fast-food outlets are offering more Russian dishes in response to market demand. Restaurants are also an attractive area of investment for successful Russian businessmen seeking to diversify their holdings. International cuisine ranges from typical European fare (Italian and French) to the Asian options of Chinese, Japanese, Thai, and even Tibetan.

Similar to leapfrogging Asian tiger economies of the 1960s,[5] the former Soviet Union was ripe for a leap directly from the nineteenth century to the twenty-first. With unprecedented growth, the Russian restaurant industry certainly acts as if it is making up for lost time. Today, the only barrier of entry to the market is the price of real estate. Moscow's four thousand restaurants for a population of 11 million leaves considerable room for expansion given the restaurant numbers in Paris (14,000) and

New York (17,000). With no recent acceptable indigenous models to follow for creating a restaurant industry, Russia is moving headlong toward the Western mode of developing a modern food-service industry. Ironically, studies indicate that up to a third of Russians cannot afford basic food items, while another third of the population visits cafés and restaurants on a regular basis. Astonishingly, anywhere from 35 to 80 percent of Russians consider themselves middle class—reflecting either a misinterpretation of the term or a highly fluctuating economy, both of which may be true.[6] The rise of a middle class and the nouveaux riches, or New Russians—including people in business, finance, services, and the Mafiosi—has created a market for consumers who wish to have experiences unfathomable in Soviet times. Many New Russians are enamored with Western styles, adopting Western consumption patterns and accumulating luxury goods.

Russian tourists who flooded into Europe and Asia in the 1990s were exposed to and experienced firsthand the varieties of eateries worldwide. Some ideas, like beer halls, are adopted as is, whereas many other concepts, the theme-restaurant for example, are adapted to Russian tastes and sensibilities. Most distinct among these new restaurants are the curious Soviet kitsch nostalgia restaurants. Found mainly in St. Petersburg and Moscow, Russia, and Kiev, Ukraine, these establishments are decorated with Communist paraphernalia, curios, and flotsam, including red velvet banners with Socialist slogans, propaganda posters, busts of Lenin, portraits of Stalin, and menus written on party letterhead. While tourists and Russian youths find the ambiance entertaining, dedicated Communists would surely lose their appetite in the face of such irreverence. They are especially popular with middle-aged folks, those who understand the irony but did not waste their lives trying to build Communism. The cuisine in these "Soviet" restaurants is a combination of favorite dishes from the former fraternal Socialist republics: the best of Uzbek, Georgian, Ukrainian, Baltic, and Russian cooking, all under one roof.

The historical and cultural context for restaurants in Russia during the Soviet period is unique and unprecedented. Artificially restrained and developed by the state, restaurants were not interested in meeting consumer demand. Now, post-Socialist Russia is concerned with *creating* demand, especially for the New Russians. Caviar and cabbage still symbolize the dichotomy of economic classes in the new Russia. Could it be that in the twenty-second century, inhabitants of Russia will look to the nouveau riche of the 1990s, only a fraction of the population, as a source for cultural inspiration?

The current restaurant craze in Russia had its beginnings in 1986 with a little-noticed loosening of the Socialist central economy. In the Soviet period, state restaurants were often associated with special occasions, such as weddings, or with gatherings of the political elite. That attitude has been slow to change. The *perestroika* campaign of Gorbachev, beginning in 1986, was an attempt to restructure the Communist system, not overturn it. One of the first tangible results of reform was the proliferation of service-sector cooperatives, particularly in the food-service industry. Semiprivate cooperative restaurants, usually family-affiliated operations, offered an interim dining experience. They fell delectably between the exclusive state restaurants and hotel dining facilities on the one hand, and the public canteens and the cafeteria (*stolovaya*), with its torpid atmosphere, service, and fare, on the other. Businessmen and the younger generation found in the cooperatives a new place for a speedy lunch or an evening of entertainment and diversion. The cooperatives of Moscow also set the standard for properly prepared and modestly priced dining. The success of the cooperatives, coupled with improving trade relations in the early 1990s, encouraged multinational corporations to quickly appear on the scene as joint-venture restaurants. These consisted of both high-end and fast-food operations, opening in or near hotels and catering to foreign nationals accustomed to high-quality cuisine.

## Menu Format

Russian restaurants, even when they are trying to present another ethnic or national cuisine, usually follow a similar menu format. A typi-

"Earn the praise" propaganda poster, 1957.

cal Russian restaurant menu offers cold appetizers, hot appetizers, a first course (usually soup), a second or main course, garnitures or side dishes, and desserts. An extensive list of alcoholic beverages is common, including vodka, Crimean wine, brandy, and champagne. Whiskey, gin, and beer and wine from abroad are making major inroads in the beverage market. Many menus even contain sections for cigarettes and cigars. As of yet, there is no such thing as a nonsmoking section of a restaurant, since almost 50 percent of Russians smoke—two-thirds of the men and one-third of the women.[7] Menus can run a dozen pages or more. The routine during the Soviet period of extreme shortages was to ask the waiter what was available without even troubling oneself with the menu. However, the transportation network and nascent market economy even now provide challenges for the ambitious menus of many restaurants.

Until recently, menus varied little. The meal begins with *zakuski*, literally "small bites," which are both hot and cold hors d'oeuvres. The cold appetizers often include sturgeon black caviar and salmon red caviar, pickled and fresh vegetables, a dish of assorted smoked or cured fish, assorted cold cuts, mushrooms, and beef tongue with horseradish. These small dishes are the accompaniment for a convivial shot or three of vodka. As the clear liquid flows, the conviviality grows. Obligatory toasts to friendship, family, and peace become more gracious and complimentary with each drink. A selection of both white and black bread with plenty of fresh butter forms the base of open-faced sandwiches in the Scandinavian style. It is not unusual to find plates of fresh herb sprigs, mostly parsley, cilantro, and dill—a tradition likely borrowed from the Caucasus. Green leafy salads are not a customary dish in the Russian repertoire. Hearty salads are often a mixture of cooked vegetables mixed with mayonnaise or vinaigrette. Beet salads, potato salads, and crab and rice salads are other common offerings. The simple dish of fresh tomatoes and cucumbers, which has come to symbolize the frontier of Soviet northern greenhouse horticulture, is still a mainstay on the menu.

Hot appetizers can be considered a meal in themselves, especially when paired with the cold *zakuski*. The saying "the appetite comes with eating" certainly has a literal and figurative sense in regard to Russian dining.[8] Buckwheat crepes (*bliny*) are among the best-known Russian dishes worldwide. *Zhul'en* is a very rich hors d'oeuvre served in timbales (small ceramic or metal pastry mold) made with béchamel sauce, melted cheese, and slivers (julienne) of either mushrooms or chicken. *Pirozhki*, small meat or vegetable pies, are savory pastries that are found in some variation in almost every cuisine worldwide. *Calzone, empanada, samosa, knish*, or *kreatopitakia*, to name a few, are similar global variants to the Russian savory pirozhok.

The first course (*pervoe*) is invariably a hot soup of borscht, cabbage soup (*shchi*), or boiled dumplings in broth (*pelmeni*). Soup for Russians is nutritionally and spiritually crucial to their diet. When you consider that essentially nine months of the year are winter, soup invokes memories of the domestic pottages of cabbage, potatoes, carrots, and onions of the countryside and the traditional hot meal of the day. Shchi is the quintessential Russian soup made with both fermented and fresh cabbage, beef, mushrooms, tomatoes, onions, turnips, and garlic. Borscht is basically the same soup with the addition of beets and perhaps a bell pepper. The cold beet soup known in the United States most likely derives from Eastern European Jewish cookery. Both borscht and shchi have extreme variations, but one can always count on them being topped with fresh dill and sour cream. Pelmeni are small meat dumplings (similar to tortelloni, a larger version or tortellini) served dry or in a clear broth. If eaten without bouillon, they may be topped with sour cream, mustard, or vinegar.

Russian main courses, known as the second course (*vtoroe*), would generally be familiar to Americans. Dishes of beef, pork, chicken, lamb, and fish—baked, boiled, braised, or fried—are most common. The differences between Russian and American entrées are found in the portion size and in their significance to the meal as a whole. As in Italy after antipasto and pasta, the Russian main course tends to be a smaller serving of protein, almost as an afterthought. The hot and cold zakuski are the highlight of a Russian meal, the soup is a touch of home cooking, and the entrée is a forgotten luxury. U.S. restaurants, on the other hand, emphasize the main dish with a six-to-eight-ounce serving of meat, chicken, or fish, replete with a starchy side such as potatoes or rice and one or two vegetable side dishes.

Although beef Stroganoff may be the best-known Russian dish in the rest of the world, shish kebab (*shashlyk*) is by far the most popular entrée at home, at the dacha, and certainly in restaurants. In Russia, it can be made with beef, pork, chicken, fish, and mutton. When done right, generous cubes of marinated meat on skewers are rotated over hot coals, essentially roasting, grilling, and smoking the meat simultaneously. Peppers, onions, and tomatoes are not interspersed on the skewers, as seen in food magazines, since the cooking time of the meat is much longer than it is for the vegetables. *Bifshteks* is a slice of broiled beef and can be almost any cut of steak, not tenderloin as sometimes translated on the menu (regrettably for the eager diner). A similar dish is the fillet (*file*), usually sirloin or a boneless steak cut of beef. *Escalop*, also from the French, is a thin slice of meat or fish, often pork loin in restaurants. *Zhar-*

*koe* is roasted beef and potatoes, ideally prepared and served in an earthenware container. Chicken and fish dishes are also found on most menus. Entrées are accompanied by a small serving of a vegetable side dish (*garnir*). The most common *garnir*, from the French meaning "to decorate," is the potato—boiled, fried, or pureed. Rice and braised cabbage are also common side dishes. In the Soviet period, canned green peas were the garnir of choice, although lonely slices of tomato and cucumber, about the only vegetables from the Soviet era, still linger as the main garnishes in Russian restaurants.

If the entrées are an afterthought in Russian restaurants, desserts are a mere perfunctory addendum, and usually an inferior supplement to the multiple courses preceding them. Desserts in a typical restaurant may include fresh fruit or berries, ice cream, and a pastry or two. Sponge cake and simple chocolate candies are also fairly common. Tea and coffee are served as the final course. Perhaps because of their association with decadence, desserts stagnated in the Soviet period. Also, sugar was often in short supply, which only added challenges for the pastry chef.

### Russian Restaurant Characteristics

Russian food service, much like the country itself, is undergoing a period of rebirth, seeking its identity and roots, and pursuing tremendous opportunities in a market environment. While concepts of what constitutes a pleasurable restaurant experience—food quality, atmosphere, and service—have become universal, there is still tremendous divergence between Russian and American expectations when dining out.

Foreigners at upscale restaurant in Crimea.

Limiting a description to only Russian fine-dining options (as opposed to fast food, cafés, and international chains), one of the first things a foreign visitor notices is the exorbitant menu prices, commonly two to three times more expensive than similar items in the United States. Russian diners who can afford to frequent these types of restaurants make up only a very small portion of the entire population. Furthermore, Russians embrace a carpe diem attitude, whether because of their one thousand years of national history or the fear that their good fortune will evaporate tomorrow. In general, those who have the money today spend it freely and guiltlessly, without assigning a relative value to the experience. A good indicator of whether a restaurant is formal, exclusive, or even private is the presence of a doorman, a holdover from prerevolutionary Russia. During Soviet times, they were a reminder in the Orwellian sense that some animals are more equal than others.

Patrons of Russian restaurants tend to be men aged 25 to 50. Children and the elderly are a rare sight. It used to be that outside of special occasions such as weddings or birthdays, women dined out only when accompanied by men. Though women in Russia joined the workforce earlier in the twentieth century and in proportionately larger numbers than in the United States, only recently have some women's incomes permitted them the luxury of dining out without a male companion.

For Russians, the atmosphere is the most important element to ensure an overall positive dining experience. Next come the quality and presentation of the food, and finally, if present, the level of service. The full evening's entertainment is the restaurant, and dining out is not something scheduled before a movie or after an opera. Only recently have restaurants moved away from the enormous hall-style interiors to either a modern or a rustic ambience. Casinos, pool halls, and even bowling alleys have incorporated restaurants into their operations. The entertainment can be as simple as recorded music and a dance floor, or more elaborate to include live music or a variety show. One Moscow restaurant even held cockfights in the late 1990s, much to the horror of unsuspecting Western visitors. Whatever the diversion, atmosphere is the primary factor for distinguishing between a good restaurant and a great one.

Service in Russia, by reputation, leaves much to be desired. Waiters, until recently, were a distinct profession, and they were usually decked out in tuxedos with a starched white towel draped over the arm. Women and young people are beginning to fill the ranks, but the waitstaff is still poorly trained and the turnover is high. This is not surprising since wages are low, tipping is a new and rare phenomenon, and the new-money patrons tend to treat the waitstaff as lowly servants. Like in Europe, a surcharge may be included on the bill, so extra tips for the staff are not always expected. The staff's livelihood is not dependent on tips like it is in the United States, so any extra money left on the table is referred to as tea money (na chai).

## Fast-Food Restaurants

The arrival of Western fast-food restaurants in Moscow and St. Petersburg in the late twentieth century was among the first visible signs of a growing consumer market in the former Soviet Union. The concept appeared destined for success in this huge, untapped market. Though fast food in its most basic sense was nothing new to Russia, the idea of prompt and friendly service in a sparkling atmosphere with the focus on the customer appealed to many people accustomed to the days of scarcity for the masses and exclusivity for the party elite. Soviet customer service consisted of distributing the remains of shoddy goods and services picked over by workers, managers, and the privileged. Western restaurants, in some respects, leveled the playing field for the consumers—that is, those with sufficient disposable income.

In 1990 Pizza Hut, helped by its parent company, PepsiCo, became among the first Western joint-venture fast-food restaurant in Moscow and the USSR, along with McDonald's. Pepsi had been part of the Soviet market since the early 1970s when U.S. president Richard M. Nixon and General Secretary Leonid Brezhnev negotiated a deal to allow Pepsi to be produced on Soviet territory in exchange for PepsiCo's importing Stolichnaya vodka to the United States. The first Russian Pizza Hut was opened on Kutuzovsky Prospect near several diplomatic apartment complexes where many foreigners resided. The first McDonald's restaurant opened to much fanfare on Pushkin Square, one of the most prestigious locations in Moscow, a few short blocks from the Kremlin. In part to skirt anti-American sentiment and globalization critics, McDonald's in the USSR was headed by the Canadian franchise arm. Today there are more than 125 McDonald's restaurants in 30 Russian cities, with 65 stores in Moscow alone. By the early 1990s, a flood of other Western companies, including Baskin Robbins, Sbarro, and Dunkin' Donuts, made their move to capitalize on the untapped market of fast-food dining in the crumbling Soviet Empire. Today, T.G.I. Friday's, American Bar and Grill, Patio Pizza, Planet Sushi, Patio Pasta, and Presto Pizza are among the more obvious choices for fast and familiar Western-style food.

Those who decry American cultural imperialism or the demise of indigenous culture should take heed at the Russian response to Western fast food. There are many signs of Russia developing a vibrant and profitable culinary culture in response to the forces of globalization. The most visible example is that of McDonald's entry into the Moscow market. The Russian feeling of cultural superiority speedily asserted itself through the concept of *nashe,* or "ours." This process of negotiation between local (Muscovites) and global (McDonald's) resulted in an indigenous rival, Russkoe Bistro,[9] a fast-food restaurant with hearty Russian fare and even a shot of vodka. Supported by the mayor of Moscow (the city government owns a 20% share), Russkoe Bistro was able to counter McDonald's burgers and fries with pirogi, *rasstegai* (savory pies with a filling visible through an open top), *kulebyaki* (savory pies with mushrooms or meat filing), soups, salads, *kvas* (a traditional soft drink), Russian vodkas, and fruit-based liqueurs (*nalivki*). Most Russkoe Bistros are franchised. Although there is a standardized training program for service, the menu and quality of food are inconsistent from franchise to franchise.

Rostick's, a Russian-Venezuelan joint venture, has become one of the most popular fast-food franchises in Moscow for fried chicken, french fries, fried meat pies (*chebureki*), pelmeni, soups, and desserts. These restaurants are also one of the few places that attract family dining by offering a children's menu with a toy and providing a playground. For higher-quality fast food, another Moscow favorite is Yolki-Palki, appealing to young people and tourists, although not a bad place for a quick business lunch. The heart of the Yolki-Palki is the appetizer buffet on a reconstructed wooden cart, but the effect is lost in the atmosphere—the waitstaff wear folk costumes and the interior is designed to look like a peasant's cottage. There is a fine assortment of Russian salads, fish, boiled potatoes, cooked cabbage, pickles, mushrooms, and jellied meats (*kholodets*), among others. Kvas is the main drink, but beer is the only alcohol served.

Coffeehouses and teahouses, beer gardens, and pubs have mushroomed in recent years. For their owners, these are generally less expensive to operate and less risky financially because of higher profit margins on the beverages, a limited food menu, and lower labor costs. German-, Czech-, Irish-, and Baltic-style beer halls are extremely popular, aided by an all-out media blitz by the beer industry in post-Soviet Russia at the expense of the vodka market. Beer advertisements (and profits) are so prevalent that they have been banned from TV, except late at night. Shokoladnitsa, Coffee Bean, Coffee House, Zen Coffee, and others add to the coffee craze of a younger generation. The antithesis of the Soviet experience with only instant coffee, these establishments cater to the increasingly sophisticated palates of those who have traveled abroad and know the difference between a latte and a cappuccino. The popularity of these cafés may also be explained by the opportunity they offer the average Russian who could hardly afford a meal at a restaurant. For a few dollars, patrons can pretend to participate in the modern gastronomic lifestyle so prevalent in the media, film, television, and popular culture.

The feeling of nostalgia over the changed culinary cultural landscape has led to the founding of the first Russian chapter (convivium) of the Slow Food movement. Slow Food is an international group originating in Italy, which bills itself as a movement for the protection of local culinary traditions diametrically opposed to the idea of fast food. Vilyam Pokhlebkin, regarded as the father of Russian culinary history, echoes the feeling that cultural authenticity has been lost in Russia. He blames current trendy imports from the West, poverty, and changes in taste for the "culinary betrayal of our national interests."[10] He argues that today Russian cuisine consists of two extremes with no middle ground—one for the destitute, victims of the last decade's reform, the other for the new elite. Those extremes sound eerily similar to both Soviet and tsarist eras as well. In reference to varieties of haute cuisine, he calls them "cosmopolitan cocktails…. One is poor and vulgar, without taste and cheap. The other is sophisticated, original, tasty, and expensive…. And both are alien, from outside the homeland, not our own." While some countries boast of French influence on their cuisine, Pokhlebkin cites Francophilia as one of the reasons for the decline of Russian cuisine. Yet Pokhlebkin thinks that even bananas and oranges of the 1980s were an unnecessary addition to the national diet. To which point in time should the Slavs return to find their pure culinary traditions? Back to Kievan Rus' or Novgorod? Before the influence of the Byzantine Greeks, Mongols, Turks, German, or French? Although some Russians share his resentment of the debasing of Russian cuisine, most are thrilled to sample the new world of gastronomy inaccessible to the masses for almost a century.

### Reemergence of a Russian National Cuisine

An examination of Russian cuisine in a national and international context reveals forces of globalization that are too subtle or gradual in the West to be noticed by most people. Precisely because Russia was devoid of restaurants and stocked grocery stores in the Soviet period, the changes over the past decade appear extreme. The external push by American and Western hospitality firms to enter the Russian market has been met by hungry and affluent consumers, whose choices had been manipulated or ignored under the Socialist system. Some argue rather convincingly that

Russia was never a consumer society in the same fashion of the West.[11] When Russia instituted free-market reforms after independence, the average Russian consumer had no inkling of the opportunities or responsibility that the market would provide. A confluence of factors—globalization, a Soviet legacy of cultural construction, and the appearance of a middle class—has allowed consumption to advance at a dizzying speed to great, uncharted depths. The result is a complicated tale of state, economic, and individual actors engaged in the commodification of culinary culture. Although it is difficult, if not impossible, to define the essential characteristics of Russian cuisine, it is clear that various players, particularly restaurateurs, are busy constructing a new national cuisine for Russia as part of a larger process of defining the new post-Communist, post-Soviet Russia.

Restaurants in the twenty-first century have achieved unimaginable heights of economic and social influence. For better or for worse, restaurants offer the framework for a comparative study of cooking and cuisine—the public fare of restaurants is taken as the standard unit of comparison between national cuisines.[12] Why is this increasingly the case in modern societies? No doubt because of the growing number of dining experiences outside the home. Meanings once associated with domestic cookery and identity are now shifting to the commercial and public sphere or are being lost altogether.

## Fine Dining

Justified or not, opinions of a nation's cuisine are often first formed by a restaurant experience. Some Russian restaurants are sleek enough to catch the attention and admiration of not only urban sophisticates and the nouveaux riches but of Western gastronomes, too.[13] These trendsetters spread the word about restaurants to the rest of Russia and to the world. Restaurant cuisine is repeatedly portrayed as essential, authentic, and genuine Russian cuisine to both the foreigner abroad and to the Russian in Russia by the media and the food-service industry.

How do restaurants, with their menu, interior design, entertainment, and mode of service, represent Russianness? Given that Russian restaurant cuisine was kept on hold during the Soviet period and domestic cookery was greatly hamstrung, the Russian immigrant experience in America may provide some clues as to how the industry might have developed in a capitalist market. A Jewish immigrant community from the USSR developed in the 1970s in Brooklyn's Brighton Beach. Brighton Beach, to this day, has some of the best delis and restaurants in New York. Yet the émigré approach to food in many restaurants there is like the Red Army's approach to military hardware—emphasis on quantity and not quality. The food of Brighton Beach, it may be argued, is not typically Russian but, in fact, typically Soviet. Its selection and presentation mirror the illustrations in the *Book of Delicious and Healthy Food*. Tabletops are crowded with fine crystal and china; assorted zakuski plates; flowers; caviar; bowls of fruit; and bottles of wine, brandy, champagne, and vodka. The food products portrayed in the book roar with images of bounty and progress. Could it be that the Communist culinary utopia was actually realized on the shores of New York and not in agrarian Russia? On the other hand, the development of a vibrant and innovative Moscow restaurant industry in the early twenty-first century only underscores the city's ability to bypass decades of stagnation. Whereas Brighton Beach retains a 1970s aura, Moscow has some of the most novel and chic dining facilities in the world. What the two restaurant scenes have in common is that nostalgia sells. Some restaurants in Brighton Beach have created what was aspired to, but never possible in the Communist era. Conversely, Moscow has claimed and combined various folk and haute dishes, added a few international touches, and created a new Russian cuisine that would probably be unrecognizable as national cuisine in tsarist times. Certainly, times change and so does a cuisine. The significance of these creations in the Russian Federation, however, is the effect they have on current Russian identity.

With the absence of a Communist state to construct culture, some restaurateurs and chefs in today's Russia make up the ranks of cultural nationalists. One restaurant that best typifies cultural commodification and identity construction is 1, Red Square. Located in the very heart of Moscow, in the State History Museum, the restaurant specializes in extravagant historical dinners. As its menu explains, the chef attempts to restore "the best traditions of Muscovite hospitality" by culling authentic recipes from the museum archives.[14] Diners can sample coronation menus, royal banquets, and feasts of the Moscow aristocratic society. The chef at 1, Red Square also offers pickled mushrooms—prepared in peasant style from a provincial source and stored on a lake bed. The menu promises patrons will discover "unknown pages of Russian culinary art," and each course is accompanied by enthralling historic commentary. At least one restaurant has identified the golden age of national cultural splendor—nineteenth-century Russia. The chef fits ideally with the notion of the artist as a cultural nationalist, dramatizing the "rediscovered myths and legends ... and projecting them to a wider audience."[15] In a nod to the Slavophiles, Russian folk music is also performed to balance the high and low cultures.

Another example of a blatant attempt to carve a new identity is Café Pushkin, named for Russia's greatest poet. Built along Las Vegas or Disney lines, whereby an artificial setting of props and architecture becomes a so-called real experience, Café Pushkin is a reconstruction of a pre-Revolutionary three-story mansion—though hundreds of such buildings already exist in Moscow, simply in need of renovation. But the point of this and other modern restaurants is to start from a blank slate, relying more on imagination and desire than historical accuracy. Café Pushkin is decorated in the high Petrine style of St. Petersburg, the center of glory for nineteenth-century Russian culture and cuisine. Classical music floats from the balcony and the menus contain facsimiles of newspapers written in old Cyrillic, assisting the patron in traveling back in time and reclaiming a missing heritage. Yet while the political, entertainment, business, and media elite gather here for power meetings, meals, or coffee, they are on some level also unconsciously participating in the redefinition of what it means to be Russian. Muscovites and Russians in Café Pushkin are not only traveling back in time in their mind, they are marking their future.

There are a few other Moscow establishments worth mentioning, without attempting to draw conclusions about their meaning and influence. Tsarskaya Okhota (tsar's hunt) presents an elaborate version of Russian nineteenth-century aristocratic cuisine, as can be found in passages by Gogol or Chekov. Frequented by bankers, actors, and foreign dignitaries, it is one of the many operations by the leading Moscow restaurateur, Arkadiy Novikov. Beloe Solntse Pustyni (white sun of the desert), named for a 1970 legendary Soviet film about the Red Army fighting Central Asian partisans, is essentially the re-creation of a movie set with Central Asian haute cuisine. Another theme restaurant is Uzbekistan, a favorite even in Soviet times, made to resemble the interior of a madrassa or mosque.

Besides Uzbek restaurants, the favorite "Eastern" cuisine in the former USSR is Georgian. Among the most outstanding Georgian restaurants in Moscow is Genatsvale. Wine is served in earthenware vessels, heartfelt toasts abound, and the pearls of Caucasian cuisine are served here, the house specialty being Black Sea anchovies. Another immensely successful theme restaurant by Novikov is Kavkazskaya plennitsa (she's taken captive in the Caucasus), which is also based on a movie: the popular Soviet comedy from the 1960s. The film-set atmosphere of the dining room depicts a Georgian mountain village, complete with a waterfall and live trout swimming in the ersatz stream. Moving beyond the imperial borders, Japanese restaurants are numerous and sushi has become so popular that supermarkets carry it. Even Santa Fe, which serves Mexican food, has a sushi bar upstairs.

At its heart, the restaurant is business, and not an easily profitable one at that. It has gradually become more a place for leisure, exploration, and style. Few restaurateurs consciously consider how they might influence or assist in creating a national cuisine. Most are simply attempting to produce a decent product and a respectable profit. Restaurants of the twenty-first century have become a source of entertainment, a vehicle of fashion, and a stage for the public presentation of self. With intent or not, restaurants in today's world have become "ephemeral postmodern shrines of culture."[16] This mocking description refers to the undue influence restaurants have on a gullible public, which believes that some traditional elements and techniques of national cuisine are preserved or revived on the menu.

Taking its culinary cues from Tokyo, Hollywood, and its own rich peasant and imperial heritage, Moscow can condense a century's worth of progress into only a decade, which is not surprising in a global era. The culinary culture that is being created in Moscow is circulated to the periphery as well as to other Russian-speaking areas through travel and a Moscow-centric media. The attempts, whether spontaneous or directed, to commodify culture and construct a new Russian identity in restaurants are proceeding apace. Sooner rather than later, a clearer picture should emerge, illustrating the extent of Moscow's cultural influence and reach, and the effect of forging a Russian identity on the plate.

## CENTRAL ASIA

Central Asian cuisine, if it has a reputation at all beyond the borders of the former Soviet Union, is considered a poor cousin to Turkish food. Anyone who has traveled to the area has undoubtedly experienced Soviet-era service and low-quality dishes in the few restaurants operating before independence of the five Central Asian states. The restaurants present a very meager imitation of the diverse local cuisine. Scratching only the surface may give the impression that the region offers little more than pilaf, shashlyk, and a few miscellaneous noodle dishes. Nothing could be further from the truth, reinforcing the argument that restaurants are a poor source for judging a nation's culinary culture.

### Roots of Hospitality

Central Asia has a rich tradition of hospitality, expressed through food in its teahouses and *caravansarais* along the Silk Road for over a millennium. A caravansarai is a way station that provided shelter for trade caravans, a hostel, and a place for nourishment for road-weary travelers and their camels. The Silk Road attracted merchants moving east and west laden with goods for exchange and sale from the second century A.D. until the fifteenth century A.D. In Central Asia, all the roads converged, bringing the area into contact with Chinese, Indian, Persian, Slavic, and Middle Eastern traders and cultural influences. The teahouse (*chaikhana*), based on similar establishments in China, remains to this day a social institution where a community or neighborhood gather over green tea and traditional Central Asian dishes of pilaf, shashlyk, and noodle soup (*laghman*).

The chaikhana is the foundation of Central Asian culinary culture, especially in Uzbekistan. Always shaded, preferably situated near a cool stream, the chaikhana is a gathering place for social interaction and fraternity. Robed men congregate around low tables, centered on bedlike platforms adorned with local carpets, to enjoy a meal and endless cups of green tea. In addition to providing nourishment, shade, fellowship, and relaxation during the sweltering summer months, the chaikhana helped preserve many aspects of Central Asian heritage and cultural identity obscured by 150 years of Russification. Most every neighborhood has a mosque and a community teahouse, both influential social institutions. The chaikhana functions as a quiet retreat, a social center, a sacred place, a restaurant, and a men's club. The village or community elders gather here to share news, discuss business, make decisions, and comment on family and cultural matters. At times, the entertainment may include betting on animal fights, which can include rams, cocks, and quails. The teahouse has maintained the Central Asian social order of patriarchy for centuries and helped to preserve certain aspects of Central Asian identity obscured by colonial powers.

*Chaikhana*, Bukhara, Uzbekistan.

*Chaikhana* public qazans, on road to Chirchiq, Uzbekistan.

The institution of the teahouse gained currency in China during the
Sung dynasty (tenth through the thirteenth centuries) as a place of relaxation, fellowship, and refreshment. The teahouse architecture is fairly
standard throughout Central Asia with a noticeable Chinese influence.
Often a two-story covered terrace runs around the perimeter of the central
building. Intricate wood construction, ornate columns, carved decorative
window frames, and brightly colored painted ceilings are traditional chaikhana touches. Other cultural elements include Uzbek silk for tablecloths
or pillow coverings and assorted cushions for reclining. Many chaikhana
cooks accept special orders in advance. For an additional price some places
provide a wok, firewood, cooking utensils, and dishes for those who bring
their own food. Customers have the option of preparing it themselves or
entrusting it to the cook.

### Russian Cultural Influence on Dining

Tsarist armies conquered the area in the nineteenth century, and then
Russians solidified a grip during Soviet rule in the twentieth century. As a
result, Russian restaurant culture was grafted onto existing Central Asian
traditions. The menu began to follow the European model with salads,
soups, entrées, and desserts. The typical Central Asian custom was tea,
and then a multiple-course meal, followed by more tea. As a rule, the
Russians built military garrisons and administrative urban areas adjacent
to the existing ancient Central Asian towns. The primary concern was

control of the borders of the empire, and the Russians did not particularly attempt to Europeanize the local society and culture. The Soviet experience, however, beginning right after the Russian Revolution of 1917, turned Central Asia on its head. Collectivization of agriculture, forced domestication of nomads, a program of social and cultural engineering, and a totalitarian political reign of intimidation and exploitation fundamentally changed the identity of Soviet Central Asia. Sadly, the variety and choice of foodstuffs in Central Asia during the Soviet period decreased as the central planners invested in cotton fields. At the same time, the amount of fruits, vegetables, and nuts expanded to the northern regions of the USSR through export from Central Asia.

The restaurant industry in Central Asia of the twenty-first century is following the Russian model of development, even though Russian political and cultural dominance diminished with the independence of the Central Asian states in 1991. The popularity and proliferation of Uzbek restaurants in today's Russia have certainly provided a model for commercial success in Central Asia itself. The main restaurants before independence were located within the blocky, crumbling Intourist hotels. Dancing, music, and floorshows, like in Russia, were an expected part of the dining experience. The menu would feature both Russian and Central Asian dishes, and the local cooking schools taught concurrent tracts of European and Eastern cuisine.

The restaurant culture in a Western sense has still not firmly taken hold in the region, partially because of the general decrease in the standard of living since the demise of the Soviet Union. Kazakstan has tremendous foreign investment because of its oil reserves, but in general, Central Asia has not had the economic success of Russia. The percentage of citizens with enough disposable income for dining out is significantly smaller than in Russia. Restrictions on private property, oppressive taxes on business, and the absence of an entrepreneurial atmosphere discourage the opening of new restaurants. However, the main reason for the lack of restaurants is that domestic cookery is still a strong and preferred tradition. Wives, mothers, grandmothers, and other women of the household spend a considerable portion of their day shopping for and preparing meals at home. There are fewer women in the workforce, and those who work are also expected to prepare the family meals. Because Central Asian cuisine is so labor intensive and the distribution system is heavily regulated by the state, it has yet to become profitable to open a great number of new restaurants featuring local cuisine. Furthermore, for Western tastes, Central Asian cuisine tends to be too heavy in the use of oil and animal fat. More importantly, foods prepared in commercial kitchens for sizable groups can in no way compare to the outdoor cookery of pilaf made in large woks over open flames, shashlyk smoked over coals, and samsas (savory pastries) baked in tandoor ovens.

### Contemporary Central Asian Restaurants

Central Asians, like Russians under Communism, went out on the town only for very special occasions. The consequence is that most restaurants valued elaborate banquets and floor shows over decent service and well-prepared and elegantly presented dishes. Private enterprise, to use the term loosely, is barely a decade old, and old habits die hard. Continuing economic hardships and the lack of a middle class make for a weak restaurant business. In the smaller cafés and roadside eateries, there is often no written menu. Many newer restaurants are relatively expensive, since it is difficult to secure a reliable source of foodstuffs. But the food is generally superior to what was served only a few years earlier. Often the cost of a variety show is added to the bill. A floor show is a unique experience, a hodgepodge of taste with contortionists, Vegas-style singers, dancers, strippers, and magicians.

In general, restaurant dishes have been artificially assigned to courses of the Russian model: hot and cold appetizers (*zakuski*), first course (*pervoe*) or soup (*sup*), main course (*vtoroe*), and dessert. Sometimes the diner is simply told the final amount of the bill; other times a sum total is scribbled on a notepad. Only recently have restaurants begun to present an itemized check. Appetizers generally consist of caviar, samsa, horse meat, tongue, assorted fish, spicy Korean vegetable salads, and seasonal fruit. The primary soups are laghman (mutton, vegetables, and thick noodles), *shurpa* (with potatoes instead of noodles), *monpar* (pasta bits like thick noodles), and borscht. Pilaf, shashlyk, cutlets, and *manti* (mutton- or pumpkin-filled dumplings) are the usual main course. Tea and coffee are served at the end.

Pilaf, manti, and kebabs are available on almost every other street corner throughout Central Asia. Most street vendors start out with a set quantity in the morning and serve until they sell out, so meals around the clock cannot be taken for granted. The food stalls in the bazaars and markets usually have the freshest products and offer the best snacks. Some homes near a market in larger cities open their courtyards for a home-restaurant experience. Roadside grills on the major highways are even more ubiquitous than in Russia. Also, long-distance bus trips usually stop at small cafés dependent on traffic for their survival. The food in cafés and cafeterias is basically the same fare as found in the outdoor stalls, but usually with a place to sit and perhaps a menu.

The major urban areas of Central Asia—Tashkent, Almaty, Astana, and Bishkek—offer a variety of European, Italian, Indian/Pakistani, Japanese, Korean, and Russian food, as well as interpretations of their national cuisine. Local Russians run and staff many of the restaurants, with menus and bills in Russian. There are also Western-oriented cafés, diners, and fast-food places in most major metropolitan areas. In Turkmenistan, the range of cuisine is rather narrow: Turkish, Iranian, Russian, or European. Kyrgyzstan generally offers European, Turkish, Chinese, Dungan, and Uighur food. Dungans are ethnic Han Chinese who have accepted the Islamic faith, and the Uighurs are a Turkic people living in western China with similar foodways of Central Asia.

In the neighboring countries of China and Pakistan, restaurants are more consumer oriented and offer a greater variety of dishes. Uighurs mainly live in Xinjiang, or Chinese Central Asia. A freer economic climate for small enterprises allows Turkic eateries to flourish in China. The Turkic cuisine in Xinjiang is more diverse and refined than across the border in former Soviet Central Asia, though most of the core dishes are similar. Beijing and Xian both have "Muslim" neighborhoods where a substantial number of Uighur and Hui restaurants operate. A greater diversity of produce and foodstuffs, combined with a modified market economy in China, has allowed restaurants and cafés to cater to the demands of the paying public. Afghanistan, also a part of Central Asia, has been beset by civil strife and war for the better part of two decades, and restaurants there are rare.

In the near term, there will always be Western-style restaurants that accommodate foreign visitors, expatriates, and the local cosmopolitan elite, as might be expected in countries with developing economies. For the long term, if the economic conditions improve, Central Asia has the potential to become one of the more diverse and interesting restaurant cultures in the world. In addition to the indigenous cuisine and obvious residual Russian impression, the cultural input is also coming from Turkey, Iran, China, and the West. Central Asian cuisine as it is known today will be altered over the coming decades with the opportunity of producing dishes with an amazing combination of East and West, business and hospitality, flavor and variety.

## NOTES

1. See David Bell and Gill Valentine, eds., *Consuming Geographies: We Are Where We Eat* (New York: Routledge, 1997) and Caroline Humphrey, *The Unmaking of Soviet Life: Everyday Economies after Socialism* (Ithaca, NY: Cornell University Press, 2002), 41.

2. Vilyam Pokhlebkin, *Kukhnya veka* [Cuisine of the Century] (Moscow: Polifakt, 2000).

3. Lynn Visson, "Kasha vs. Cachet Blanc: The Gastronomic Dialectics of Russian Literature," in *Russianness: Studies on a Nation's Identity: In Honor of Rufus Wellington Mathewson, 1918–1978*, ed. Robert L. Belknap (Ann Arbor, MI: Ardis, c1990), 63.

4. Catriona Kelly and David Shepherd, eds., *Constructing Russian Culture in the Age of Revolution, 1881–1940* (New York: Oxford University Press, 1998), 291.

5. Indonesia, Singapore, Malaysia, Thailand, South Korea, and China are described as having tiger economies, which pursue an export-driven model of economic development. With the injection of large amounts of foreign investment capital, these economies grew substantially between the late 1980s and early-to-mid-1990s.

6. Poll numbers on this question vary dramatically. The 34.8 percent number was reported by the Carnegie Endowment for International Peace, *Russian Attitudes toward Democracy, Markets, and the West*, Meeting Report, vol. 3, no. 10, 2 April 2001, http://www.ceip.org/files/events/mcfaulstateofstate.asp?pr=2&EventID=300, while another poll finds the figure closer to 80 percent: American Enterprise Institute, "The Russian Economy: Strategic Trends, Problems, and Opportunities," January 2004, http://www.aei.org/events/filter.,eventID.741/summary.asp.

7. World Health Organization, *Highlights on Health in the Russian Federation*, (Copenhagen, Denmark: World Health Organization, 1999), 18, http://www.euro.who.int/document/e72504.pdf.

8. This proverbial saying gained popularity in the mid-seventeenth century, based on the writings of the sixteenth-century French satirist Francois Rabelais. The adage is found in many Slavic and European languages—meaning that desire or facility increases as an activity proceeds.

9. The etymology of the word *bistro* has several competing stories. One is that Russians who chased Napoleon's armies back to Paris in 1815 were heard to shout "*bystro*," the Russian word for "quickly" or "hurry up." According to *Larousse Gastronomique*, however, it may also be related to a word in French dialect, "bistreau, or cowherd, and by extension, a jolly fellow—an apt description of the innkeeper. The most likely origin is an abbreviation of the word bistrouille" (37). Whatever the origins, the word *bistro* now refers to a casual dining place and has returned to the Russian language with a French pronunciation.

10. Vilyam Pokhlebkin, *Kukhnya veka* [Cuisine of the Century] (Moscow: Polifakt, 2000), 373.

11. Kelly and Shepherd, *Constructing Russian Culture*, 291.

12. Raymond Grew, *Food in Global History* (Boulder, CO: Westview Press, 1999), 80.

13. The social role of gastronome is that of theorist and propagandist about culinary taste. See Steven Mennell, A. Murcott, and A. van Otterloo, *The Sociology of Food: Eating, Diet, and Culture* (London: Sage, 1992), 84.

14. A. N. Filin, "Red Square, 1," http://www.redsquare.ru/english/index.htm.

15. John Hutchinson, *Modern Nationalism* (London: Fontana Press, 1994), 45.

16. Grew, *Food in Global History*, 12.

# 7

# Special Occasions

Food, festivals, feasts—there are few other elements of culture that can so concisely define an ethnic or national group. In every corner of the world, communal meals maintain a special place during social events, informal gatherings, and holy days. Whether in a religious or secular occasion, food may play a symbolic, sublime, or purely functional role. Holidays are a major force in synthesizing traditions of a cultural group—traditions that were formed over the centuries and passed down from generation to generation. Sacrificial offerings, fasts, and feasts are part of the key ritual aspects of the main representative religions of Eurasia: Christianity, Islam, Judaism, and Buddhism. Increasingly, religious holidays have emerged with renewed significance as the countries of the former USSR continue their quest for identity and social direction. Yet many holidays celebrated today in Russia and Central Asia are holdovers from the Soviet era. Moreover, a full set of new state holidays has been instituted to foster national pride in the 15 emergent countries from the remnants of the Soviet Union.

Even during the Communist reign of the twentieth century, religiously devout people in the USSR celebrated their holidays, be it Easter, Ramadan, or Passover. Throughout the past century, other holidays were incorporated or replaced by new Soviet festivals. In addition to a substantial overhaul of the Russian language and a switch from the Julian to the Gregorian calendar after the 1917 revolution, the Soviets also tinkered with religious and pagan holidays to reduce the cultural distress of completely removing these sacred traditions. Thus, Soviet New Year's celebrations absorbed Christmas traditions, Socialist Labor Day on May 1 supplanted Easter, and birthdays were more lavishly celebrated than the Christian Orthodox Name Days. Religious holidays have now rebounded, yet many secular Soviet ones remain deeply embedded too. As a result, there are more holidays and more merriment now in Russia and Central Asia. Religion of any ilk was quashed in Soviet times; therefore, in the initial glow of independence, those suppressed faiths have experienced a resurgence. Some holidays persevered and the foodways associated with those holidays remained, even if the public and religious significance was diminished.

Eighty percent of Russians identify themselves as Eastern Orthodox Christians. Another eighty-five million people in the 15 former Soviet republics, roughly 25 percent of the total, claim Islam as their belief. Muslims make up 70–80 percent of the population in Central Asia. Such statistics can be misleading at first blush. The number of believers is often based on the people who are historically considered Christian and Muslim, not necessarily those who are fervent believers. Most of the 80 percent who profess the Christian faith, for example, do not attend church services. Also, many post-Soviet Muslims neither attend mosque nor observe Ramadan, as required by Islam. Most also drink alcohol.

## RUSSIAN CELEBRATORY MEALS

The typical Russian celebratory meal requires much planning and preparation. The region is well acquainted with famine and hardship, and consequently feasts are intensely appreciated. Finding all the necessary ingredients, not to mention budgeting for them, demands great sacrifice and scheduling. The hosts of a family celebration may spend a week or more getting ready for the big day. Whether in Russia or Central Asia, there are certain residual Soviet commonalities for any feast, reinforced through stereotypes portrayed on television and film. Apartments are generally small, rarely containing a separate dining area. For more intimate gatherings, guests may dine in the kitchen. For larger gatherings, the living room, which often doubles as a bedroom with a foldout couch, is transformed into the dining room with a large folding table dominating the space. No expense is spared for the sake of effect and result. The hosts intend not only to impress their guests but also to ensure an unforgettable experience. The white tablecloth-laden table is usually wholly covered with small plates of appetizers (*zakuski*), salads, cold cuts, pickled vegetables, and bread. Selections of vodka, wine, or champagne are proudly displayed. The finest crystal and china, usually stored in the living-room cabinets, are dusted and shined for maximum pageantry. Once everyone is seated, a glass is raised in honor of the host or honored guest. Diners help themselves to the hors d'oeuvres and the plates are passed family style. The evening is often a noisy affair as dishes clang, music or television drones in the background, conversation builds, and more toasts are offered and accepted. A main hot course follows the toasts. Dessert brings the eating to a close, and hot tea with dessert completes the evening.

Toasting in the former Russian Empire remains a high art form and a mandatory ritual for almost all occasions. Toasts are offered as a show of gratitude and honor, or as a memorial, functioning almost as a public prayer. They can be honorific, solemn, humorous, or irreverent, depending on circumstance and mood. Toasts may be as simple as "To your health" or as elaborate as a compelling story or tale, bordering on sermon length with a bit of wisdom or a pithy lesson to share. Georgians are renowned for their eloquent and protracted toasts, usually made with local and homemade wine instead of vodka. The toastmaster has attained the status of a profession in Georgia. The silvery tongue of an accomplished *tamada* is in high demand during ceremonies and celebrations. This tradition and the title have been adopted in the rest of the former Soviet Union, albeit less formally. Either the host or the most elderly member of the gathering offers the first toast.

A toast is generally a bottoms-up belt of 2–3 ounces of straight vodka, followed by an immediate bite of zakuski, food that serves as a solid chaser. Most often, a pickle or a piece of bread removes the edge of the vodka shot. While the women generally sip their drink, the men will down the whole glass in one draw, be it vodka, brandy, or wine. The party almost always continues until all the bottles are drained. Although beer consumption has gained on vodka in post-Soviet times, beer is not served at meals and toasting with it is rare. Mugs are reflexively clinked only as a collective show of inebriation.[1] The meal remains the focus of all celebrations, and drink merely assists in high spirits and in structure (to signify the beginning of the meal, to punctuate notable moments with toasts, and to close the evening).

## CENTRAL ASIAN SPECIAL OCCASIONS

In Central Asia, the meal described for Russia would not be uncommon, considering 150 years of Russian and Soviet cultural influence. However, for most home meals during special occasions, the routine may differ from that of Russia. If guests are invited, the occasion becomes even more special following the Eastern tradition of hospitality. Guests arrive, remove their shoes, and wash their hands. Only men shake hands. Women, when greeting, put their right hand on the heart and bow slightly. Dozens of dishes are set on a low table or on a tablecloth draped across the floor. This table setting (*dastarkhan*) is the embodiment of Central Asian hospitality. The diners sit or recline on colorful pillows around the tablecloth. The evening begins with tea and perhaps a prayer. Breads, nuts, and sweets are offered to stimulate the appetite. After the first serving of tea, the leisure commences. Toasts may be offered if the hosts drink alcohol. Pilaf (*palov*), the ubiquitous dish of privilege for Central Asians, is served on most holidays and special occasions. The meal proceeds at an unhurried pace, and many dishes may follow the main course. The evening ends much as it began, with tea and a prayer.

Hospitality and tradition define Central Asian culinary culture. All special meals emphasize the significance of welcoming guests and paying respect to elders. The nomad will slaughter the sheep and the city dweller will spread out the dastarkhan. Food served at home almost always involves great sacrifice on the part of the host. In yurts, the honored guest usually sits opposite the doorway, with the men to his right and women and children on the left. Many urban homes have a special guest room for entertaining. Nomads place the dastarkhan on the floor in the center of the yurt or outside on the grass, lined with pillows. City dwellers may sit on the floor around a low table surrounded by cushions for support. Sometimes a low table is placed on a bedlike platform (*takhta*) covered with carpets. Family and social life revolve around the takhta. Otherwise the dastarkhan is simply placed in the middle of an unfurnished room.

## RELIGIOUS FEASTING AND FASTING

The relationship between food and faith is a voluminous subject. Since recorded history, the main periodic rites for civilizations commemorated the most significant events in the existence of the cultural group. These affairs, of course, were intimately associated with sustenance and survival, namely the planting and harvesting seasons in spring and autumn. The arrival of spring (which in many cultures marked the beginning of the new year) and the fall harvest festival have been incorporated as holidays into most organized religions. As religions grew more elaborate and ceremonial, certain foods became associated with each holiday. Many of these customs survive in some form even today, oftentimes adapted from earlier cultural or pagan traditions. One food historian posits that the profession of cookery arose from the practice and preparation of the sacrifices to the gods with the advent of organized religion.[2] The numerous temple specialists were essentially cooks, taking the responsibility of food distribution to the public realm. Whatever the origins of the profession, food and the abstention from food are part of the major ritual components for almost all of the world's religions.

In the Christian tradition, the Orthodox faith has the most rigorous fasting rules, while Protestants fast according to only congregational or individual discretion. The Russian Orthodox Church requires a minimum of 220 fasting days in the year, including every Wednesday and Friday, several one-day fasts, and several other extended fasts. Wednesday fasts are in remembrance of Christ's betrayal, and Fridays commemorate his crucifixion and death. The fasting periods leading up to the major holidays are broken with religious feasts. Generally, meat, eggs, and dairy products are prohibited, although fish is also banned during some fasts. The rationale behind the fasts is to make people receptive to God's grace and to bolster resistance to gluttony. While fairly regularly observed from the tenth to the nineteenth century in the Slavic areas, Christian religious fasting and dietary restrictions were almost obliterated during the Soviet period. Since independence, Russian restaurants have made a concerted effort to include Lenten choices on their menus, and grocery stores regularly advertise Lenten foods.

Ramadan (*Ramazan*) is the best known of the Islamic fasting periods, although some customs dictate additional days of fasting throughout the year. The ninth month of the Islamic lunar calendar, Ramazan commemorates the revelation of the Koran, Islam's holy book, to the prophet Mohammed. Since the months are tied to the lunar system, Ramazan usually begins 10 days earlier than the previous year. Devout Muslims should abstain from all food and drink from dawn to dusk, and refrain from smoking and sexual intercourse for the entire month. After sundown the feasting begins, and it ends again just before daybreak. As with Orthodox fasting, the Muslims of the former Soviet Union are adopting some Ramazan traditions, but far fewer than the numbers who observed these rites before the Russian Revolution.

Since many Jews of the Russian Empire either assimilated into the local culture over the past several centuries or emigrated to other countries, defining a single Judaic tradition for the region is nearly impossible. Jewish fasts include Yom Kippur (Day of Atonement), Tisha b'Av (observing the destruction of the Jewish Temple), and five minor fasts. For Yom Kippur and Tisha b'Av, Jews refrain from food and drink for 25 hours, from sundown until sundown. Fasting in the Jewish tradition is observed for atonement of sins or when coming to God with exceptional requests.

Tibetan and Mongolian Buddhist traditions spread north into Siberia beginning in the early seventeenth century. Buddhists are mainly found in the Siberian republics of Buryatia, Altai, and Tuva. The autonomous Kalmyk Republic, on the northern shores of the Caspian Sea, stands as Europe's only Buddhist region. The Buddhist faith now claims nearly one thousand lamas (monk or religious teacher) and a million followers in Russia.[3] Fasts are traditionally observed on full-moon days and during a few other holidays. Some liquids may be consumed, although solid food is not allowed. The goal of a fast is to clear the mind as a process of physical purification.

## ORTHODOX CHRISTIAN HOLIDAYS

The Russian Orthodox Church still retains the older Julian calendar system to mark the main periods of feasting and fasting. A distinction is made between moveable feasts, which are based on the scheduling of Easter, and fixed feasts and saints' days that fall on a particular day of the month. Christmas is second only to Easter in religious significance and is celebrated on January 7.[4] In the recent past, Orthodox Christmas was celebrated only by the deeply religious. This holiday also provides a nice contrast with the secular commercialization of Christmas in the form of Russian or Soviet New Year's festivities, where the focus has fallen on Santa Claus (Grandfather Frost), gift giving, and merrymaking.

On Orthodox Christmas Eve, everyone looks to the night sky for the appearance of the first star, which signifies the beginning of the holiday. After at least a day of fasting, the holy supper commences only after the holy liturgy. From an Orthodox tradition dating back to the fourth century A.D. in Constantinople, the fast should be broken by *sochivo*, *kut'ya*, or *kolivo*, different names for a special kind of porridge (*kasha*) made with grains, dried berries, walnuts, poppy seeds, and honey. Therefore, Christmas Eve has become known as Sochel'nik. The Christmas Eve dinner does not include meat. The main dishes are kut'ya and *uzvar*, a soup of dried apples, pears, and plums. Grains symbolize hope; honey, happiness; and poppy seeds, peace. After the meal, the family attends the Christmas service, returning home between 2 and 3 A.M.

On Christmas Day, the family prepares a feast, which, according to Orthodox tradition, should consist of 12 dishes, representing the 12 apostles. Traditionally, meat dishes were common at the Christmas table since animals were slaughtered in the winter. According to rural lore, pork is eaten at Christmas because a pig made too much noise in the manger, disturbing the baby Jesus from restful sleep. The pig's stubble also pricked the Lord's delicate hand when he tried to pet it. The 12 days of Christmastide (*svyatki*) came after Christmas Day and meat could be consumed every day. Roasted duck and piglet are among the many traditional Russian winter-holiday dishes, but beef and fish are also fairly common. Kut'ya is again served, washed down with *sbiten'*, an ancient Slavic hot drink made with honey and spices. Cookies are also an integral part of Russian Christmas. Fir cones (*yelovye shishki*) are an appropriate cookie to serve at the meal since the Russian Christmas tree is usually a fir or spruce tree. Christmas caroling is rewarded with *kolyadki*, cookies given to the carolers as they proceed from house to house.

Maslenitsa has become the Russian equivalent of Fat Tuesday or Mardi Gras, the pre-Lenten festival of Shrove Tuesday, arriving in February or March, depending on the Easter date. The Russian painter Boris Kustodiev captures the spirit of this holiday with his 1916 snowy masterpiece, *Maslenitsa*. The root of the word comes from *maslo* (butter or oil). During the Soviet period, this holiday was transformed to Provody Zimy (farewell to winter), a feast with pagan origins and celebrated early in the Lenten season. Fairs, carnivals, vendors, and music filled the streets, even during the Soviet period. One day of Maslenitsa is designated as *tyoshchiny bliny*, or "pancakes at mother-in-law's." Maslenitsa is also a celebration of newlyweds, keeping with the spirit of Maslenitsa—the hope of spring and new beginnings.

In general, Maslenitsa is a holiday of gluttony and excess that dates to the pre-Christian era. It is an end-of-winter holiday in honor of the sun god Yarilo, also the god of erotic sexuality, similar to Dionysus. The pancake (*blin*) represents the sun, and dozens of bliny are consumed throughout the week. Bliny are eaten with liberal amounts of butter, sour cream, caviar, smoked fish, and jams. They are made with buckwheat or wheat flour, or a mixture of both, with yeast or baking soda as the leavening agent. Orthodox Christianity adopted this holiday and it was given an additional meaning as the last week before Lent. Maslenitsa is celebrated eight weeks before Easter, easing the transition to the prolonged fast of Lent. The final Sunday of Maslenitsa is the Day of Forgiveness.

The longest and most strict abstention from certain foodstuffs occurs during Lent (Velikiy Post), roughly stretching from Maslenitsa until Holy Week, sometimes lasting up to 49 days. Lent, a Middle English word for "spring," is a solemn period of penance and fasting. According to proper Orthodox etiquette, on the first and last day of Lent no food is allowed at all. Fasting typically involves abstaining from meat, dairy, and alcohol rather than abstaining from all food. Vegetables are eaten every day for sustenance. For the other days Lenten fasting rules are as follows: Mondays, Wednesdays, and Fridays—no hot food, only bread, water, fruit, and cooked vegetables with no oil; Tuesdays and Thursdays—hot food with no vegetable oil; Saturdays—grains, vegetables, and mushrooms; and Sundays—vegetables only, though vegetable oil and occasionally wine are allowed. Fish is allowed only twice: on Palm Sunday (Verbnoe Voskresen'e) and for Annunciation.

There are many dishes associated with the Russian Lent season. The large number of fasting days contributed to the development of a variety of vegetable salads and fish dishes. Beet salad and borscht are common standbys. Mushrooms take the place of meat in cutlets, rice pilaf, and soups such as *shchi*. Potatoes and pickled or salted herring are always a treat, served with fresh onion slices and when allowed, oil. *Pokhlyobka* and *tyurya* are traditional Lenten soups. *Pokhlyobka* is a catch-all term for a variety of meager pottages or soups made of cabbage, potatoes, onions, carrots, and barley. Tyurya is a watery soup made with bread, cabbage, and onion, as frequently connected to sustenance and peasant cuisine as it is to Lent.

The final week before Easter is Holy Week (Strastnaya nedelya). Maundy Thursday (Velikiy Chetverg) is the day for washing up, cleaning the house, and decorating the eggs. Saturday is a day of complete fasting until the midnight Easter service. Early on Saturday, food preparation begins for the Easter feast later that night. More frequent visits to church services, partaking of communion, and participating in confessionals are expected during Lent. This is the one time of year when every Orthodox Christian should make a confession, which should be done on an empty stomach.

Easter (Paskha), also known as the Feast of the Resurrection, is the foremost celebration in every parish and home. Easter was always considered the most sacred holiday in Christian history, even though Christmas has generally surpassed Easter in non-Orthodox countries. Easter so dominated the Slavic cultural calendar that it was marked by nonreligious and non-Christian people even during the Soviet era. The religious meaning of Easter, of course, was downplayed by the government, but state bakeries carried *kulich* (traditional coffee cake–type bread) during the holidays.[5] The Saturday-night service culminates with the candlelight procession, in which believers file around the church in the early-morning hours just before dawn. The traditional Easter greeting is *"Khristos voskres"* (Christ has risen), to be answered with the reply *"Voistinu voskres"* (He has risen indeed), followed by three kisses.

The ritual foods of Easter are painted eggs, kulich, and *paskha,* a sweet cheese spread molded into different shapes. People bring their food to church before the Easter service so it can be blessed. The eggs are traditionally painted with liquids made from onion skins for a reddish brown color, from beets for bright pink, and from scraps of silk and other easy-to-fade fabrics to achieve other colors. By the time A Gift to Young Housewives was written by Elena Molokhovets at the end of the nineteenth century, there were already several brands of commercial egg-coloring kits available in Russia.[6] Many more are on sale now, but most people continue to use onion skins because the natural pigments produce the most beautiful, authentic color associated with Easter eggs. The reddish color symbolizes the resurrection, the single most important event for those of the Christian faith. Easter eggs were a traditional gift exchanged with friends and family during the holiday. Another tradition was to give chocolate eggs as well as wooden, carved, or painted ones, handmade by craftsmen. That tradition culminated in the world-famous, ornate Faberge eggs, made as presents to the tsar's family from 1895 to 1916.

Elena Molokhovets lists 17 different recipes for paskha in her book alone. The most basic kind is made by mixing *tvorog* (similar to cottage cheese or farmer's cheese), cream, sugar, butter, hard-cooked egg yolks, raisins, and almonds. The mixture is pressed into a special wooden or plastic mold, most often in the shape of a truncated pyramid to symbolize the holy tomb. Paskha is usually spread on slices of kulich. Kulich is prepared from a very rich dough that does not skimp on eggs, sugar, and butter. It is supposed to be very tall and light, so the yeast dough requires several risings. While baking, the kitchen door is shut and protected against drafts, as it is believed that any bursts of air—even loud sneezing and screaming—could negatively affect the end result. Any cylindrical metal baking forms can be used to make kulich. Resourceful homemakers in the Soviet Union saved tall tin cans throughout the year to ensure kuliches of various shapes and sizes as Easter treats. To maintain the ritual, the top of the kulich should be glazed and topped with round multicolored sprinkles.

Orthodox tradition also requires the presence of a lamb on the Easter table to represent the sacrificial death of Jesus. At the very least, butter may be molded into the shape of a lamb, although this tradition has mostly been forgotten. Apart from the ritual foods, the table is laden with meat dishes: ham, leg of lamb, and poultry. The traditional Easter feast consists of cold foods since the table is set before the church service, well in advance of mealtime. Fish was not traditionally served at Easter, but it too has made its way onto today's holiday table. The main consideration is a highly adorned and vibrant table, beautifully decorated with flowers and painted eggs set on specially grown grass of the first spring. Today the standard Russian Easter meal begins with zakuski and vodka and concludes with kulich and paskha.

## ISLAMIC HOLIDAYS

The Islamic calendar begins in A.D. 622 to mark the Hijra, Mohammed's flight to Medina. A.H. 1 (*anno Hegirae*) began on July 16 of that year. The calendar is based on the Koran (chapter [sura] 9, 36–37) and its observance is a sacred duty for Muslims. Since the calendar follows a lunar cycle, Muslim holidays cannot be assigned to a specific day of the month. The Islamic calendar year lasts about 355 days, so the timing of each holiday varies every year.

Ramadan (Ramazan) is the most renowned Muslim holiday, a month-long ceremony of prayer, fasting, and charity occurring in the ninth month of the year. No food or drink is allowed during daylight hours. All foods, however, are permitted from sunset to sunrise. The Koran dictates to "eat and drink until the black and white thread can be discerned at dawn." Ramadan (*Uraza* in Uzbek and Tatar) is a working holiday, but work schedules may be seriously disrupted or altered. In Central Asia, Ramadan is a time of spiritual purification, remembering the deceased, visiting and helping the sick and aged, making donations and giving alms, and performing charitable work. Although relatively few people in Central Asia strictly obey the sun-up-to-sun-down fast, it is considered impolite to eat on the streets during the holy month. Due to the slow business, some cafés and restaurants close during the day, while others completely shut down during this period. 'Id al-Fitr (Hait or Uraza Bairam), in Central Asia, is the three-day feast marking the end of the 30-day fast of Ramadan. Everyone makes or buys sweets and exchanges them with family, friends, and neighbors.

In Uzbekistan, the largest festival and holiday is Qurban-Hait (also Qurban Bayram or Id Al-Adha), eagerly awaited all year. Qurban-Hait occurs 70 days after Ramadan, to celebrate God's mercy in providing the

Pilgrimage picnic, Osh, Kyrgyzstan.

sacrificial lamb. The holiday has special importance for the pilgrims performing the hajj, or journey to Mecca. After independence in the 1990s,
small numbers of Muslims from Russia and the Central Asian countries
began to take part in the hajj, a feat nearly impossible in the Soviet era.

The day and evening before Qurban-Hait is called Arafa, or preparation day. Pilaf and *khalvaitar* (sweet wheat porridge) are the traditional
dishes of the holiday, and families share their food with neighbors. On
the first day of Qurban-Hait, males attend mosque and return home with
presents and hearty greetings for family and friends. This holiday in Central Asia usually involves the sacrifice of a one-year-old sheep or goat, to
both consume and give away as charity. Qurban-Hait has also evolved as
a formal time to remember the dead. Families should visit a cemetery, pray
for the deceased, and take care of their loved ones' graves.

Nauruz Bayram is the ancient, pre-Islamic holiday celebrating the
coming of spring on March 21, the vernal equinox. Although sometimes
called the Muslim New Year, it has no basis in Islam. Nauruz has its origins
in an Iranian folk holiday with roots in Zoroastrianism.[7] The celebration
of Nauruz was revived in the waning days of the USSR, because much
like Maslenitsa in Russia, the holiday had a tenuous religious significance.
Traditional dishes in Uzbekistan include *koq samsa, koq chuchvara, halim,
nishalda,* and *sumalak. Koq* means "green" in Uzbek, and the savory pastries and the small ravioli-like dumplings are made with all the spring
greens that abound in the mountain valleys. Wheat porridge (halim) is
made from boiled meat and wheat grains, seasoned with ground black

pepper and cinnamon. Nishalda, a meringue flavored with licorice root, is also popular during Ramadan.

Sumalak is an elaborate ritual dish made exclusively by women during the 24 hours before Nauruz. Wheat is soaked in water for three days to sprout the grains. The green sprouts are then put through a meat grinder. Oil, flour, and sugar are added and cooked over low heat. The eleventh-century linguist Mahmud Kashgari links the root of the word *suma* with an ancient Turkic meaning of "swollen wheat."[8] Sometimes a bread is also made from the dried, crushed wheat sprouts. Women sit around the stove or kitchen table as it cooks. They gossip, dance, sing, and tell tales while taking turns stirring the pot. There are numerous folk traditions and superstitions surrounding sumalak, most of which are associated with fertility, friendship, and tolerance. Seven blessed stones are placed in the pot with the sumalak.[9] Sumalak is first offered to women without children before sharing with the mothers present. Earrings are made from wheat grass, and male infants are placed on a bride's lap to increase fertility. During the celebration of the sumalak, unmarried girls pray to the seven stars for familial success, while female elders plant new trees with young unmarried women.

## JEWISH HOLIDAYS

In contrast to the Gregorian calendar, which is based on the solar cycle, and the Islamic calendar, which is lunar, the Hebrew calendar was established on both lunar months and a solar cycle (to delineate the years). The major Jewish holidays follow the Hebrew calendar, yet the two main culinary elements of Judaism are Kashrut, the dietary law, and the observance of the Sabbath. Food, however, plays a symbolic and social role in all Judaic holidays. The Jewish traditions in the former Soviet Union are extremely diverse and particular to each family. Therefore, it is highly speculative to collectively describe the ceremonies and foods of the Jews of the ex-USSR. The largest Jewish group arose in Germany during the last millennium and spread throughout Central and Eastern Europe, including the Russian Empire. Their food reflected the European diet, including boiled chicken and bouillon, minced meats, and fish. The best-known dishes are *gefilte* (literally "stuffed") fish, salted herring, *cholnt*, and *tsimes*. Gefilte fish is a labor-intensive, exceedingly tasty poached fish dish made with minced whitefish (*sig*), carp (*karp*), and pike (*shchuka*) together with unleavened bread (matzo) and seasoning. Cholnt (also *cholent* or *chelnt*) is a slowly braised meat, bean, and potato stew, whereas *tsimes* is a dessert dish of stewed carrots and plums. With few exceptions, most of the Jews in Russia are *Ashkenazi*, those with German or East European origins, as opposed to *Shephardic*, Jews who trace their lineage to Spain and North Africa.[10] In broad terms, Shephardic cookery, greatly influenced by Turkic cookery of the Ottoman Empire, includes olive oil, peppers, eggplant, and rice.

Kashrut involves daily prohibitions of certain foods or combinations of food (mixing meat and milk, for example). Based on verses in the Torah, food is considered kosher (from the Hebrew word *kasher*, meaning "fit") if it fulfills the requirements of Jewish dietary law. According to the book of Leviticus, dietary law reinforces ritual purity and holiness. These restrictions were further developed in the oral law and extensively codified by later rabbis.[11] There are various explanations for kashrut—hygienic reasons, symbolic aims, or as a basis for Jews to distinguish themselves from other religious and cultural groups. Others prefer to view the holy practice as simply beyond human understanding. In brief, kosher animals must have cloven hooves, must chew their cud (i.e., sheep, goats, cows, and deer), and must be butchered by an ordained slaughterer. Dairy products from kosher animals are allowed, but Orthodox Jews must not mix dairy and meat, either in a dish or during its preparation. This involves maintaining separate kitchens, utensils, cookware, and dishes for meat and dairy products. Fish must have both fins and scales, thus removing catfish, crabs, lobster, shrimp, and eels, among others, from Orthodox menus.

The Sabbath (Shabbat) is a day of respite, observed from Friday at sundown until Saturday at sundown. No work, or even cooking (for most Jews), is allowed on the Sabbath. Hence, the special meal must be prepared in advance. The Sabbath feast is observed 52 days during the year, resulting in more sacred meals than in any other religion or tradition. The Sabbath is considered among the most important holy days in the Jewish calendar since it was the first holiday mentioned in the Bible. On Saturday evenings, the family enjoys the best dishes it can afford. In general, the three ritual dishes include *challah* (braided sweetened bread made from a rich egg dough), a stew of meat and vegetables, and wine.

On Friday afternoon, the family sets a beautiful table and prepares a celebratory meal. After a brief evening service, a leisurely dinner is enjoyed. The head of the household delivers a prayer, Kiddush, over wine sanctifying the Sabbath. The usual prayer for eating bread is recited over two loaves of challah. Dishes are, by and large, soups, stews, or slow-cooked items that may easily be reheated, one form of work permitted on the Sabbath. In addition to cholnt, fried, boiled, or braised fish with various stuffings; herring; and salad dishes are served. Saturday afternoon after the Shabbat services, the family prays again and sits down to another unhurried meal. A sweet raisin-and-apricot *kugel* (a casserole or pudding dish), fruits, berries, and nuts often grace the table. Shabbat ends on Saturday night when three stars are visible.

Rosh Hashanah is the Jewish New Year's, commemorating the creation of the earth, year one according to the Hebrew calendar. The food should be neither dark nor cloudy in color, neither spicy nor marinated—to ensure a sweet and successful New Year. Some of the main dishes for Rosh Hashanah in the NIS include fish, symbolizing bounty; head of sheep or fish, to lead in the coming year; carrot slices resembling gold coins; round challah with raisins for health; fruits and vegetables in hope of an abundant harvest; and finally, apples and honey, so the year will be sweet and favorable.

Chanukah, or the Festival of Lights, celebrates the wondrous story of the Maccabee brothers, who defeated the Assyrians in 164 B.C. and rededicated the Temple in Jerusalem. The eight-day festival is highlighted by the daily lighting of a candle held by a menorah, since, according to legend, one day's worth of oil miraculously lasted for the eight days. Some traditional dishes include potato pancakes (*latkes*); bliny with sour cream, butter, goose fat, and cracklings; donuts (*sufganiot*) cooked with vegetable oil; chicken or beef stew; and dairy products, especially cheese and tvorog.

Passover (Pesach) is a joyous holiday commemorating the flight of Jews from Egypt as told in the book of Exodus. The main part of the ritual, *seder*, is a ceremonial meal on the evening of the first day. The table is set with the finest tablecloth and china and adorned with a silver plate containing matzo and a specially divided platter with other symbolic foods: *haroset* (a mixture of nuts and fruits to commemorate the mortar used by slaves in Egypt); *beitsa* (a plain boiled egg signifying a new beginning); *maror* (horseradish, to symbolize the bitter days of slavery), *z'roa* (a shank bone or chicken neck to represent the Paschal lamb); and *karpas* (a sprig of fresh greens or boiled potatoes, which are dipped in salt water to signify spring and tears). Red wine (as a symbol of blessing) is the other part of the ritual. All during Passover week, leavened foods are off limits, to commemorate the flight from Egypt, when there was no time for even the dough to rise.[12] Before the preparation of the holiday meal, the house receives a thorough scrubbing in accordance with scripture to remove all possible traces of leavened bread. Other dishes served in Jewish homes across Russia and the former Soviet Union during Passover may include gefilte fish, chicken soup, chicken pilaf, or fried chicken.

## SECULAR AND NATIONAL HOLIDAYS

During the seven decades of the Communist experiment, all holidays celebrated the glory of labor as well as specific professions, special days of

Communist history, and memorials to war, particularly World War II. Of course, the government also co-opted many religious or folk festivals and put a Socialist twist on them. Russians had previously marked New Year's Day after the fall harvest, on September 1, until Peter the Great decreed the observance of New Year's Eve on December 31, 1700, to bring Russia in line with the West. He also encouraged the European tradition of decorating a Christmas tree. Russians to this day continue to celebrate New Year's Eve much like a combination of the Christmas and New Year's holidays in the West. Christmas trees, Santa Claus or Grandfather Frost (Ded Moroz), the exchange of presents, and a large family meal are all included in the celebration. But they also ring in the New Year with champagne and fireworks all in the same day.

On New Year's Eve, people usually leave work early and spend the rest of the evening preparing the food and setting the table. Most foods have been purchased and stockpiled in advance to reduce the workload and extend the often-meager family resources. New Year's is considered a family holiday. Young people are discouraged from going out with their friends, but like teenagers everywhere, to little effect. This is one of the few times during the year when dinner is served in the living room. In the background, the movie *The Irony of Fate* (*Ironiya sudby*) is shown on television, a Soviet tradition retained to this day. In some ways, this 1975 film has the same association with New Year's in Russia as the movie *It's a Wonderful Life* has with Christmas in the United States. *The Irony of Fate* is a romantic comedy that takes place on New Year's Eve, a mild satire on the Communist standardization of life, hard-drinking men, and other Soviet realities.

Russians believe that the new year will unfold in direct relation to the manner in which it was celebrated. Therefore, no effort or expense is spared for the grandest of contemporary holidays. The table features all the favorite and traditional Russian dishes, including a wide array of appetizers, salads, and bread. A standard menu often includes red and black caviar, *salat Oliv'ye*, *salat vinegret*, trays of assorted smoked fish and cold cuts, and pickled cucumbers and other brined vegetables. By the time the main course arrives, hunger has long since passed. Dessert and tea are obligatory at the end of every festive meal, and New Year's is no exception. The meal usually runs up to and beyond the stroke of midnight. Right before the clock strikes 12 A.M., a toast with vodka, wine, or brandy is raised to the old year—an appreciative farewell. The first toast of the New Year is made with champagne (actually sparkling wine from southern Russia, Ukraine, or Georgia), proclaiming "With the new year comes new happiness" (*s novym godom, s novym schast'em*).

Red Army Day and International Women's Day are two closely related Socialist holidays that continued their importance in the post-Communist era. The Day of the Defenders of the Fatherland, formerly known as Soviet Army Day, is celebrated on February 23. Since military service was mandatory for all Soviet males, it approximates a combination of Memorial Day and Father's Day in the United States. Women congratulate the men on their service, but except for small military parades, it is usually just a holiday of intoxication. Women's Day, however, is an international holiday celebrated initially in 1911 as a Socialist and suffragist movement in Germany, Austria, Denmark, and some other European countries.[13] March 8 is the only day of the year when men can be found in the kitchens preparing breakfast and other meals. Women's Day, too, has American equivalents—roughly Valentine's Day and Mother's Day rolled into one. Men shower the ladies with candy, flowers, and gifts.

May 1 was known as the International Day of Workers' Solidarity, only recently officially renamed Spring and Labor Day. During the Soviet era, it was observed with official public rallies and parades on Red Square in Moscow and the main squares in every town. Although it was a nonworking holiday, colleagues and schoolmates still assembled in the morning for the mandatory parade. The first of May is still among the most favorite holidays because it usually involves outings and picnics since the weather in central Russia is generally mild by early May.

The Celebration of Victory Day in the Great Patriotic War, the Russians' name for World War II, is marked on May 9, the day of Soviet triumph over Nazi Germany in 1945. The Soviet Union lost up to 30 million soldiers and civilians in that war, and those years are still deeply ingrained in the Soviet psyche. The day begins with a morning parade of the armed forces and veterans, although there are fewer and fewer survivors every year. Most people revere the holiday even if they do not go out of their way to celebrate it at home. For others, it serves as another excuse, perhaps appropriate, for a drinking party. The 1st, 2nd, 8th, and 9th of May are nonworking days. Add in the weekends, and the first half of May becomes a prolonged vacation. In 2005, Russia abolished the November 7 holiday (commemorating the October 1917 Bolshevik Revolution) and Constitution Day on December 12, and reduced the first of May holiday from two days to one. In return, Russians enjoy extended New Year's and Christmas holidays, essentially recognizing the fact that the country shuts down for a fortnight in January, regardless of the official calendar.

Some of the older seasonal celebrations in Uzbekistan and Central Asia, directly related to food and survival, are experiencing a cultural revival:

Erga urug kadash (planting festival), Khosil bairami (harvest holiday), Mekhrjon (bounty of nature celebration), Uzum saili (grape day), and Kovun saili (melon day). These days are marked with feasts, folk songs, and prayers. The Central Asian republics continue to celebrate the Soviet holidays of New Year's Day, International Women's Day, May 1, and May 9. They have also added Nauruz, Islamic holidays, independence days, constitution days, and a handful of nation-building holidays.

## LIFE EVENTS AND FAMILY CELEBRATIONS

Ask Russians what their favorite celebrations are, and the answer varies little: New Year's, May Day holidays, and birthdays. For children, the birthday party is the most important festive occasion of the year, rivaled only by New Year's. The importance fades as one ages, but birthday celebrations are almost never forsaken. The parents organize the children's parties, which are usually held at home. For the adults, as in other parts of Europe, the birthday person (or if male—his wife or mother) is responsible for throwing a party for friends and family. This includes doing all the shopping, cooking, and cleaning up. Most people have parties at home (except the wealthiest minority, who can afford to organize extravagant banquets with concerts and fireworks). Along with the obligatory cake with candles, an elaborate

Birthday picnic, Black Sea shore.

meal is customarily served. Gifts are expected, and flowers are traditional for women and girls. In general, Russians love giving and receiving flowers, and floral shops are a lucrative business—one of the first nonindustrial sectors to boom after the initial liberalization of the economy.

Birthday parties took the place of Name Days—the feast day of a saint after whom a person is named—which were discouraged and almost forgotten during the Soviet times. Name Days are slowly coming back, but birthdays are not fading either. For a Name Day party, the honoree was presented with a *karavay* (a celebratory round loaf of bread). The tradition remains in a game that is still common at birthday parties. Children sing a song about baking a karavay and perform a ring dance (*khorovod*) around the honoree.[14] Then the birthday child is supposed to choose the person he or she likes the most to take his or her place in center circle to sing and dance. In old Russia, all major events were celebrated with a karavay.

Traditionally the late fall, after harvest, was the time for weddings in Russia. Today weddings take place any time of year, although the Orthodox Church forbids them during Lent and other fasts, on certain days of the week, and before major religious holidays. The number of couples having a church wedding has been increasing every year since independence, but the majority still opts for a civil ceremony, which can take place any day. More and more frequently, couples live together without any ceremony at all. When finally engaged, the future groom traditionally received crescent-shaped pies with a sweet or savory filling.

The somber civil wedding ceremony takes place in one of several Palaces of Weddings or a more modest Civil Registry Office with an officiating woman-registrar giving a canned speech about the role of family in society. For an additional cost, a small orchestra performs Mendelssohn's "Wedding March," a recessional from Shakespeare's *A Midsummer Night's Dream*, and other classics.[15] The bride wears a white dress and a veil; the groom, simply a suit and tie. The ritual, whether civil or religious, involves an exchange of rings. An Orthodox religious ritual also includes a crowning ceremony to underscore the importance of the event. The crowns are symbols of the glory and honor that God bestows on the couple during the sacrament. They are also a sign of martyrdom, since the individual must make some sacrifices for the union to succeed. A walk around the altar represents a promise of faithfulness until death, and drinking wine from one cup symbolizes an agreement to drink from the same cup of life.

After the ceremony, the couple, family, and close friends usually go to a reception in taxis or limousines decorated with conjoined rings on the roof as well as dolls in wedding attire attached to the front bumper. Receptions are most frequently held at home or, if a couple can afford it, at

Wedding with bread and salt tradition.

a restaurant. The menu mainly depends on the budget. The bride and groom and their parents sit at the head of a table. Customary dishes include a variety of salads and cold cuts, smoked fish, meat or poultry for the main course, and a wedding cake for dessert. The bride typically cuts the cake; the groom serves the first piece to her, then she to him. Western-style receptions with the bride and groom cutting a tall cake simultaneously are becoming common too.

Traditionally, the bride and groom start the dancing, then the groom dances with his mother-in-law and mother, and the bride with her father-in-law and father. Special guests are presented the ceremonial karavay on an embroidered towel with a small wooden container of salt on top—hence the Russian word for "hospitality," *khlebosol'stvo* (bread and salt). For a wedding, karavay are baked at the houses of both the bride and the groom. The newlyweds are often presented with a richly decorated *krendel'* (pretzel-shaped fancy bread). One enduring tradition at every wedding reception is for the guests to complain that the food and drink are bitter by yelling out "*Gor'ko!*" This is a call for the newlyweds to kiss, thus "sweetening" the food.

Weddings in Central Asia may follow some Russian/Soviet traditions, but every cultural group has its own unique way of celebrating this special day. Families with nomadic roots, living in Western-style dwellings, may erect yurts to celebrate weddings and funerals. In Uzbekistan, prior to the wedding, representatives from the groom's family visit the bride's house to formally ask for her hand. The event is culminated in a ritual called *non sindirish* (breaking of bread). The date of the wedding is agreed upon. At the end of the evening, the bride's family presents each representative with a dastarkhan, two flatbreads, and sweets, as well as gifts for the groom's family. The party continues at the groom's house, where the presents are examined and the treats enjoyed. The couple is now considered to be engaged. On the day of the wedding two pilafs are cooked: one at the groom's house and one at the bride's house. The typical Uzbek wedding pilaf contains rice, mutton, chickpeas, raisins, onions, carrots, barberries, cumin, and turmeric for a golden color. Tajik wedding pilaf is very sweet—with sugar, dried fruit, and orange peel—to ensure the sweet life for the couple. The bride ceremoniously leaves her house for the groom's house, and the main party continues there.

Another special domestic ceremony in Uzbekistan takes place in conjunction with the Islamic holiday Qurban-Hait. Any bride married in the previous 12 months opens her home to everyone, especially the neighborhood women and young girls. For three days after Arafa, visitors judge the skills of the new wife in hospitality and cooking. The new wife passes on her secrets to and shares her talents with the younger pupils. The table is continuously set with elaborate sweets and tea prepared by the new wife and her family. Elders pay particular attention to the way the hostess pours the tea. The tea ceremony involves pouring the hot tea from a small pitcher into a handleless cup (*piala*). The first two cups are returned to the teapot. Only the third cup is suitable for drinking. If the hostess pours

New bride's table, Tashkent, Uzbekistan.

too much tea into the piala, it is a sign of disrespect, for the tea will not remain hot. This custom requires her to be attentive and offer guests just the right amount of tea so it is always fresh and hot.

Moving into a new apartment is always a major event in the former Soviet Union, where a chronic housing shortage has persisted throughout the twentieth century, especially in the main metropolitan areas. A housewarming party follows the similar pattern of holiday meals, in which the hosts make all the arrangements and invite guests to share in their happiness. A full lunch or dinner is the norm, and it usually involves toasting and drinking. Russians mark major new purchases with a custom called *obmyvat'* (to clean or bathe), related to the tradition of launching a new ship with a bottle of champagne. A bottle is opened and glasses poured. The owner will offer a toast to the new item, be it a car or a washing machine, to ensure its proper care and functioning. The same holds for a new home or an apartment. A drink may even be sprinkled onto the floor for good fortune and, inevitably, a special meal follows.

Funerals in Russia are not only a time for mourning but a period of elaborate food and drink rituals. In the Russian Orthodox tradition, the day of death, the day of the funeral, and the 3rd, 9th, and 40th days after death are all considered days of mourning. In addition, several Parents' Days are assigned by the church throughout the year to remember the dead. On all of these days it is customary to visit the graves and leave some food on the grave as a symbolic offering to the loved ones.

On the day of the funeral the family prepares and serves a special dish—a variation of *kut'ya* (also called *kolivo*): a sweet kasha made with wheat or rice. Grain symbolizes eternal life, and sweetness (usually honey, sugar, raisins, jam, etc.)—heavenly peace. After the funeral, family and close friends gather at home for the funeral banquet (*pominki*). A table setting is prepared for the deceased person and a chair is left empty in memory of the departed. People talk about the life and good deeds of the deceased and drink to his or her memory and for the peace of his or her soul. "May the earth be fluffy for him/her" (*Pust' zemlya emu/ei budet pukhom*) is a customary wish for the deceased. Along with kut'ya, bliny, and *kisel'* (a thickened drink made with fruit or berries) are the traditional mourning dishes. The rest of the menu varies depending on individual tastes and budget. A similar banquet is repeated on the 40th day from death.

In Central Asia, a pilaf ritual takes place on three main occasions: the wedding day, 20 days after a death, and the one-year anniversary of a death. It involves not only relatives and friends but the entire neighborhood (*mahalla*). On the eve of the event, a carrot-cutting (*sabzi tugrar*) party takes place, usually with a concert (for weddings only) and a feast, during which the roles for the next day are assigned by the elders. The pilaf is cooked just before dawn so it is ready by the time the morning prayer is over. Wedding and funeral feasts are prepared and served by men only. Folk music calls the neighborhood to the table. The ritual begins with bread and tea, and then pilaf is served. Each platter is to be shared by two guests. Once guests are finished with the food, they leave and their places are taken by new arrivals.

## RECIPES FOR SPECIAL OCCASIONS

### Kut'ya (Sochivo, Kolivo) (Orthodox Christmas and Funeral Dish)

- 1 cup hulled wheat (sold as wheat berries in many health-food stores with bulk supplies)
- 3/4 cup poppy seeds
- 2 oz. slivered almonds or other nuts, coarsely ground
- 2 oz. raisins
- vanilla extract, honey, and sugar to taste

Boil wheat berries until tender, at least 3 hours, keeping covered with water. Blanch poppy seeds, drain, and grind in food processor. Combine drained wheat berries, ground poppy seeds, nuts, and raisins. Add a tablespoon or so of honey, sugar, and vanilla extract to taste. Serve cold in a plain bowl.

### Grechnevye Bliny (Russian Buckwheat Pancakes/Crepes)

- 2 cups buckwheat flour
- 4 cups milk
- 5 eggs, separated
- 1 teaspoon salt
- 1 1/2 packages dry active yeast
- 4 tablespoons unsalted butter, melted
- 2 tablespoons sugar
- 2 cups all-purpose flour

Mix buckwheat flour with 1 cup of cold milk. Stir in 2 cups of warm milk to the flour mixture. Mix in the yeast and only 1/2 teaspoon of sugar. Cover and set aside in a warm place for 30 minutes. Blend the egg yolks with the remainder of the sugar, melted butter, salt, and all-purpose flour until smooth and add to the buckwheat mixture. Adjust consistency with remaining milk. Cover and set aside for 45 minutes. Fold whipped egg whites into the batter a little bit at a time. Drop 2–3 tablespoons of batter onto a hot, buttered skillet. Cook for 1 1/2 minutes; flip and cook other side for 30–60 seconds. Serve with the usual garnishes of sour cream, fish, jam, caviar, tvorog, and so forth.

## Potato *Tsimes* (Jewish Meat and Vegetable Stew)

- 1 1/2 lbs. kosher beef, cubed
- 1 lb. carrots, julienned
- 10 oz. potatoes, diced
- 7 oz. onions, chopped
- 7 oz. pitted prunes
- 3 1/2 oz. vegetable oil
- sugar, salt, pepper to taste

Fry beef in hot oil until caramelized. Add chopped onions to meat and sauté. Add julienned carrots and cover with water by 1–2 inches. Cook on low heat until almost tender. Add diced potatoes, prunes, and a dash of sugar. Cook until meat is exceedingly tender. Add salt and pepper to taste.

## *Salat Oliv'ye* (Russian Potato Salad)

- 3 medium-sized carrots, boiled
- 2 medium-sized potatoes, boiled
- 2 eggs, hard cooked
- 1 can (15–16 oz.) of sweet peas
- 3–4 medium-sized pickled cucumbers
- 1 fresh cucumber
- 1 medium-sized onion, finely chopped
- 2 tablespoons mayonnaise
- 8 oz. bologna, cooked chicken, or beef (optional)

Peel and dice vegetables and eggs, add together in bowl with finely chopped onion. Combine mixture with meat and mayonnaise and stir. Chill, garnish with parsley and dill, and serve in bowl.

### Salat Vinegret (Russian Beet Salad)

- 3 large potatoes, boiled
- 2 medium-sized beets, boiled
- 2 pickles or 1/2 cup of sauerkraut (kvashennaya kapusta), drained
- 2 medium-sized carrots, boiled
- 1 medium onion, finely diced
- 2 tablespoons vegetable oil
- salt to taste

Peel and uniformly dice cooled potatoes, beets, carrots, and pickles. Combine with onions. Add vegetable oil and salt and mix gently.

### Koq Chuchvara (Uzbek Green Dumplings)

#### Dough
- 4 cups flour
- 1 egg, boiled and chopped
- 1 cup water
- 1 teaspoon salt

#### Filling
- 1 1/2 lbs. mixture of greens and herbs: sorrel, spinach, mint, cilantro, dill, basil, thyme, parsley, celeriac, garlic, green onion, rocket, arugula, shepherd's purse
- 12 oz. onions, finely diced
- 4 oz. butter or animal fat
- 1 egg, boiled and chopped
- black pepper, salt to taste

Chop the herbs and combine well with onions, boiled egg, butter, and seasonings. Make stiff dough out of flour, salt, egg, and water; let stand for 30–40 minutes. Roll out dough into 1/12 inch thick layer and cut into 2×2 inch squares. Place a touch of filling in the center, fold dough corner to corner, and pinch edges—completely enclosing filling. Boil in salted water until they float, no more than 4 minutes. Serve in broth or drained with yogurt or sour cream; sprinkle with black pepper.

### Bairam Palovi (Uzbek Wedding Palov)

- 5 cups rice
- 3 lbs. mutton or beef

- 2 lbs. carrots, cut in matchstick strips
- 2 1/2 quarts water
- 5 onions, sliced
- 3/4 cup raisins
- 1 cup chickpeas, canned
- 4 1/2 cups vegetable oil
- salt, black pepper, cumin, coriander, turmeric, and barberries to taste

Cut meat in small pieces and sear in hot oil. Add sliced onions. After a few minutes put in carrot strips and mix. Add 2 1/2 quarts water, chickpeas, raisins, salt, and spices; simmer for 25–30 minutes. Add rice and more water to 1/2 inch above surface of rice. Cook uncovered until water evaporates. Cover and cook on low heat 30–40 minutes or until meat is tender and rice is fully steamed. Stir mixture, remove the meat, and cut into uniform sized pieces. Serve rice in a mound on a large platter topped with the meat pieces.

## Kisel'

- 2 cups fresh raspberries, cranberries, or strawberries
- 5 cups water
- 5 tablespoons sugar
- 1 teaspoon cornstarch
- 1/4 teaspoon fresh lemon juice, or to taste
- 1/8 teaspoon salt

Simmer half of the berries for 10 minutes in 4 1/2 cups of water. Strain the liquid through a sieve into a bowl and mash the berries. Add sugar to the strained juice and bring to a boil until the sugar is dissolved. Mix cornstarch and salt in 1/2 cup of cold water. Add cornstarch mixture to saucepan. Stir rapidly until it boils, thickens, and becomes smooth. Pour saucepan contents through sieve and add the other half of fresh berries to the juice. Stir in lemon juice. Chill and serve in tall glasses.

## Kulich (Easter Cake with Walnuts and Raisins)

- 8 cups flour
- 1 1/2 cups sugar
- 6 eggs
- 1 1/4 cups milk
- 10 oz. butter

- 2 oz. dry yeast
- dried apricots, raisins, candied citrus peel (optional)
- salt, cardamom, vanilla, ginger powder to taste

Mix flour, sugar, butter, spices, and yeast. Add dried fruit, milk, and eggs. Leave the batter in a warm place for up to 1 hour. Place in a tall, round cake tin and bake at 325 degrees for 40 minutes. Glaze the cooled kulich with meringue or thin icing and decorate with colored round sprinkles.

### Paskha (Easter Cheese Spread)

- 2 lbs. tvorog (Quark or farmer's cheese found at specialty stores)
- 6 1/2 oz. butter
- 11 oz. sugar
- 6 hard-cooked egg yolks
- 1/2 teaspoon vanilla extract
- 3/4 cup almonds, ground
- grated zest of 1/2 lemon
- 1/2 cup raisins
- extra raisins, chopped candies, and fruit for garnish

Combine tvorog, butter, sugar, yolks, and vanilla in a food processor. Transfer mixture to a large bowl and add almonds, lemon zest, and 1/2 cup raisins; mix well. Line a clean, unused flower pot (or similar tomb-shaped container) with wet cheesecloth. Place the cheese mixture into the lined pot, fold the ends of the cheesecloth over the top, and weight the top directly on the cheese to force out excess liquid. Place the pot above a bowl to catch the excess liquid and refrigerate overnight. Remove paskha from the mold and discard the cheesecloth. Decorate with additional raisins or candied fruit, pressing some into the paskha to form the Russian letters XB (Khristos Voskres—Christ has risen). Serve paskha with kulich.

## NOTES

1. Clinking glasses has several reputed origins. In ancient Greece, to prove wine was safe, a host would pour some of his guest's wine into his own cup and drink it first. If the guest trusted his host, however, he would merely touch his cup against the other. Some cultures believed that clinking glasses would drive away evil spirits, since bells and other similar sounds were thought to scare away demons.

2. Michael Symons, *A History of Cooks and Cooking* (Urbana: Illinois University Press, 2000), 240–63.

3. The Washington Times, "Buddhism Flourishes in Siberian Republics," via Victor Loginova Agence France Presse, 27 September 2003, www.washtimes. com/world/20030927-112321-7610r.htm. For specific information about Buryat cuisine, see three works by Sharon Hudgins, *The Other Side of Russia: A Slice of Life in Siberia and the Russian Far East* (College Station: Texas A&M University Press, 2003), 123–43; "Raw Liver, Singed Sheep's Head, and Boiled Stomach Pudding: Encounters with Traditional Buriat Cuisine," *Sibirica: Journal of Siberian Studies* 3, no. 2 (October 2003): 131–52; and "Spicy Siberia: Hot Foods in a Cold Climate," *Chile Pepper* 9, no. 6 (November/December 1995): 16–23, 34–36.

4. The difference between the Julian and Gregorian calendars reached 13 days by 1918, when the Communists adopted the Gregorian calendar. Thus, the Russian Bolshevik Revolution of October 25 came to be celebrated on November 7 and Orthodox Christmas now falls on January 7 instead of December 25. Most Western European nations shifted to the Gregorian calendar system between 1582 and 1753.

5. *Kulich,* like the word *paskha,* has Greek roots, reflecting the deep cultural influence of the Orthodox Church and the Byzantine Greeks. *Kóllix* is a circular or oval loaf of bread.

6. Joyce Toomre, *Classic Russian Cooking: Elena Molokhovets' A Gift to Young Housewives* (Bloomington: Indiana University Press, 1992).

7. Zoroastrianism is based on the concept of struggle between light (good) and dark (evil) religion, founded in Persia in the sixth century B.C. by Zoroaster.

8. Mahmud Kashgari, *Divanü Lügat-it Türk* [Encyclopedia of the Turkish Language], trans. Besim Atalay, ed. Robert Dankoff, TDK Publ. 521, 4 vols. (Duxbury, MA: Basildigi yer Harvard Universitesi Basimevi, 1982–85).

9. Seven was known as a "perfect" number among peoples of southwest Asia, symbolizing righteousness and completeness. Ancient Sumerian and Babylonian civilizations identified seven planets and framed seven days of the week around them. During the hajj, or annual Islamic pilgrimage, Muslims stone the statues of devils three times using seven stones each time.

10. The Karaites, who once had a thriving population in both Crimea and Lithuania, and the Jewish community of Bukhara in Uzbekistan both trace their roots to non-European ancestry.

11. Judaic oral law is recorded in the Mishnah and the Talmud, the remaining books of the Old Testament.

12. As the Jews fled Egypt through the desert, they had no time to bake bread, so they took with them unleavened bread known as matzo. In observance, all leavened products are forbidden during the entire week of Passover, as commanded in Exodus 12:15, "Seven days you shall eat unleavened bread; on the very first day you should remove leaven from your houses."

13. This date was chosen by German women because, on that date in 1848, the Prussian king, faced with an armed uprising, had promised many reforms, including an unfulfilled one of votes for women.

14. *Khorovod* literally means "to lead the choir" and is related to the Greek round dance *chorea* (*choreia*, *khoreia*).

15. Richard Wagner's "Wedding March" from the romantic opera *Lohengrin* (1850), also known as "Here Comes the Bride," is often used for heralding the entrance of the bride. Felix Mendelssohn's "Wedding March" (1826) has become the traditional wedding music for the exit of the bridal party. In 1893, George V of England chose this combination for his wedding and it has since become the standard wedding processional and recessional in Western weddings.

# 8

# Diet and Health

All societies accept the direct link between food and health. Traditional diets of many cultural groups that developed over generations and even millennia are disappearing with globalized commerce and the availability of foodstuffs year round. Diets worldwide are rapidly changing with the introduction of convenience foods, industrially processed products, and nutritional supplements and quick fixes. In Russia and Central Asia, food is not only treated as a source of nourishment and fuel, but it is also valued for its preventative and curative role. Eating healthfully keeps a body fit and free of disease. Should they fall ill, Russians and Central Asians have numerous cures using a wide range of foods and medicinal herbs. In fact, in the Middle Ages, food and medicine were so closely related that the words *recipe* (*retsept* in Russian) and *receipt* in many European languages meant a formula or set of directions for a medical prescription.[1] In English, the medical sense of the term survives today only in the pharmacist's abbreviation *Rx*. The variety, purity, and freshness of food in the former Soviet Union unfortunately are not enough to ensure proper health. Despite the conscious and continual efforts of mothers, wives, and grandmothers in the NIS to feed and care for their families, health has generally deteriorated over the past decade. Food, however, is only one part of the equation for good health.

Russians and Central Asians have several health-related problems in common: a short life expectancy, cardiovascular disease, and general nutritional deficiencies, as well as high rates of tobacco and alcohol use. Specific nutritional problems include the lack of affordability of certain healthful and essential food items, the suspect quality of some foodstuffs, and the absence of public awareness of what constitutes a healthful and balanced diet. Much of the overall decline in health, without a doubt, may be attributed to the social and economic disruptions since 1991. The Soviet experiment can be credited with improving the general diet of the lowest economic classes, but not until well into the 1960s. The nutritional perspective, though, was narrowly Marxist with an emphasis on feeding the public mainly to ensure a productive and efficient workforce. Soviet nutritional models favored a high-meat, high-protein, and high-calorie diet. The Russian approach later added a Western perspective, in which nutrition is frequently reduced to the purely molecular level of vitamins and minerals, and the primacy for good health is placed on consuming a proper balance of the basic food groups. Pre-Soviet nutritional philosophies in Russia, where food was often scarce, generally stressed quantity over quality. Central Asians, on the other hand, loosely maintained a diet based on the ancient Greek humoral practices as propagated by the Iranian philosopher ibn Sina in the eleventh century. This theory holds that the body has four humors (blood, yellow bile, black bile, and phlegm) that determine health and disease. The humors were, in turn, associated with the four elements: air, fire, earth, and water, which were neatly paired with the qualities hot, cold, dry, and moist. According to that theory, a proper and evenly balanced combination of humors characterized the health of the body and mind; an imbalance resulted in disease. Combining local wisdom with traditional Chinese thought, Central Asians consider food to have either "hot" or "cold" qualities in regard to both medicinal and nutritive functions.

Folk beliefs about diet and health still persist in Russia and Central Asia. Traditional dietary advice paints a truer picture of a culture than an examination of the cold, ever-changing science of nutrition does. The word *diet* is derived from the Greek *diaita*, meaning "a mode of life," or "a lifestyle." In current usage it has come to mean the habitual consumption of food and drink. In affluent societies, the term has an even narrower connotation, more commonly associated with restrictions on, or reductions of, certain foods and drinks. With the development of nutritional science over the past two centuries, much of the conventional wisdom, both good and bad, about eating habits is vanishing. With the exception of crude observation and basic trial and error, numerous folk recommendations for maintaining health or curing disease have little or no scientific basis. Many curative diets are nonetheless effective, even if modern science cannot necessarily identify the cause and effect.

## RUSSIA

Food in Russia and the USSR was frequently scarce. The common adage that "over the course of its recorded history, Russia has averaged one bad harvest out of every three" may indeed contain a grain of truth. Within the past century alone, Russia has endured massive crop failures in the 1890s, in 1921, in 1932–33, and again in 1946–47, plunging the country into famine and hunger. The recurrent societal upheavals are a major part of the Russian psyche and certainly affect the Russian attitude toward food and diet.

### Food-Related Health Problems

By the mid-1990s, the government of the Russian Federation began to realize the real dangers that food insecurity, malnutrition, and poverty can pose to a country. It ordered the State Institute of Nutrition of the Russian Academy of Medical Sciences to draft a policy and a plan of action to counter some of the main causes of poor nutrition, such as the lack of access to sufficient amounts of food, an inferior diet, and bad sanitary conditions. Anemia and cardiovascular diseases are two of the main manifestations of an unbalanced diet in the country. While it may be some time before the government has the will and wherewithal to implement a comprehensive health policy, at least the issue has received some attention at the highest level.

Life expectancy in Russia has dramatically deteriorated in recent years. Many factors contribute to this decline, including decreasing per capita incomes; use of tobacco and alcohol; lack of exercise; poor nutrition; the degeneration of the health-care system; and social stress caused by years of economic and social instability. Still, the overriding reason for the declining health and the growing rate of mortality in Russians is their high alcohol consumption. Not only does abuse of alcohol lead to the development of health-related conditions, but it also contributes to the high incidence of violent crimes and deadly accidents at home, at work, and on the road.

Life expectancy in Russia is lower today than it was during the Khrushchev era. While many like to blame the mortality crisis on the new economic conditions, the fact is that life expectancy has been falling for 40 years, not just the last 15. In 1965, life expectancy among Russian men was only 2.3 years less than life expectancy among American men. By 2003, Russian men were dying 15.4 years earlier than their American counterparts.[2] According to the 2002 census, Russian citizens have the shortest lifespan in Europe by more than a dozen years.[3] Even people in Central Asia and the rest of the NIS live longer than their Russian neighbors.[4] The current average male life expectancy in Russia is only 58 years, meaning that most Russian men never see their official retirement age of 60. As a result, almost 53 percent of the population is now female, and women have been increasing their numbers compared to men for the past 30 years.[5] Western increases in life expectancy may be linked to increased expenditures on health, the protection of the environment, the promotion of a healthful way of life, and improved medical care. Without an orchestrated approach to the issue of health, Russia will not reverse the trends.

Among industrialized nations, Russia has the highest rate of cardiovascular disease in the world. Heart disease, as in the United States, is the main cause of death in Russia. While two-thirds of those deaths in Russia might be attributed to smoking or drinking (or both), at least a portion are due to, or exacerbated by, poor eating habits over a lifetime. If the men die early because of heart disease, it is the Russian women who are more prone to be overweight or obese. The general trend is that the incidence of extra weight increases with age.[6]

Overall, the intake of macronutrients (proteins, carbohydrates, fats) and micronutrients (vitamins and minerals) is deficient for most Russians. Specifically, great quantities of dairy, meat, sugar, and alcohol have precipitated a decline in Russian health in recent years as well as contributing to obesity in elderly women.[7] Some of these food choices are holdovers from Soviet nutritional norms, whereas others are the result of economic realities. The daily consumption of vitamins and minerals is well below the norms set by the World Health Organization. The diet is generally high in fat and cholesterol and low in fiber, fruit, and vegetables.

Despite the prodigious natural resources and the potential wealth of Russia, 46 million people, or roughly 31 percent of the population, live below the poverty line as defined by the Russian Government.[8] Many people are now dependent on state-subsidized bread and food (mainly potatoes) from private plots. Meat production has sharply declined since 1991 and imported meat prices are too high for the average consumer. Therefore, the proportion of energy obtained from fat and protein has also decreased. To compound health matters, the price of alcohol has remained relatively flat, while the cost of foodstuffs has skyrocketed. The primary nutritional shortfalls in the Russian diet are the B complex vitamins, vitamin C, calcium salts, and iron. The unfortunate combination of lifestyle and diet is a recipe for cardiovascular disease. The combination of excess alcohol, tobacco, salty foods, saturated fats, eggs, and whole milk is like playing Russian roulette with the heart.

## Food Beliefs and Practices

Quantity and freshness have priority over quality and finesse on the Russian table. Although restaurants and cafés are numerous in the big cities, hearty homemade meals are the ideal in both the countryside and in urban areas. A well-balanced meal should have a main course of fish or meat for flair, a starch (potatoes, pasta, or rice) for energy, and vegetables (often in the form of a cooked vegetable salad) for vitamins. Soup and tea are the bookends of a meal. Dessert would make it complete in the minds of most Russians.

Many people believe that they are harming their digestion and internal organs unless they eat soup regularly. In fact, the Russian word for food (*pishcha*) derives from the verb *pit'* (to drink), suggesting that many of the early Slavic dishes were primarily liquid. To eat a poor diet of sandwiches and snacks is called *vsukhomyatku* (dry). Soup is still considered the most

Eating soup, Moscow.

healthful of foods, essential for good digestion. Many Russians believe that Western-style fast food instead of the traditional soup-centered meal is contributing to the declining health of the nation, especially in children. Although major multinational corporations are heavily promoting concentrated bullion cubes, most Russian women are accustomed to making a natural meat broth for soup or other dishes. Some people claim that most vegetables actually become more nutritious after being cooked in a soup. Nutritional science, however, has shown that vegetables lose some of their B and C vitamins through boiling. Furthermore, overcooking serves only to break down cellulose and gelatinize the starches in vegetables, not to improve the nutritional qualities.

A folk expression explains the Russian approach to meals: "Eat breakfast yourself, split lunch with a friend, and give dinner to an enemy." In other words, to maintain a proper weight, eat a large breakfast, a small lunch, and little to no dinner. It is considered healthful to eat a filling breakfast, which, along with bread and dairy products, should include protein—eggs, hot dogs, or another type of sausage. This Soviet nutritional norm was chiefly promoted during the intense period of industrialization when productive labor was the key to building Communism. At least one hot meal a day is crucial to maintaining good digestion and health. Lunch, according to an earlier Russian tradition, was the main meal of the day, a custom that disappeared with most people going to work and being stranded in a city in the middle of the day. A light lunch is usually taken at work; therefore, few people follow the recommendation for a light dinner.

The daily menu of most Russian families includes a meat or sausage dish. Therefore, the typical diet is very high in protein and animal fat, mostly from low-quality processed, smoked or cured meats. Yet fat is an essential source of energy that also helps to absorb vitamins A, D, E, and K. One undesirable change in the post-Soviet era is the decline of fish consumption in favor of meat consumption. The reasons are ecological, economic, geographic, and demographic, but the results are detrimental to the health of the people whose ancestors consumed large quantities of fresh fish on a regular basis for generations.

Most people consume dairy products (usually fermented) daily, including cheese, dairy drinks (kefir, prostokvasha, ryazhenka), farmer's cheese (tvorog), and, more recently, yogurt. Russians are firm believers that these products help digestion and are among the most healthful foods available. The expression "krov' s molokom" (blood with milk) is a Russian euphemism meaning "the picture of health." Children are encouraged to drink milk and eat as many dairy products as possible.

The most common vegetables are potatoes, cabbage, onions, tomatoes, and cucumbers. People grow vegetables on their dacha plots, mostly for personal consumption rather than for sale. Vegetables are almost always cooked (and often overcooked), except for tomatoes, cucumbers, and radishes, which are used in fresh salads. Green leafy salads have never caught on in Russia. This might be due to a variety of factors: an unsuitable climate for producing great quantities of leafy greens, the lack of a ready supply of clean water for washing raw vegetables, or simply a preference for higher-calorie dishes that were necessary in premodern times for energy in cold environments. A salad accompanies most meals and it is usually dressed with sour cream or sunflower oil. It may also be as simple as sliced tomatoes and cucumbers sprinkled with salt. For centuries Russians have relied on fermented cabbage (*kvashenaya kapusta*) to fill the vitamin void during the brutal winters. Although mostly water with few calories, fermented cabbage is very flavorful and also contains potassium, vitamin A, calcium, and folate in sufficient quantities to supplement a traditionally nutrient-poor winter diet. The fresh cabbage core, or heart, is a beloved treat for children and adults alike. Potatoes contain vitamins $B_6$ and C. Beets are full of folate, potassium, and phosphorus. The leafy tops are used in soups and stocks and contain beta-carotene, calcium, and iron.

Apples are the most widely consumed fruit. Fruit and berries are typically used to make preserves such as jams and marmalades. Children are especially encouraged to eat fresh fruit. Cherries are a good source of vitamins A and C and potassium, and sour cherries contain more beta-carotene than either sweet potatoes or broccoli. The bountiful assortment of berries is similar to that of Scandinavia, Canada, and the northern United States. Berries are a delicious, low-calorie food, as well as a great source of fiber and nutrients and the antioxidant vitamins E, beta carotene (a form of vitamin A), and especially vitamin C. Most of the vitamin C in berries is destroyed by the intense heat required for making preserves. The pectin, or fiber, is retained, which helps control blood cholesterol levels, although some of the benefits are negated by the high sugar content.

Russians love bread and might deny themselves other nutritious foods by filling up on bread. For some people, it is an economic necessity for survival, as bread is a cheap filler; but mainly bread is a choice based on tradition and taste preference. Bread—either white or black—is a necessary accompaniment to any meal, especially soup. It is also a fundamental part of a common snack: the open-faced sandwich of cold cuts or cheese, usually with the bread liberally buttered.

Frying as a cooking method was not widely practiced in traditional Russian cuisine, as baking, boiling, and steaming were preferred in the Middle Ages. In addition, Russians used few fats beyond butter, hemp oil, and imported olive (Provence) oil.[9] Russians therefore never learned how to fry properly with vegetable and animal fats via French influence, adversely affecting the health of the population.[10]

Russians say that "sugar and salt are the equivalent to white death." However, that common belief does not translate into dietary change. Russians love salty foods such as pickles, sauerkraut, and cured meats, which results in a very high sodium intake—yet another contributing factor to the high incidence of heart disease. Another reason for heavy sodium consumption is that Russians do not like heavily spiced foods and sometimes compensate for the lack of flavor in their food with liberal salting.

Tea and coffee are almost always sweetened and rarely consumed without accompanying sweets, such as chocolate, candy, cookies, or jam. Tea with dessert typically ends meals, and people also drink tea a couple of times or more a day. Almost no house, regardless of the income, is ever without a variety of sweets for the daily tea-drinking ritual.

Sauerkraut (vitamins C and A) and kvas (vitamin B) were considered the best combination for overall health and defense against many diseases. Many common Russian foods contain significant amounts of B complex vitamins, yet Russians are still generally deficient in this area. Bread is high in $B_{12}$, and meat, fish, chicken, grains, cereals, potatoes, and

Propaganda poster, "Say no to drink," 1954.

yogurt contain $B_6$. How can the deficiency be explained? Vitamin B is water soluble and stored in the body in only very small amounts. Alcohol interferes with the absorption of many vitamins, especially thiamine and others in the B group. Not only does alcohol destroy the body with its poison, alcoholism is a major underlying cause of malnutrition.

More than 50 percent of the population drinks unsafe water, which contributes to intestinal disorders. Therefore, many Russians believe it is unhealthful to drink a lot of water. Certainly it is not customary to drink water during a meal. Cold water is believed to be particularly harmful after a rich meal, coagulating the fat in the stomach and intestines. Few people drink tap water, and anyone who can afford them uses filters or buys purified water, even for use in cooking and making tea. Others boil their water or buy mineral water for drinking. Natural mineral waters are very popular and considered medicinal. Water is sold in pharmacies as well as grocery stores. The most highly regarded therapeutic water in the former Soviet Union is Borjomi, which comes from an ancient natural spring in the neighboring country of Georgia. It contains a number of essential vitamins and minerals and is believed to be beneficial for the treatment of a variety of gastrointestinal and liver disorders, colds, and the flu; it is generally helpful for digestion, well-being, and even good skin. The water is so popular that counterfeiting became a real problem in recent years to the point that the company had to introduce several levels of protection and distinguishing marks to help consumers identify the authentic product.

Russians believe very strongly in the healing attributes of honey. Many use it regularly as a health food to strengthen the body's immune system and prevent respiratory and gastrointestinal diseases. Honey is the most commonly used treatment for colds and coughs (sometimes mixed with tea, warm milk, mineral water, or lemon juice). Its proponents claim that honey even helps to heal ulcers, heart disease, and tuberculosis. Other bee products are also believed to be highly curative. Propolis, or "bee glue," is a resinous substance produced by bees for use in the construction of their hives. It has a cult following among people who consider it to be an effective antioxidant and antimicrobial agent.

Food allergies are hardly endemic in Russia like they are in the United States. There may be cases, but few people talk about allergies or acknowledge them as a condition that needs medical treatment. Some general food beliefs are that cucumbers, pickles, and salted herring are not to be eaten together with milk for fear of indigestion. Another dangerous combination is water and melon, said to cause diarrhea.

Children and the infirm are fed porridge (*kasha*), because of its nutritive and alleged healing properties. Kasha might also turn out to be the only hot meal of the day. As in most societies, children receive the choicest servings of food. Great emphasis is placed on children's nutrition, even to the point of overfeeding, since plump children are synonymous with healthy children. During the Soviet period, the state made infant nutrition one of its priorities. There were strict guidelines enforced by pediatricians and child-care facilities. All newborns received free dairy products, specially formulated, prepared, and distributed at children's dairy kitchens, located in every urban district. These still exist, but most now operate on a commercial basis, and only underprivileged children receive free food. Mothers are encouraged to breast-feed, but most do not. Doctors' recommendations to breast-feed are drowned out by the din of advertisements by the baby-food manufacturers. It is generally believed that the poor state of environment, malnutrition, and high levels of stress in mothers are responsible for poor lactation in Russian women. In Russia, children are given supplemental food much earlier than recommended in the United States: fruit juices and water (a few drops at a time) within just a few weeks of birth. These recommendations have recently been revised. The official position of the medical establishment now is to wait 4–6 months before adding any supplemental food to the infant's diet, but old habits die hard, especially when enforced by the grandmothers who rely on their own experiences.

There is a growing realization among Russians about the dire situation of their health, including an obsession with thinness in women. More and more people are concerned with their weight, rather in connection with their appearance than in regard to health risks. The number of fitness centers grows daily, as does the popularity of various fad diets and exotic lifestyle regimes. Bookstores overflow with works on new-age lifestyles, low-carbohydrate or blood-type diets, and Chinese and Tibetan medicine. Still, only a privileged few can afford to worry about such things.

## CENTRAL ASIA

Traditional medicine and nutrition in Central Asia fall somewhere among folk medicine, myth, and science. The inextricable relationship between diet and health forms the basis for the humoral theory of medicine, which still holds considerable sway in individual food choices in the region. Although there are variations of the theory worldwide, Hippocrates of the fifth century B.C. is generally credited with setting down the four-humor theory. Galen refined it in the second century A.D. and it had much influence in Europe in the Middle Ages. Ibn Sina, Central Asia's best-known philosopher, wrote the *Canon of Medicine* in the eleventh century, which may be the most widely read medical text in the world. The fifteenth-century Latin version of the *Canon* became the standard medical textbook in Europe until the seventeenth century. For more than a millennium, his works on health have been the benchmark for herbal and dietetic medicine.

The humoral theory was such an accepted part of daily life that traditional Central Asian medicine and nutrition cannot be understood without it. For ibn Sina, food and diet are central to the treatment of diseases, a viewpoint condensed simply to "most illnesses arise solely from long-continued errors of diet and regimen." This means that disease can be prevented or treated by using the various properties of food to adjust the body's balance. A healthful diet requires varying the menu not only according to season but also by the age, gender, physical constitution, and characteristics of the diner as well. Thanks in part to ibn Sina's writings, the layman in Central Asia can still classify most foodstuffs as having hot or cold properties.

The diet and lifestyle of the citizens of Central Asia have received scant attention in the West since independence in 1991, and even less consideration from within the countries themselves. Tajikistan spent much of the 1990s embroiled in civil war and recovery. Turkmenistan is essentially closed to foreign researchers and has yet to produce any reliable nutritional studies of its own. Therefore, the overall picture in Central Asia is incomplete and probably in a tremendous state of flux with the introduction of market economy changes. Although not as dire as in Russia, diet and nutrition in Central Asia, especially in the cities, must be considered poor. The major health-related problems in Central Asia are low life expectancy, cardiovascular diseases, high rates of tobacco and alcohol use, and general nutritional deficiencies.

## Food-Related Health Problems

The declining economic situation for most of the population in the post-Soviet era is a major hindrance in procuring both a variety and sufficient quantity of foodstuffs. Smoking is extremely widespread, especially among men, and alcoholism is not uncommon.

Combined with diets high in fat and low in antioxidants, the conditions for cardiovascular disease are ripe.[11] Central Asia is well below the recommended average daily calorie consumption for the European region. Acute malnutrition among children remains high, resulting in disorders caused by lack of micronutrients such as iron and iodine. Carbohydrates in the form of bread and potatoes make up a larger part of the diet as the consumption of fats, milk products, fish, and eggs have declined. Still, the saturated fatty acids of animal fat make up a large portion of total calorie intake.

According to recent reports by the World Health Organization, the Central Asian republics, while still in need of improvement, experienced some positive health results since the early 1990s.[12] Kyrgyz appear to have the best relative health in the region. In general, they eat a more healthful diet, smoke less, and are less frequent drinkers. Muslims in Central Asia, according to recent research, were significantly less likely to drink frequently or smoke.[13] The Kazak diet remains true to its nomadic origins—high in meat and salt and low in vegetables and fruits. Vitamin A and C deficiencies are common in Kazakstan and Kyrgyzstan because the people eat fewer fruits and vegetables than do Uzbeks, Tajiks, and Turkmen. One concern in Tajikistan is the prevalence of thyroid deficiencies due to lack of iron in the diet. Turkmen depend heavily on bread for calories, with only seasonal consumption of vegetables and fruit, resulting in a deficiency of protein and fat. Overall per capita food consumption in Uzbekistan actually increased between 1992 and 1996, except for milk products. Uzbek consumption of meat increased, while bread intake has remained relatively stable since 1992.

### Food Beliefs and Practices

Central Asians believe that oils and fats should reach the smoking point in the pan before cooking, to enhance the flavor. People also believe that this process burns off the impurities, minimizes the negative effects on the body, and even kills bacteria. There are many other Central Asian methods to assist the body in digesting large amounts of saturated fat in the diet. Hot green tea drunk before, during, and after a fatty meal not only aids absorption but also cools the body temperature because of perspiration. Sweets, fruit, and fresh greens such as dill and cilantro, onions, radishes, and other vegetables aid in the digestion of fatty foods. Fruit is a rich, natural source of vitamin C, which aids protein digestion. Fats, green vegetables, and sugars all require either an alkaline or a neutral medium for their digestion and therefore should be eaten together. Finally, red wine vinegar, used as a seasoning, also helps digest greasy dishes. The vinegar supposedly contains enzymes that aid the digestive process. Cold water should never be mixed with fatty food or drunk after eating fruit.

Spices and herbs are important not only for the flavor they bring to dishes but also because it is believed that they enhance the appetite and provide additional vitamins and minerals. Cumin, the most prevalent spice in Central Asia, is considered the "natural refrigerator," since it is believed that meat sprinkled with ground cumin and salt will not spoil for up to a week, whereas refrigerated meat lasts from three to five days before spoilage begins. In a diet rich in meat and starch and low in vegetables (especially during the winter), herbs and greens are a significant source of nutrients. Hot peppers, although rich in vitamins C and A, are considered harmful in large quantities because they can irritate the lining of the digestive tract. Chiles actually contain more vitamin C than citrus fruit, and chiles are certainly more common in Central Asian markets than citrus fruits.

Herbs and peppers are dried at home for use during the winter months. In the spring and early summer, lush mountain vegetation appears—in particular, multihued wildflowers, rhubarb, and edible leafy greens. These plants contain numerous vitamins, minerals, antioxidants, and bioflavonoids, not to mention that they are an inexpensive source of nutrition and add unusual flavor notes to any dish. A wide assortment of herbs and plants is collected to make green dumplings (*koq chuchvara*). This seasonal favorite is considered a delicious way to vitamin-load after a long winter of nutritional deficiency. The filling can be made with any mixture of available leafy greens or herbs.

Rice is not as processed as in the West (neither hulled, washed, nor bleached) and therefore retains much of its natural nutrition. Rice includes significant amounts of B vitamins and iron, forms a complete protein when combined with beans and other legumes, provides energy, and contributes to protein synthesis. Citrons, similar to lemons, are native to Central Asia. The peel may be used as a seasoning and the juice is indispensable for acidity and vitamin C.

Green tea was used in Chinese medicine to treat headaches, general body aches, poor digestion, depression, and to increase life expectancy. A pinch of black pepper in tea is used to treat colds. Green tea also acts as an antioxidant and contains vitamin C, riboflavin, vitamin D, vitamin K, and carotenoids. Given the meager diet of the nomads, it is not surprising that tea quickly became a cultural superfood of Central Asia.

## NOTES

1. The word *recipe* in English can be found in written sources as early as the fourteenth century, meaning "medical prescription," from the Latin imperative *recipe*, meaning "take!" The first instance of using *recipe* instead of *receipt*, mean-

ing "instructions for preparing food," was recorded in 1743. AllWords.com English Dictionary, http://www.allwords.com/ and Online Etymology Dictionary, http://www.etymonline.com/.

2. Paul Globe, "Eye on Eurasia: Why Russians Are Dying," *United Press International*, 9 October 2004.

3. Russian men live about 58 years on average and women 72. "Russians Have the Shortest Life Time [sic] in Europe," *The Russian Journal*, 12 February 2004.

4. World Health Organization, "Highlights on Health in the Russian Federation," http://www.euro.who.int/document/e72504.pdf.

5. Rosbalt News Agency, "First Results of 2002 Census Published," *Pravda* 29 October 2003.

6. David Sedik and Doris Wiesmann, "Globalization and Food and Nutrition Security in the Russian Federation, Ukraine, and Belarus" (ESA working paper no. 03–04, United Nations, 2003).

7. David Sedik, Sergey Sotnikov, and Doris Wiesmann, *Food Security in the Russian Federation* (Rome: Food and Agriculture Organization of the United Nations, 2003).

8. FIAN International, "The Right to Adequate Food (Art. 11) and Violations of This Right in the Russian Federation," (presented to the UN Committee on Economic, Social and Cultural Rights, Heidelberg, Germany, April 1997), http://www.infoe.de//report.html#Heading17.

9. Provence oil is also described as sunflower oil flavored with anise seeds.

10. Vilyam Pokhlebkin, *Moya kukhnya i moyo menyu* [My Food and My Menu] (Moscow: Tsentrpoligraf, 1999), 53–61.

11. William C. Cockerham, Brian P. Hinote, Pamela Abbott, and Christian Haerpfer, "Health Lifestyles in Central Asia: The Case of Kazakhstan and Kyrgyzstan," *Social Science & Medicine* 59, no. 7 (October 2004): 1411.

12. The statistics from this section are from the following WHO reports: World Health Organization, *Highlights on Health in Kazakhstan*, Copenhagen, Denmark: World Health Organization, 1999, 18, http://www.euro.who.int/document/E72497.pdf; World Health Organization, *Highlights on Health in Kyrgyzstan*, Copenhagen, Denmark: World Health Organization, 19, http://www.euro.who.int/document/e72499.pdf); World Health Organization, *Highlights on Health in Tajikistan*, Copenhagen, Denmark: World Health Organization, 1999, 18, http://www.euro.who.int/document/e72505.pdf; World Health Organization, *Highlights on Health in Turkmenistan*, Copenhagen, Denmark: World Health Organization, 2000,18–19, http://www.euro.who.int/document/e72506.pdf; and World Health Organization, *Highlights on Health in Uzbekistan*, Copenhagen, Denmark: World Health Organization, 1999, 18, http://www.euro.who.int/document/e71959.pdf.

13. Cockerham, Hinote, Abbott, and Haerpfer, "Health Lifestyles in Central Asia," 1419.

# Glossary

**ayran**   Central Asian yogurt and water.

**belishi**   (Russian *belyashi*) Kazan Tatar dish of fried dough with mince-meat and onion filling, similar to *chebureki*.

**blinchiki**   Paper-thin crepes made with little flour and served as a dessert or as a tea accompaniment.

**bliny**   Thin pancakes or crepes made from buckwheat flour or wheat flour, or a combination of both.

**borscht**   Russian soup usually containing beet juice as a foundation.

**brynza**   Popular salted cheese made from sheep's milk, most closely re-sembling feta cheese.

**chaikhana**   Central Asian teahouse, literally means tea room.

**chebureki**   Deep-fried Crimean Tatar savory pastry with a mutton-and-onion filling.

**chernozem**   Fertile agricultural soil of Ukraine and southern Russia, lit-erally "black earth."

**collective farms**   *Sovkhoz* (state farms) and *kolkhoz* (collective farms) created by the Soviet state to control agricultural production and dis-tribution.

**dacha**   Russian country house that often includes a garden plot where city dwellers may grow their own food.

**dastarkhan**   Sometimes translated as "tablecloth," it refers to the prolific assortment of prepared dishes laid out for the honored guest in Central Asia.

*Domostroi*   Russian household management manual written in the sixteenth century, which also includes recipes and other information about domestic cookery.

**golubtsy**   (Ukrainian *holubtsy*) Ukrainian specialty with seasoned mince-meat and rice wrapped in young cabbage leaves, either stewed or baked, and garnished with sour cream.

**halva**   Confection made from flour, sugar, milk, and nuts.

**kasha**   Boiled buckwheat groats; also meaning any hot cereal.

**kazy**   Horse meat sausage common in Central Asia.

**kefir**   Effervescent fermented-milk drink originating in the Caucasus.

**khlebosol'stvo**   Russian word for "hospitality"; derives from the roots *khleb* (bread) and *sol'* (salt), which were traditionally presented to guests as a sign of welcome, warmth, and generosity.

**kompot**   (compote) Drink made by boiling water with fresh or dried fruits and sugar.

**kumiss**   Fermented mare's milk made by nomads throughout Central Asia.

**kvas**   Fermented beverage similar to beer, made from rye or barley.

**laghman**   Central Asian thick noodle dish served as soup or as separate noodles with meat, peppers, tomatoes, and onions.

**lapsha**   All-encompassing term for "noodle," but specifically refers to a flat noodle similar to linguine or fettuccini.

**manti**   Central Asian steamed dumpling dish served as a main course. It is usually filled with mutton and onions, though sometimes made with pumpkin.

**non**   Central Asian flatbread.

**palov**   Pilaf.

**pelmeni**   Siberian dumplings made with beef and pork filling, eaten all over the former Soviet Union.

**pirog**   Russian pie usually made with a savory filling.

**pirozhki**   Baked or fried yeast dough with fillings of meat, mushrooms, buckwheat, potatoes, liver, cheese, eggs, and vegetables—particularly cabbage. It may be served with soup or eaten as a snack or appetizer.

**prostokvasha**   Similar to clabber, fresh milk that has soured and thickened.

**qazan**   Wok.

**salat Oliv'ye**   Famous cold Russian salad of boiled, diced potatoes and carrots, onions, peas, pickles, and chicken, mixed with mayonnaise; named for nineteenth-century French chef Olivier. Also called stolichny salad.

**salo**   Cured pork fat of Ukrainian fame.

**samsa**   Central Asian savory pastries made with onions and either a meat or pumpkin filling, baked in a tandoor oven.

**shashlyk**   Russian word for "shish kebab," based on Turkic roots.

**shchi**   Russian cabbage soup.

**sumalak**   Sprouted wheat porridge served on special occasions in Central Asia, typically during Navrus.

**syrniki**   Pancakes made from tvorog and fried in butter, from the word "cheese" (*syr*).

**tabaka**   Georgian dish of whole butterflied chicken, pressed down with a weight to ensure even cooking, and panfried or roasted. It is served with a plum sauce, *tkemali*.

**tandir**   Central Asian tandoor clay oven, either cylindrically shaped or with an arched ceiling like a pizza oven, in which food is cooked over intense heat. Derived from Hindi *tandur, tannur*, from Persian *tanur*, or from Arabic *tannur*.

**tkemali**   Georgian wild plum sauce, a universal condiment for chicken, vegetables, grilled lamb, and other dishes.

**tvorog**   Fresh cheese curds roughly comparable to farmer's cheese found in the West.

**ukha**   Russian fish soup, made by simmering whole fish in seasoned broth.

**vareniki**   Boiled Ukrainian dumplings filled with potatoes, mushrooms, *tvorog*, cabbage, meat, cherries, plums, or berries.

**vinegret**   Russian salad containing potatoes, pickled cabbage, beets, carrots, and onions.

**vobla**   (roach fish) Perhaps the most emblematic Russian fish. Salted and dried, it is sold in markets as an accompaniment to beer.

**zakuski**   Russian hors d'oeuvres.

# Resource Guide

## SUGGESTED READING

### Russia

Balzer, Marjorie Mandelstam, ed. *Culture Incarnate: Native Anthropology from Russia.* Armonk, NY: M.E. Sharpe, 1995. Anthropological study of the many ethnic groups that make up Russia—from the Volga Basin and the North Caucasus to Siberia and the Mongolian border.

Bennett, Vanora. *The Taste of Dreams: An Obsession with Russia and Caviar.* London: Headline, 2003. Part history, part travelogue about caviar and the historical context that makes it a status symbol around the world.

Billington, James H. *The Icon and the Axe: An Interpretative History of Russian Culture.* Magnolia, MA: Peter Smith Publisher, 1994. A classic introduction to Russian cultural and intellectual history from the ninth century A.D. to the Brezhnev era.

Csaki, Csaba. *Food and Agricultural Policy in Russia: Progress to Date and the Road Forward.* Washington, DC: World Bank, 2002. A standard World Bank report that concludes that most agricultural policy is made at the regional level. It discusses the obstacles toward private market development.

Davidson, Alan. *The Oxford Companion to Food.* Oxford: Oxford University Press, 1999. Brief country culinary profiles including Russia; separate entries for many traditional foods mentioned in the primary article provide additional information.

Friedrich, Paul, and Norma Diamond, eds. *Encyclopedia of World Cultures*, Vol. 6, *Russia and Eurasia/China.* Boston, MA: G.K. Hall, 1994. Fifteen hundred summary descriptions of cultures around the world, cross-referenced and arranged by geographical regions.

Hudgins, Sharon. *The Other Side of Russia: A Slice of Life in Siberia and the Russian Far East*. College Station: Texas A&M University Press, 2003. A contemporary review of Siberia from American eyes, filled with food references, a description of the ethnic Buryats, and special attention on the cities of Vladivostok and Irkutsk.

Kaiser, Daniel, and Gary Marker, eds. *Reinterpreting Russian History*. New York: Oxford University Press, 1994. A reader in Russian history with new focus on gender and cultural history, as well as the economy, society, and everyday life.

Lovell, Stephen. *Summerfolk: A History of the Dacha, 1700–2000*. Ithaca, NY: Cornell University Press, 2003. A charming social and cultural history of the dacha, exploring the origins of these country villas, its role under Communist rule, and its vital post-Soviet function for familial survival.

McKee, W. Arthur. "Sobering Up the Soul of the People: The Politics of Popular Temperance in Late Imperial Russia." *The Russian Review* 58, no. 2 (1999): 212–233. A fascinating look at temperance movements led by Orthodox leaders leading up to the Russian Revolution.

OECD Centre for Co-operation with Non-Members. *Review of Agricultural Policies. Russian Federation*. Paris: Organisation for Economic Co-operation and Development, 1998. An agricultural perspective on the transition to a market-oriented economy in Russia, underscoring its enormous potential as a significant part of Russia's economic and social structure.

Rorlich, A. A. *The Volga Tatars: Profile in National Resilience*. Stanford, CA: Stanford University Press, 1986. An overview of history, culture, and politics of Tatarstan from ancient times to the Soviet era.

Saffron, Inga. *Caviar: The Strange History and Uncertain Future of the World's Most Coveted Delicacy*. New York: Broadway Books, 2002. A captivating work on the commerce of caviar, with all its culinary, natural, and cultural history.

Sedik, David, Sergey Sotnikov, and Doris Wiesmann. *Food Security in the Russian Federation*. Rome: Food and Agriculture Organization of the United Nations, 2003. A review of food security and the nutritional status and diet of the Russian population.

U.S. Foreign Commercial Service. *Russian Federation Hospitality and Restaurant Industry Food Service Sector Report 2000*. Washington, DC: U.S. Foreign Commercial Service, 2000. Government report outlining the current state of the Russian hospitality industry and the potential for American firms to conduct business in this sector.

Wehrheim, P., K. Frohberg, E. Serova, and J. von Braun, eds. *Russia's Agro-Food Sector: Towards Truly Functioning Markets*. Boston: Kluwer Academic Publishers, 2000. This work follows the transition of Russia's agro-food sector from the centrally planned system of the communist era to the post-Soviet market-oriented attempt.

White, Stephen. *Russia Goes Dry: Alcohol, State, and Society*. Cambridge, MA: Cambridge University Press, 1996. A case study of Gorbachev's antialcohol campaign and all its economic and societal ramifications.

Zelnik, Reginald. "Wie es eigentlich gegessen: Some Curious Thoughts on the Role of Borsch in Russian History." In *For Want of a Horse: Choice and Chance in History*, ed. John M. Merriman. Lexington, MA: Stephen Greene Press, 1985. A parody of approaches to Russian history using food as a metaphor. His final analysis is that the history of food has little significance in and of itself, without cultural context.

Ziker, J. "Raw and Cooked in Arctic Siberia: Diet and Consumption Strategies in Socio-ecological Perspective." *Nutritional Anthropology* 25, no. 2 (2002): 20–33. Research on diet in Northern Russia and how the change to a market economy has affected nutrition and consumption strategies.

Zohoori, N., D. Blanchette, and B. Popkin. *Monitoring Health Conditions in the Russian Federation: The Russia Longitudinal Monitoring Survey 1992–2003*. Chapel Hill: University of North Carolina, 2004. A survey designed to measure the effects of Russian reforms on the economic well-being of households and individuals, monitoring such factors as health, diet, and household expenditures.

## Central Asia

Akiner, Shirin. *The Formation of Kazakh Identity: From Tribe to Nation-State*. London: The Royal Institute of International Affairs, 1995. Analyzes Kazak national identity through their nomadic and Islamic traditions, including the impact of the Tsarist and Soviet periods.

Allworth, Edward, ed. *Central Asia, 130 Years of Russian Dominance, A Historical Overview*. Durham, NC: Duke University Press, 1998. A collection of essays that explores the Central Asian culture and the Russian influence on its development.

Allworth, Edward. *The Modern Uzbeks: From the Fourteenth Century to the Present; A Cultural History*. Stanford, CA: Hoover Institution Press, Stanford University, 1990. A historical overview of Uzbeks and Uzbekistan, including a new chapter covering the dramatic years from 1989 to 1993.

Babu, Suresh, and Alisher Tashmatov, eds. *Food Policy Reforms in Central Asia: Setting the Research Priorities*. Washington, DC: International Food Policy Research Institute, 2000. One of the few resources on food policy in Central Asia, identifying information gaps and setting priorities for policy research to help reform the region's sectors of food, agriculture, and natural resources.

Bacon, Elizabeth E. *Central Asians under Russian Rule: A Study in Cultural Change*. Ithaca, NY: Cornell University Press, 1980. A classic survey of the cultural changes for Central Asian nomads and city dwellers during both the Russian and Soviet empires.

Benson, Linda, and Ingvar Svanberg. *China's Last Nomads: The History and Culture of China's Kazaks*. Armonk, NY: M. E. Sharpe, 1998. Explores the Kazaks of Xinjiang in western China, examining their political, social, and cultural history up to the foundation of the People's Republic of China in 1949.

Buell, Paul, Eugene Anderson, and Charles Perry. *A Soup for the Qan*. London: Kegan Paul, 2000). A remarkable dietary guide and cookery manual from the fourteenth century for the Mongol emperor of China written by the imperial physician. It reveals the foodways of China and medieval Eurasia.

Gleason, Gregory. *The Central Asian States: Discovering Independence*. Oxford: Westview Press, 1997. A postindependence look at the culture, economy, and politics of Kazakstan, Kyrgyzstan, Tajikistan, Turkmenistan, and Uzbekistan.

Gross, Jo-Ann, ed. *Muslims in Central Asia: Expressions of Identity and Change*. Durham, NC: Duke University Press, 1992. A collection of scholarly essays on the formation of ethnic, religious, and national identities in Muslim societies of Central Asia.

Hopkirk, Kathleen. *A Traveller's Companion to Central Asia*. London: John Murray Publishers, 1993. A general history of Central Asia covering the major events of the past two centuries.

Mack, Glenn. "Central Asia." In *Encyclopedia of Food and Culture*. ed. Solomon H. Katz. New York: Charles Scribner's Sons, 2002. A description of Central Asian foodways in the extremely thorough three-volume set covering almost every conceivable aspect of food.

Melvin, Neil. *Uzbekistan: Transition to Authoritarianism on the Silk Road*. Amsterdam: Harwood Academic Publishers, 2000. An introduction to Uzbekistan for nonexperts, covering history, politics, economics, and foreign relations.

Pandya-Lorch, R., and M. Rosengrant. "Prospects for Global Food Security: A Central Asian Context." *Food Policy* 25, no. 6 (2000): 637–46. An analysis of Central Asian food security if recommended policies are properly implemented. It also discusses food safety and trade.

Rudelson, Justin Jon. *Oasis Identities: Uyghur Nationalism along China's Silk Road*. New York: Columbia University Press, 1997. An elegant anthropological approach to the study of Uighurs in China, with an undercurrent theme of who owns history.

Saroyan, Mark. *Minorities, Mullahs, and Modernity: Reshaping Community in the Former Soviet Union*. Berkeley: University of California, 1997. A formidable collection of essays and lectures on the region's religious traditions, cultures, and politics.

Schoeberlein-Engel, John. "The Prospects for Uzbek National Identity." *Central Asia Monitor* vol. 4 no. 2 (1996): 12–20. An insightful examination of identity as the Uzbeks cobble together a history and culture from a variety of traditions.

Soucek, Svatopluk. *A History of Inner Asia*. Cambridge: Cambridge University Press, 2000. A general history of Inner Asia defined as the countries of Uzbekistan, Kazakstan, Kyrgyzstan, Tajikistan, Turkmenistan, Xinjiang, and Mongolia, covers from the Islamic conquest to the present.

Starr, Frederick, ed. *The Legacy of History in Russia and the New States of Eurasia*. Armonk, NY: M. E. Sharpe, 1994. A review of foreign relations and political identity of the new Central Asian states, with a backdrop of past relations among the post-Soviet nations.

Zanca, Russell. "'Take! Take! Take!' Host-Guest Relations and All That Food: Uzbek Hospitality Past and Present." In "Food and Foodways in Eastern Europe and Postsocialist Eurasia." Special issue, *Anthropology of East Europe Review* 21, no. 1 (spring 2003). An insightful, witty peek into Uzbek hospitality, bread, pilaf, tea time, and external influences on diet from an anthropological perspective.

## COOKBOOKS

### Russian

Boeckmann, Susie, and Natalie Rebeiz-Nielsen. *Caviar: The Definitive Guide*. New York: John Wiley, 2000. Half of the book is devoted to caviar recipes, but it also includes serious discussion on all aspects of caviar, including the possibility of sturgeon extinction due to pollution and overfishing.

Chamberlain, Lesley. *The Food and Cooking of Russia*. New York: Penguin Books, 1983. One of the most enduring Russian cookbooks in English.

Cheremeteff Jones, Catherine. *A Year of Russian Feasts*. Bethesda, MD: Jellyroll Press, 2002. An award-winning book that is part cookbook and part food memoir.

Frolov, Wanda. *Katish: Our Russian Cook*. New York: Random House, 2001. The tale of a Russian émigré hired as a cook in Los Angeles during the 1920s. Mainly a narrative but several recipes are included in the final chapter.

Goldstein, Darra. *A Taste of Russia: A Cookbook of Russian Hospitality*. Montpelier, VT: Russian Information Services, 1999. With more than two hundred recipes, this best-selling Russian cookbook includes cultural asides and compelling historical notes.

Kropotkin, Alexandra. *The Best of Russian Cooking*. New York: Hippocrene International Cookbook Classics, 1993. Three hundred Russian recipes that include both the classics and the lesser-known offerings.

Papashvily, Helen, and George Papashvily. *Russian Cooking.* Foods of the World Series. New York: Time-Life Books, 1969. The best cultural overview of the diverse culinary world of the Soviet Union with several traditional recipes.

Petrovskaya, Kira. *Russian Cookbook.* New York: Dover Books, 1992. More than two hundred recipes adapted for American kitchens, includes traditional dishes and some historical notes.

Sogolow, Rosalie. *Memories from a Russian Kitchen: From Shtetl to Golden Land.* Santa Barbara: Fithian Press, 1996. Much more than a cookbook—includes a collection of touching stories about daily life in the Soviet Union.

Toomre, Joyce, trans. and ed. *Classic Russian Cooking: Elena Molokhovets' a Gift to Young Housewives.* Bloomington: Indiana University Press, 1992.

Visson, Lynn. *Russian Heritage Cookbook: A Culinary Heritage Preserved through 360 Authentic Recipes.* New York: The Overlook Press, 1998. The author attempts to rescue one part of Russian heritage lost during the Soviet experiment—the cuisine, based on recipes from the old Russian émigré community in New York City.

Volokh, Anne, and Mavis Manus. *The Art of Russian Cuisine.* New York: Collier Books, 1989. With almost five hundred recipes for classic Russian dishes, this book also provides a respectable history of Russian food and foodways.

von Bremzen, Anya, and John Welchman. *Please to the Table: The Russian Cookbook.* New York: Workman Publishing Company, 1990. One of the best comprehensive approaches to the wonderful diversity of culinary culture in the USSR, including four hundred recipes sprinkled with anecdotes and lines from Russian literature.

Ward, Susan. *Russian Regional Recipes: Classic Dishes from Moscow and St. Petersburg; The Russian Federation and Moldova; The Baltic States; Georgia, Armenia and Azerbaijan; and Central Asia and Kazakhstan.* London: The Apple Press, 1993. A colorfully illustrated cookbook that traces the various influences that shaped Russian cuisine.

### Central Asian and Other Regional Cuisines

Alford, Jeffrey, and Naomi Duguid. *Flatbreads and Flavors: A Baker's Atlas.* New York: William Morrow and Company, 1995. Introducing flatbreads from the farthest corners of the world, including Central Asia, this amazing cookbook also includes another 150 recipes for traditional accompaniments.

Batmanglij, Najmieh. *Silk Road Cooking.* Washington, DC: Mage Publishers, 2002. One hundred fifty vegetarian recipes from the Silk Road, with stories, pictures, histories of ingredients, and words of wisdom from the author's favorite poets and writers of the region.

Chen, T.S., and P.A. Pak. *Traditional Korean Cooking*. Almaty. Kazakstan: Ta-
vana, 1994. Contains about six hundred Soviet Korean recipes, including some from China and Japan. In addition, the authors have included a
short ethnographic sketch of Korean culinary culture in Central Asia.

Cramer, Marc. *Imperial Mongolian Cooking: Recipes from the Kingdoms of Genghis
Khan*. New York: Hippocrene Books, 2000. Over one hundred recipes are
preceded by a thoughtful introduction; the book closes with a glossary of
spices and ingredients.

Goldstein, Darra. *The Georgian Feast: The Vibrant Culture and Savory Food of the Republic of Georgia*. Berkeley: University of California Press, 1999. A delicious
history of Georgia and its culinary culture with over one hundred recipes.

Ilkin, Nur, and Sheilah Kaufman. *A Taste of Turkish Cuisine*. New York: Hippocrene Books, 2002. A history of Turkey's culinary traditions accompanies
the 187 recipes, as well as glossaries of commonly used ingredients and
Turkish cooking terms.

Mack, Glenn, and A.S. Madrakhimov. *Uzbek Cuisine*. Tashkent, Uzbekistan:
Mekhnat, 1996. Uzbek, English, and Russian cookbook with color illustrations for every recipe.

Nelson, Kay Shaw. *Cuisines of the Caucasus Mountains: Recipes, Drinks, and Lore
from Armenia, Azerbaijan, Georgia, and Russia*. New York: Hippocrene
Books, 2002. A niche cookbook that covers all areas south of Russia and
north of Iran.

Visson, Lynn. *The Art of Uzbek Cooking*. New York: Hippocrene Books, 1998.
The first U.S. English-language cookbook on Uzbek cuisine.

Zahny, Bohdan. *Best of Ukrainian Cuisine*. New York: Hippocrene International
Cookbooks, 1998. Updated with a list of menu terms in Ukrainian and
English and includes both traditional and contemporary cuisine from all
regions of the Ukraine.

## WEB SITES

*Central Eurasian Studies World Wide Resources for the Study of Central Eurasia*. Provides basic information on Central Asia studies, encompassing all fields of
the social sciences and humanities wherever in the world people engage in
such study. http://cesww.fas.harvard.edu/.

*Economic Research Service (ERS) of the U.S. Department of Agriculture*. http://www.
ers.usda.gov/Data/InternationalFoodDemand/.

*Food and Agriculture Organization of the United Nations*. Nutritive factors utilized
in food balances. http://www.fao.org/es/ESS/xxx.htm.

Islamic calendar and holidays. http://moonsighting.com/holidays.html and
http://www.islamicfinder.org/.

Russian customs, holidays, and traditions. http://russian-crafts.com/russian-tradi
tions.html.

*Russian Foods.com.* The Russian department store and gourmet food network—online grocery store with a large selection of Russian souvenirs, music, videos, and a large collection of authentic Russian cooking recipes. http://www.russianfoods.com/.

*Russian Longitudinal Monitoring Survey.* (RLMS) 2002 data. http://www.cpc.unc.edu/projects/rlms/data.html.

Russian Orthodox Calendars: *Russkoe Pravoslavie,* http://www.ortho-rus.ru/titles/home-calendar.htm; *Pravoslavny Kalendar,* http://www.days.ru.

*Traditional Cultures in Central Asia: Food.* http://depts.washington.edu/uwch/silk road/culture/food/food.html.

Uzbek Cookery. Online version of 1996 cookbook, *Uzbek Cuisine,* http://www.angelfire.com/ct/DIVA/UzbekCuisine.html.

## VIDEO/FILM

*Beyond Communism. The People of Perestroika: Central Asia and Kazakstan.* VHS. Evanston, IL: Journal Films, 1993. This work looks at the importance of Central Asia because of its oil reserves, especially in Kazakstan; the importance of the Silk Road in European history; and the marvelous diversity of over eighty nationalities in Central Asia.

*Beyond Communism. The People of Perestroika: The Russian Federation.* VHS. Evanston, IL: Journal Films, 1993. Video examines how the Russian people live in this time of rebuilding from Communism.

*Central Asia: Kyrgyzstan and Uzbekistan.* VHS. Victoria, Australia: Lonely Planet, 1997. Travel video highlighting nature, animals, as well as a trip on a Red Army helicopter, on horseback, meeting nomadic shepherds, and sharing a meal eating a sheep's eye.

*Disappearing World: The Herders of Mongun-Taiga, the Tuvans of Mongolia.* VHS. Newton, NJ: Shanachie Entertainment, 1998. Along the Siberian-Mongolian border in the Sacred Wilderness, the descendants of aboriginal Siberian people continue to live in yurts. These nomads herd yaks, sheep, horses, and goats. Under these harsh conditions, they must produce all their basic necessities.

Dvortsevoy, Sergey. *Chastie* [Paradise]. VHS. Brooklyn, NY: First Run/Icarus, 1995. This feature film offers a glimpse of one family's life on a steppe in South Kazakstan. Uses English subtitles to translate their infrequent verbal exchanges in scenes filmed with a mostly stationary camera. Shows food preparation, meals, child care, shoe repair, and the tending of livestock—including piercing a camel's nose to insert a lead rope.

*The Face of Russia.* VHS. Chicago, IL: Home Vision Entertainment, 1998. PBS series on Russia's cultural history by one of America's preeminent Russian scholars, James H. Billington.

*Geography of the World—The Middle East and Central Asia: Land and Resources.* VHS. Chatsworth, CA: AIMS Multimedia, 1999. An informative program covering the agriculture, transportation, and natural resources of the area. For grades 6–12.

*Geography of the World—The Middle East and Central Asia: The People.* VHS. Chatsworth, CA: AIMS Multimedia, 2000. Learn about the rich diversity of lifestyles in the Middle East and Central Asia in this program, which also clears up common misconceptions about Muslim and Arab customs. For grades 6–12.

*Globe Trekker: Central Asia.* VHS. Victoria, Australia: Lonely Planet/555 Productions, 2002. Informative and lighthearted travel video about Central Asia.

*Globe Trekker: Russia—Moscow, St. Petersburg, and Murmansk.* VHS. Victoria, Australia: Lonely Planet/555 Productions, 2000. New look at Russia through its main cities and a side trip to Northern Russia on the Barents Sea near the Arctic Circle.

Goldin, Sidney. *The Feast of Passover [Di Seder Nakht].* VHS. Waltham, MA: Standard Film Exchange, 1931. This historic Jewish American short film depicts a seder in the midst of North American prosperity and a traditional Passover celebration in Russia, with the same cast featured in both scenes. A humorous twist ending reflects the inescapable hand of modernity. In English, Hebrew, and Yiddish.

Roberts, Sean. *Waiting for Uighurstan.* VHS. Directed by Sean Roberts. Los Angeles: The Center for Visual Anthropology, 1996. This documentary chronicles the experience of three Uighurs who live in Kazakstan. Cut off from their homeland for over 20 years, they only reestablished ties with their family and friends in Xinjiang in the mid-1980s.

*Rural Russia.* VHS. Sacramento, CA: Artistic License Inc., 1999. Survey of Russia's remote countryside where there are no highways, shopping malls, airports, or supermarkets—just family, friends, and 8 million square kilometers of wilderness.

*The Silk Road: An Ancient World of Adventure.* VHS. New York: Central Park Media, 2000. A stunning documentary follows the storied route of Marco Polo as he traveled between Venice and China in the thirteenth century. Includes topics of world history, geography, religion, art, and economics.

*World Geography Module 2: Russia, the Caucasus, and Central Asia.* VHS. Falls Church, VA: Cerebellum Corp., 2003. Examines the diverse histories, cultures, economics, and physical characteristics of distant (and not-so-distant) regions of the world.

# Selected Bibliography

Abbott, Pamela. *Living Conditions, Lifestyles, and Health in Armenia, Belarus, Georgia, Kazakhstan, Kyrghyzstan, Moldova, Russia & Ukraine: Social Trends 1990–2002.* Vienna: Institute for Social Research, 2003.

Allsen, Thomas T. *Culture and Conquest in Mongol Eurasia.* Cambridge, England: Cambridge University Press, 2001.

Anderson, Benedict. *Imagined Communities: Reflections on the Origin and Spread of Nationalism.* New York: Verso, 1991.

Appadurai, Arjun. "How to Make a National Cuisine: Cookbooks in Contemporary India." *Comparative Studies in Society and History* 30, no. 1 (1988): 3–24.

————. *Modernity at Large: Cultural Dimensions of Globalization.* Minneapolis: University of Minnesota Press, 1996.

Beardsworth, A. D., and E. T. Keil. *Sociology on the Menu: An Invitation to the Study of Food and Society.* New York: Routledge, 1997.

Belasco, Warren, and Philip Scranton. *Food Nations: Selling Taste in Consumer Societies.* New York: Routledge, 2002.

Belknap, Robert L., ed. *Russianness: Studies on a Nation's Identity: In Honor of Rufus Wellington Mathewson, 1918–1978.* Ann Arbor: Ardis, 1990.

Bell, David, and Gill Valentine, eds. *Consuming Geographies: We Are Where We Eat.* New York: Routledge, 1997.

Bourdieu, Pierre. *Distinction: A Social Critique of the Judgement of Taste.* Cambridge, MA: Harvard University Press, 1984.

Braudel, Fernand. *The Structures of Everyday Life: The Limits of the Possible.* Civilization and Capitalism: 15th-18th Century. Reprint edition. Berkeley, CA: University of California Press, 1992.

Chang, K. C. *Food in Chinese Culture: Anthropological and Historical Perspectives.* New Haven, CT: Yale University Press, 1977.

Cockerham, William C. *Health and Social Change in Russia and Eastern Europe*. New York: Routledge, 1999.

Cook, Ian, and Philip Crang. "The World on a Plate: Culinary Culture, Displacement and Geographical Knowledges." *Journal of Material Culture* 1, no. 2 (1996): 131–53.

Counihan, Carole. *Food and Culture: A Reader*. New York: Routledge, 1997.

Fernandez-Armesto, Felipe. *Near a Thousand Tables: A History of Food*. New York: Free Press, 2002.

Foster, Robert. "Making National Cultures in the Global Ecumene." *Annual Review of Anthropology* 20 (1991): 235–60.

Geertz, Clifford. *The Interpretation of Cultures*. New York: Basic Books, 1973.

Glants, Musya, and Joyce Toomre, eds. *Food in Russian History and Culture*. Bloomington: Indiana University Press, 1997.

Goody, Jack. *Cooking, Cuisine, and Class: A Study in Comparative Sociology*. Cambridge: Cambridge University Press, 1982.

Grant, Bruce. *In the Soviet House of Culture: A Century of Perestroikas*. Princeton, NJ: Princeton University Press, 1995.

Gronow, Jukka. *Caviar with Champagne: Common Luxury and the Ideals of the Good Life in Stalin's Russia*. Leisure, Consumption and Culture. New York: Berg, 2004.

Harrison, Simon. "Cultural Difference as Denied Resemblance: Reconsidering Nationalism and Ethnicity." *Society for the Comparative Study of Society and History* 45, no. 2 (2003): 343–61.

Herlihy, Patricia. *The Alcoholic Empire: Vodka and Politics in Late Imperial Russia*. New York: Oxford University Press, 2002.

Hobsbawm, Eric. *The Invention of Tradition*. Cambridge: Cambridge University Press, 1992.

Humphrey, Caroline. *The Unmaking of Soviet Life: Everyday Economies after Socialism*. Ithaca, NY: Cornell University Press, 2002.

Hutchinson, John. *Modern Nationalism*. London: Fontana Press, 1994.

Ivanits, Linda. *Russian Folk Belief*. Armonk, NY: M.E. Sharpe, 1992.

Jameson, Fredric. *Postmodernism, or, The Cultural Logic of Late Capitalism*. Durham, NC: Duke University Press, 1991.

Kelly, Catriona, and David Shepherd, eds. *Constructing Russian Culture in the Age of Revolution: 1881–1940*. New York: Oxford University Press, 1998.

Kemper, Michael, Anke von Kügelgen, and Dmitrii Ermakov, eds. *Muslim Culture in Russia and Central Asia from the 18th to the Early 20th Centuries*. Berlin: Klaus Schwarz Verlag, 1996.

Kirshenblatt-Gimblett, Barbara. *Destination Culture: Tourism, Museums, and Heritage*. Berkeley: University of California Press, 1998.

Kittler, Pamela Goyan. *Food and Culture*. Belmont, CA: Wadsworth/Thomson Learning, 2001.

Laitin, David. *Identity in Formation: The Russian-Speaking Populations in the Near Abroad*. Ithaca, NY: Cornell University Press, 1998.

McGee, Harold. *On Food and Cooking: The Science and Lore of the Kitchen.* New York: Macmillan, 1984.

Mennell, Steven, A. Murcott, and A. van Otterloo. *The Sociology of Food: Eating, Diet, and Culture.* London: Sage, 1992.

Mintz, Sidney. *Tasting Food, Tasting Freedom: Excursions into Eating, Power, and the Past.* Boston: Beacon Press, 1997.

Paksoy, Hasan Bülent, ed. *Central Asia Reader: The Rediscovery of History.* Armonk, NY: M. E. Sharpe, 1994.

Pilcher, Jeffrey M. *Que Vivan Los Tamales: Food and the Making of Mexican Identity.* Albuquerque: University of New Mexico Press, 1998.

Pouncy, Carolyn Johnston, ed. and trans. *The Domostroi: Rules for Russian Households in the Time of Ivan the Terrible.* Ithaca, NY: Cornell University Press, 1994.

Rabinovich, Michael R. "Ethnological Studies in the Traditional Food of the Russians, Ukrainians, and Byelorussians between the 16th and 19th Centuries: State of Research and Basic Problems." In *European Food History: A Research Review,* ed. H. J. Teuteberg, 224–235. New York: Leicester University Press, 1992.

Schultze, Sydney. *Culture and Customs of Russia.* Westport, CT: Greenwood Press, 2000.

Smith, R. E. F., and David Christian. *Bread and Salt: A Social and Economic History of Food and Drink in Russia.* Cambridge: Cambridge University Press, 1984.

Spang, Rebecca. *The Invention of the Restaurant: Paris and Modern Gastronomic Culture.* Cambridge, MA: Harvard University Press, 2000.

Symons, Michael. *The History of Cooks and Cooking.* Urbana: Illinois University Press, 2000.

Tannahill, Reay. *Food in History.* Revised edition. New York: Crown Trade Paperbacks, 1995.

Toomre, Joyce, trans. and ed. *Classic Russian Cooking: Elena Molokhovets' a Gift to Young Housewives.* Bloomington: Indiana University Press, 1992.

Toussaint-Samat, Maguelonne. *History of Food.* Trans. Anthea Bell. Cambridge, MA: Blackwell, 1994.

Trubek, Amy B. *Haute Cuisine: How the French Invented the Culinary Profession.* Philadelphia: University of Pennsylvania Press, 2001.

Wallerstein, Immanuel. "Culture as the Ideological Battleground of the Modern World-System." In *Global Culture: Nationalism, Globalization, and Modernity,* ed. Mike Featherstone, 31–55. London: Sage Publications, 1990.

Williams, Robert. *Russia Imagined: Art, Culture, and National Identity, 1840–1995.* New York: Peter Lang Publishing, 1997.

Wu, David, and Sidney Cheung, eds. *The Globalization of Chinese Food.* Honolulu: University of Hawaii Press, 2002.

Zubaida, Sami, and Richard Trapper, eds. *A Taste of Thyme: Culinary Cultures of the Middle East.* London: IB Taurus, 2000.

# INDEX

## About the Authors

GLENN R. MACK is a food historian who trained in the culinary arts in Uzbekistan, Russia, Italy, and the United States. He is the Director of Education for the Culinary Academy of Austin and founded the Historic Foodways Group of Austin. He has coauthored *Uzbek Cuisine* (1996), among other works.

ASELE SURINA is a Russian native and former journalist who now works as a translator and interpreter. Since 1999 she has worked at the Institute of Classical Archaeology at the University of Texas on joint projects with an archeological museum in Crimea, Ukraine.